THE CAPTAIN OF INDUSTRY IN ENGLISH FICTION 1821-1871

THE
Captain of Industry
IN
ENGLISH FICTION,
1821-1871

BY IVAN MELADA

ALBUQUERQUE

UNIVERSITY OF NEW MEXICO PRESS

TO DALE

TO PETER, JULIA AND SAM

AND TO MY MOTHER AND FATHER

Acknowledgments

I should like to thank Professors John Henry Raleigh, Herbert L. Sussman, and Leo Lowenthal for their encouragement and advice as readers of an earlier version of this study. I also want to express my gratitude to Professor Franklin M. Dickey who read the work in manuscript and offered valuable suggestions for improvement. To Professor Ernest W. Baughman, I am grateful for advice relating to the preparation of the manuscript for publication. For her faith and her patience and her help, only part of which included the typing of the manuscript, I owe a debt of deepest gratitude to my wife, Dale Leavesley Melada.

Contents

Introduction

I shall never forget Mr. Boulton's expression to
me: "I sell here, Sir, what all the world desires to
have—POWER."

Boswell, *Life of Johnson*[1]

URING THE SECOND HALF OF THE EIGH-
teenth century, a series of technological innovations precipitated a revolution in industry, creating a new physical force which demanded a new type of man to manipulate, organize, and control it. Henry Adams, in his analysis of the effect of the liberation of this *vis nova*, characterized the emergent type who could bring it to order as "a man with ten times the endurance, energy, will, and mind of the old type."[2] Having fixed their economic position in the late eighteenth and early nineteenth centuries, the new men, fittingly termed "captains of industry" by Carlyle, gained political stature with the passage of the Reform Bill of 1832. By the third quarter of the nineteenth century, the third generation of industrialists, along with the professional classes, achieved social recognition as members of what G. Kitson Clark has called the "new gentry."[3]

The stages of the industrialist's progress sketched above have been recorded by British novelists in the nineteenth century, and it is the representation of this process in fiction that is the subject of this study. Using a selection of novels written between 1821 and 1871, I shall trace the changing image of the industrialist in the course of his assimilation into a society traditionally dominated by the social, economic, and political interests of the landed aristocracy.

I have limited the study to a consideration of the industrial magnate who engaged in large scale enterprise. The majority of the industrialists under discussion are manufacturers of textiles, primarily cotton goods; and the remainder of the group is composed of ironmasters, colliery owners, a manufacturer of gloves and a railway contractor. Captains of finance receive only passing mention chiefly for the purposes of contrast, and the small operator, such as the owner of the sweat shop in Kingsley's *Alton Locke*, for example, is not dealt with at all.

The industrial magnate has been singled out for study because of the social implications inherent in the combined factors which distinguish him from the financier and the small manufacturer; namely, wealth coupled with the large work force necessary to produce that wealth. With respect to the first factor, the affluence of the great industrialists created in time an aristocracy of wealth which sought to share the privileges, power, and rank long the prerogative of the landed aristocracy. Part of the struggle of the new class to assert itself stems from the efforts of industrialists to make a place for themselves among the established rulers of the land. But the old aristocracy was only one element of society with which the industrialist had to come to terms. The large-scale manufacturer also had a work force of hundreds of men with which to contend. Like the aristocrat, the industrialist had a responsibility, whether accepted or neglected, toward a sizeable group of dependents; but unlike the aristocrat's dependents, the new breed of "lower orders," whose initial emergence coincided with the French Revolution and whose mass reading experience had begun in part with Tom Paine's *Rights of Man*, sought to assert its independence and equality through the trade union movement.[4] Thus the industrial magnate was challenged both by the upper and the lower ranks. This study is in part a history of the relationship of the new class to other classes in the hierarchy of English society. Emerson as well as Marx noted the tendency of the middle classes to accept the privileges of rank without attending to its responsibilities.[5] In the course of the fifty year period covered in this study, the industrial magnate in the novels learns to accept the social responsibilities of power and to be worthy of the rank to which he has aspired.

There are three points concerning method upon which it is necessary to elaborate. One involves a justification of the principle underlying organization and another, a qualification of the role of the novelist as social historian. The third is an explanation of the use to which historical novels have been put.

With respect to the problem of overall organization, the treatment of the emergence of a new class orders itself according to the logic of the following process: initial entrance, a period of struggle for assertion, and final assimilation. Chronologically the process may be roughly divided into three periods: 1800-30, 1830-50, 1850-70. The assumption that the passage of time generally supports the logic of emergence is borne out by the following example. The first generation of manufacturers of the early days of the industrial revolution were, according to one historian, rough, coarse strangers to etiquette and not far removed from the class of workmen out

of which many had arisen.[6] The second and certainly the third generations of manufacturing families that managed to survive gluts and trade
depressions were composed of individuals who acquired more refined
personal characteristics as a result of education and contact with the
world. Although the foregoing example illustrates the general historical
as well as logical pattern of the industrialist's progression from self-made
man to gentleman, it is necessary to note that the members of the new
class did not make their entrance into English society in one wave, beginning about the turn of the nineteenth century. In the fiction dealing with
the early period, 1800-30, self-made men tend to preponderate, but they
also appear in the novels of the 1850s. And conversely, the gentleman-
manufacturer who as a general rule dominates the fiction of the last
period, 1850-70, makes an appearance in a novel of the 1820s. With these
reservations in mind, I have treated the emergence and assimilation of the
industrialist as process, a method of organization that is logically natural
for such a study, and one that has general historical validity.

A second aspect of method involves the evaluation of writers' attitudes,
particularly in that part of the study (Chapters III, IV, V) in which the
social problem novel is prominent. This concern arises out of the necessity of distinguishing fact from opinion. W. A. Aydelotte has offered a
caveat for the social historian who would use social problem novels as
sources for a historical work. His advice is equally applicable to a literary
study treating matters of social history. The social problem novel, warns
Aydelotte, though it purports to acquaint the world with the immediacy
of social questions, does not offer a history of fact but a history of opinion.
As a consequence, the facts of an age presented in such works are "highly
suspect" for the purposes of the historian, "spotty, impressionistic, and
inaccurate." The novelist's involvement in social questions, continues
Aydelotte, is limited by his interests, his class background, and by the
dictates of artistic purpose. The value of this kind of novel lies not in the
facts it sets forth about social conditions, but in what it tells us about the
attitude of the novelist toward social conditions.[7] To these strictures may
be added Emery Neff's suggestion that more should be known about what
drew these writers into treating class questions.[8] For the social problem
novel, I have dealt with the question of writers' attitudes as largely a matter of either class background or humanitarian interests. The part played
by artistic purpose has been discussed, as a rule, only when it is at cross-
purposes with polemic.

A third point about method concerns the assessment of the contem-
poraneity of a writer's attitude in a novel, the action of which is set in an
earlier time. The evaluation of a writer's assumptions in this kind of novel
gives rise to two questions; namely, are the attitudes expressed in a his-

torical novel those of the time in which it is set, or are they a reflection of the spirit of the writer's time? These questions are best answered with reference to individual works.

In this study I have occasionally used novels written late in the period but set one or two generations earlier as source materials; in some cases for the earlier period, and in other cases for the later period. Such a mode of procedure might suggest a mishandling of evidence, but it is hoped that the following brief discussion of two works will serve to justify the method.

An example of the first procedure mentioned is the use of James Kay-Shuttleworth's *Scarsdale* (1874) to delineate the relationship between the aristocracy and the "millocracy" of the 1830s. In the absence of contemporary novels depicting the manufacturer in a state of transition from the yeoman class, I have had to make use of the novel in this way.[9] It has been asserted by the contemporary historian Peter Gaskell, and the modern Paul Mantoux, that a segment of the manufacturing class originated from the decayed yeomanry.[10] Thus far, Kay-Shuttleworth's novel is historically valid, and serves the purpose of the early part of the study by exhibiting a historical phenomenon. But because of his aristocratic bias I have been careful not to accept as a historical truth Kay-Shuttleworth's assumptions about class relationships of the 1830s.

The second procedure is exemplified by the use of Dinah Maria Mulock's *John Halifax, Gentleman* (1856), set in the first quarter of the nineteenth century, in order to exhibit attitudes toward social questions that are characteristic of the 1850s. Mrs. Craik is preoccupied with the theory of a gentleman, an idea which the historian Asa Briggs, writing about the continuing importance of deference in an industrial society, has called "the necessary link in any analysis of mid-Victorian ways of thinking and behaving."[11] Mrs. Craik thus reflects the spirit of her times, an age in which the idea of a gentleman received much attention as English society became increasingly complex and the status of a gentleman was in need of redefinition. It is not necessary, therefore, to take into strict account the early nineteenth-century setting of the novel.

Admittedly, the greater risk of an inexpert use of evidence lies with the first procedure. Moreover, the literary historian cannot altogether put his trust in the stated purpose of a novelist who avows that he is describing the social conditions of a bygone era. But with an exercise of judiciousness, a sense of a novelist's motives and biases, and some knowledge of the historical periods involved, the literary historian is able to employ the historical novel to illuminate a general truth about another age.

ONE

Homines Novi

Meantime the markets kept ever growing, the demand, ever rising. Even manufacture [lit. the
hand-powered process] no longer sufficed. There-
upon, steam and machinery revolutionized industrial production. The place of manufacture was
taken by the giant, Modern Industry, the place of
the industrial middle-class, by industrial million-
aires, the leaders of whole industrial armies, the
modern bourgeois.

Marx and Engels,
Manifesto of the Communist Party

ONE OF THE CONSEQUENCES OF THE INVEN-
tion of the steam engine in 1769 and of spinning and weaving machinery
between 1764 and 1785 was a social revolution, which as Friedrich Engels
observed, "changed the entire structure of middle-class society."[1] Karl
Marx, enlarging upon this social transformation, noted that "entire classes
of the population disappear and new ones with new conditions of existence, and new requirements take their place."[2]

Although the primary concern of this study is to examine the attitudes
of Victorian novelists toward the new class of industrialists as they adapted
themselves to an existing social structure that itself had to change in order
to accommodate them, the purpose of this first chapter is to analyze the
social phenomenon of their newness, while providing an historical account
of their initial emergence in the late eighteenth century. In order to ac-
complish this aim, I have established four criteria by which the newness
of the class might be judged. In this analysis I shall discuss (1) the social
origins of the early industrialists, (2) the uniqueness of their economic
and social position as a new class, (3) the qualities needed for success in

industrial enterprise, and (4) the degree of social recognition bestowed upon such representative industrialists as James Watt and Richard Arkwright by the old ruling class, the supremacy of which was challenged by men whose wealth stemmed from the economic basis of factory production instead of land. This historical introduction will seek to differentiate the industrialists from other affluent classes, and thereby assess their distinction as *homines novi*.

Our first consideration, the social origins of the early industrialists, has drawn attention to itself by virtue of the persistence of the economic historian Paul Mantoux in establishing a connection between the new class of manufacturers and that "darling of poets and social theorists," the English yeoman.[3] According to Mantoux's theory, the yeoman class, which rapidly decayed in the eighteenth century, supplied the raw material for the emergent manufacturing class.[4]

Arnold Toynbee, attempting to account for the decay of the yeomanry, records that at the end of the seventeenth century Gregory King estimated the number of freeholders in England at 180,000. Less than one hundred years later (1787), Arthur Young spoke of the class as nearly gone. The cause of this rapid disappearance following the era of parliamentary supremacy after 1688 is chiefly political, but economic reasons figure as well. He who possessed the soil possessed political power, under conditions which gave power in parliament to owners of land. The Englishman's land hunger can thus be ascribed to what Disraeli called a territorial constitution.[5] Since such was the case, both the greater gentry and the wealthy merchant class strove to invest in land the immense fortunes made in foreign trade and colonial enterprise. Pressure from this quarter together with the decline of domestic industry led to the extinction of the yeomanry.[6]

The Peel family, notes Mantoux (p. 370), affords a striking example of the process by which the moribund yeomanry transformed itself into the new manufacturing class. The father of Sir Robert Peel, the Prime Minister, was a cotton spinner and maker of printed calicoes who died in 1830, leaving a personal estate of £1,400,000. The grandfather of Sir Robert, born in 1723, was one of Arkwright's imitators and competitors. Before entering into cotton spinning he sold woolens and cottons made by himself at home. While engaged in domestic weaving, he also farmed land that had been in the possession of his family who had been peasant proprietors of the yeoman class since the fifteenth century. Thus the family had begun as farmers, become farmer-weavers, and then entered industry.

Two lesser known figures, William Radcliffe and Joshua Fielden, were not as favored by fortune as the Peels, but their histories exhibit a similar pattern. The fall of the Radcliffe family, who had been landed proprietors, had begun during the civil wars of 1642-49. The Enclosure Acts and the subsequent growth of large estates forced them from the land, and they turned to weaving. A product of several generations of weavers, Radcliffe set up for himself in 1789 and by 1801 employed one thousand workers. Joshua Fielden, on the other hand, was still a yeoman farmer in 1780; but after having set up looms in his house, he owned a five story factory by the end of the century.[7]

If it were feasible, argues Mantoux, to lay out the genealogies of late eighteenth-century manufacturers, one significant fact would emerge: "Many of them, particularly in the cotton industry, were of country stock and came of that semi-agricultural, semi-industrial class which up to that time [the late 18th century] had formed a large part, perhaps more than one-half, of the population of England. And, if we go further back still, we often arrive at the peasant stock, at the old race of yeomen, now hidden though not extinct."[8]

In his attempt to account for what became of this class, Mantoux has presupposed that the yeomen were ambitious, energetic, enterprising, and prepared to meet the challenge posed by the loss of their small holdings and the decline of home industry, by entering into the main current of the Industrial Revolution "in a spirit of adventure and conquest" (p. 373). On the other hand, Peter Gaskell, whose beau ideal of the Englishman was the country squire, presents quite another stereotype of the yeoman. Writing in 1833, Gaskell holds that the yeoman class was apathetic and utterly incapable of adapting to change:

> The yeoman had lived for generation after generation upon his patrimonial acres—rarely increasing their extent and quite as rarely lessening them. He had, however, failed to keep pace with the onward march of events—had confined himself to cultivating his land precisely in the same way in which it had been cultivated by his forefathers— viewed all innovations as rank heresy, vegetated upon his natal soil, profiting either it or the world but little; but having, notwithstanding many points about him of real value. He was strictly honest in all his dealings—though almost universally improvident, more, however, from want of mental energy and forethought than from actual extravagance— contented with his lot and a kind and hearty neighbour—but utterly unable to cope with the crisis [consolidation of small holdings and decline of domestic industry] which was opening for him.[9]

Gaskell, moreover, viewed the yeoman class as unfit to compete with those to whom the intermittent changes occurring in business were not disquieting. The yeomanry's "long course of inactivity and the little diffusion of intelligence amongst them, rendered them incapable of maintaining the struggle with men who had been accustomed to the variations of trade; and whose forethought enabled them to apply remedies, and to take such precautionary and anticipative measures as screened them from loss" (p. 44).

According to Gaskell, then, the successful manufacturer was a man already experienced in business. He was most likely either a petty manufacturer, who in addition to being a producer of goods engaged also in marketing, or a merchant who had acquired control over the means of production. In either case, the members of this class would have been the merchant manufacturers, who provided the transition between the master craftsman and the modern industrialist.

Mantoux's estimation of the yeoman class—the bold, independent peasantry of England, losing their small holdings, making their fortune in manufacturing, buying land once more from a gentry that had looked down upon them, and building stately homes as "monuments to their new wealth and their ancient pride" (p. 373)—is not without appeal by virtue of its simplicity and the suggestion of myth-making that accompanies it. The account, moreover, argues for a vitalism in the history of society in which no element becomes extinct but merely suffers a sea change and reappears prepared to respond to the changes that had made its former being obsolescent. Considering, however, the lack of clearly defined classes in such a period of social and economic flux as the Industrial Revolution, such an uncomplicated point of view regarding the social origins of the new class of industrialists would seem to belong more appropriately to the folklore of capitalism, along with the myth of the self-made man.[10]

Despite the attractiveness of the yeoman-turned-manufacturer theory, it seems more likely that inventors, industrialists, and entrepreneurs came from every social class.[11] The Duke of Bridgewater, best known for his improvements in transportation, began building canals in order to get his coal from Worsley to Manchester. The clergyman Edmund Cartwright, a classical scholar and imitator of Pope, invented the power loom and set up a factory in 1787, thereby incurring the accusation of "having deserted his caste."[12] John Roebuck was a doctor who turned to industrial chemistry and later founded the famous Carron ironworks. Richard Arkwright, the wealthiest spinner in the cotton industry, had been a barber. Peter Stubs, an innkeeper, built up an extensive file-making concern. Samuel Walker, a prominent figure in the iron industry of the North, had begun as a schoolmaster. The myth of the self-made man, it would seem, came nearest to reality in the second half of the eighteenth century, for during these years, "vertical mobility had reached a degree higher than that of any earlier, or perhaps any succeeding age."[13]

The foregoing discussion has revealed the difficulty of differentiating industrialists from other classes on the basis of social origins. But by turning to our second criterion for assessing newness, a consideration of the industrialists' economic basis, we are able to view their unique position in relation to the merchant, the laboring, and the landed classes.

The rise of the large-scale industrialist was accompanied by a change in the traditional relationship between merchant and manufacturer. At the beginning of George III's reign in 1760, merchants and landlords controlled British productive resources. As a basis for economic power, the merchants had a monopoly of trade. The merchant controlled the production of the small pre-Industrial Revolution manufacturer by regulating the supply of raw material and the output of finished goods. The accumulation of capital by manufacturers, however, together with the failure of many commercial houses during the American Revolution, led to the involvement of the new class of capitalists in banking and credit. By the 1780s and 1790s manufacturers began to extend their operations so that, in addition to production, they secured raw materials and marketed finished products on their own. Having become independent of mercantile control, the new class of captains of industry took their place by the side of land and commerce as an entirely new source of moneyed power.[14]

If, at the end of the century, the manufacturer stood in a new relation to the wealthy and powerful classes, his connection with his employees had also undergone change. Before the Industrial Revolution, in the era of the small manufacturer, it was difficult to distinguish between master and man. As the factory system developed with greater numbers of workers in large mills a gulf arose separating employer and employee.[15] This altered relationship is evident in the change in meaning of the word, "manufacture." Andrew Ure, in his *Philosophy of Manufactures* (1835), noted that "manufacture" had in the course of time lost its original meaning, "to make by hand." With the establishment of the factory system, the machines "manufactured" and by "manufacturer" was meant the owner of machinery and the employer of its operators, instead of a master craftsman who worked along with his apprentices and journeymen.[16] Marx and Engels commented upon the change from the patriarchal workshop to the factory by extending the martial metaphor, captains of industry, in order to dramatize the unenviable position of the rank and file:

> Modern industry has converted the little workshop of the patriarchal master into the great factory of the industrial capitalist. Masses of laborers, crowded into the factory, are organized like soldiers. As privates of the industrial army, they are placed under the command of a perfect hierarchy of officers and sergeants. Not only are they the slaves of the bourgeois class, and of the bourgeois state; they are daily and hourly

enslaved by the machine, the overlooker, and above all, by the individual bourgeois manufacturer himself. [17]

The gulf between the employers and employed, which was the natural consequence of the disciplined organization of industrial production on a large scale, was further widened, one observer states, by virtue of the rise of many employers from the working class:

> Many of the manufacturers had in fact come from what the "Great" were often disposed to look upon as "the refuse of mankind," and their very emergence from the ranks of common labor tended to raise higher the barriers already existing between employers and employees in manufacturing enterprises. The further separation of these two groups is another manifestation of the early differentiation of the new manufacturers from other groups.[18]

It is this last connection, the relation of the employer to his dependents, that distinguishes the early industrialist from the aristocrat. The two classes were similar in the respect that both possessed moneyed power and—unlike the wealthy merchant or later the captain of finance—the one had an army of factory workers and the other, a host of agricultural laborers as dependents. Traditionally, the landowners professed a social responsibility for their farm workers, while on the other hand, industrialists were accused of espousing a cash-nexus relationship between master and man.

Carlyle's concept of society as a group of individuals tied together by bonds of mutual obligation instead of an aggregate of atoms appealed to those of his generation who were inclined to look for this kind of society as existing before the Industrial Revolution. To such a writer as Peter Gaskell, looking back in 1833, the relationship of the landed gentleman to his dependents was that of a patriarch. Gaskell's idealized portrait of the country squire in pre-industrial rural England reflects his Tory nostalgia:

> The distinctions of rank, which are the safest guarantees for the performance of the relative duties of all classes were at this time in full force; and the "Squire," as the chief landed proprietor was generally termed, obtained and deserved his importance from his large possessions, low rents, and a simplicity and homeliness of bearing which, when joined to acknowledged family honours, made him loved and reverenced by his tenants and neighbours. He mingled freely with their sports—was the general and undisputed arbitrator in all questions of law and equity —was a considerate and generous landlord—a kind and indulgent master—and looking at him in all his bearings, a worthy and amiable man; tinged, it is true, with some vices, but all so coated over with wide-

spreading charity, that the historian willingly draws the veil of forget-
fulness over them.[19]

Only a few of the squirearchy are left in the industrial North, continues
Gaskell, implying at the same time that manufacturers are lacking in the
social attitudes of the country squire: "This race of men is now nearly
extinct from the manufacturing districts. Their possessions are passed into
new hands—their descendants 'pushed from their stools' by an order of
men having few or no traits in common with them. . . ."[20]

If Gaskell suggests only indirectly that the relationship between the
manufacturer and his employees differed from that of the squire and his
dependents, a modern interpreter of the early nineteenth century or late
Georgian period emphasizes the distance at which the employer held his
workers in contradistinction to the squire's sense of social obligation to
his inferiors:

> But they [the squirearchy] had a tradition of social responsibility that
> was almost entirely lacking in those hard-headed and self-made indivi-
> dualists [the industrialists]. No doubt in long-established family busi-
> nesses an almost patriarchal relation between the head of the firm and
> his hands was capable of establishing itself. . . . But these cases were at
> the best, exceptional, and the drift of the time was towards the segrega-
> tion of industrial employers and employed into separate class entities
> that might, or might not, be able to adjust their mutual relations on a
> peaceful basis to their common advantage, but were no more inclined
> to enter into social relations with each other than Jews and Samaritans.
> So that research may possibly be able to unearth some isolated instance
> of an employer skippering his factory's cricket team, or his wife func-
> tioning as Lady Bountiful, these things would have been viewed, even
> at the time, as exceptional. Whereas they were, on country estates, not
> only normal, but ranked among customs more honoured in the ob-
> servance than the breach.[21]

Perhaps the most strongly worded statement emphasizing the distinction between the new class and the aristocracy with respect to the relationship between the wealthy and their dependents was made by Marx and
Engels:

> The bourgeoisie, whenever it has got the upper hand, has put an end
> to all feudal, patriarchal, idyllic relations. It has pitilessly torn asunder
> the motley feudal ties that bound man to his "natural superiors," and
> has left remaining no other nexus between man and man than naked
> self-interest, than callous "cash payment." It has drowned the most
> heavenly ecstasies of religious fervor, of chivalrous enthusiasm, of
> Philistine sentimentalism in the icy water of egotistical calculation. It

has resolved personal worth into exchange value, and, in place of the numberless indefeasible chartered freedoms, has set up that single, unconscionable freedom—free trade.[22]

As a result of the changeover from small manufacturers to large-scale industrialists, it is evident that the new class stood in a new and unique relation to the merchants, the working population, and the aristocracy. But what individual characteristics set the industrialist apart as a *homo novus*? To answer this question, it is necessary to turn to a discussion of the third criterion of newness: the combination of prerequisites for success in industrial enterprise.

The men who survived in the process of changing over from small to large-scale industry had one distinguishing characteristic—an ability to put other men's inventions to work. Richard Arkwright, for example, was a master at obtaining results from others' inventions where the originators had failed.[23] Given this ability, the distinctive task of the manufacturer was that of an organizer of industrial production. As such, his energies were divided among the exigencies of accumulation of capital, management of labor, and accurate knowledge of markets.

The first problem of the manufacturer was to secure capital since, except for second-generation manufacturers (the father of Sir Robert Peel, for example), most early industrialists were not wealthy. Men who had neither capital nor patents had to begin very modestly, working with their hands and saving to accumulate capital. Their hopes to rise very often lay in forming a partnership with other men like themselves or, as in the case of Robert Owen, becoming managers and subsequent partners of a large concern.[24]

After obtaining the capital necessary to set up a factory, the manufacturer had to recruit and train workers who were not accustomed to the discipline required to make a factory productive. According to Andrew Ure, writing in 1835, the task of subjecting the new class of factory workers to this discipline was formidable, and it posed the major problem of the factory system:

> The main difficulty did not, to my apprehension, lie so much in the invention of a proper self-acting mechanism for drawing out and twisting cotton into a continuous thread, as in the distribution of the different members of the apparatus into one cooperative body, in impelling each organ with its appropriate delicacy and speed, and above all, in training human beings to renounce their desultory habits of work, and to identify themselves with the unvarying regularity of the complex automaton. To devise and administer a successful code of factory discipline suited to the necessities of factory diligence, was the Herculean enterprise, the noble achievement of Arkwright."[25]

In addition to accustoming his workmen to the new discipline of the factory, the early industrialist also had to deal with markets, since, unlike the small manufacturer, he produced too large a quantity for local, and in many cases even national consumption. As Mantoux has observed, if the large-scale manufacturer "was not a born trader, he had to become one, and learn how to extend his connections over the whole country and beyond" (p. 377).

In summing up the qualities needed for success in industrial enterprise, it may be said that the manufacturer had to perform successfully the functions of capitalist, factory manager, and merchant, thereby setting "a new pattern of the complete businessman."[26] If the factory system visited the division of labor upon the work force, the opposite seems to have been true with regard to the early millowner. Perhaps the best contemporary evidence of this new type of businessman is the testimony of Robert Owen, midway in his career which began with a clerkship in the retail trade and ended with the ownership of the New Lanark Mills. In 1791 at the age of twenty, Owen became the manager of a cotton mill employing five hundred people. Mr. Drinkwater, the proprietor, knew nothing about the mill, nor did the outgoing manager leave any instructions. In addition to the qualities discussed above, the following account illustrates the adaptability and attention to detail with which Owen distinguished himself as a successful manufacturer:

> thus uninstructed I had to take the management of the concern. I had to purchase the raw material,—to make the machines, for the mill was not nearly filled with machinery,—to manufacture the cotton into yarn,—to sell it,—and to keep the accounts,—pay the wages,—and, in fact, to take the whole responsibility of the first fine cotton spinning establishment by machinery that had ever been erected. . . . I at once determined to do the best I could, and began to examine the outline and detail of what was in progress. I looked grave,—inspected everything minutely,—examined the drawings and calculations of the machinery. . . . I continued this silent inspection and superintendence day by day for six weeks, saying merely yes and no to the questions of what was to be done or otherwise, and during that period I did not give one direct order about anything. But at the end of that time, I felt myself so much the master of my position as to be ready to give directions in every department.[27]

Robert Owen, as proprietor of the New Lanark Mills, gained social recognition in his lifetime. Through his model establishment came visitors of all degrees and countries. At one point in the 1820s Owen even fancied that he had influence among such heads of state as Castlereagh who listened patiently to his schemes for the regeneration of society. But

Owen's career was exceptional; his fame does not rest entirely upon his work as a manufacturer. For other early manufacturers, social recognition was not so readily achieved.

The great manufacturers, employing "several thousand" workmen and able to raise "single capitals of two or three hundred thousand pounds" and obtain credit at home and abroad for a year to eighteen months, excited envy indeed in the hearts of titled wealth because of the potential power inherent in such affluence. And with envy of the source of power came disdain for the means by which it was acquired.[28] Broadly speaking, the English aristocracy, to its credit, was not characterized by that class rigidity typical of its Continental counterpart which would lead it to shun industrial wealth as a means of broadening its economic base. Assuredly, in earlier times the aristocracy was not unwilling to make connections with the commercial classes. Nevertheless, the upper classes in the time of Arkwright and Watt expressed an antagonism toward those two representatives of industrial talent and wealth.

Carlyle, writing in *Chartism* (1839), eulogized Arkwright and Watt as men who, though of unheroic origin, were capable of heroic doings. Arkwright, wrote Carlyle, was no hero of romance with god-like looks and gestures but "a plain, almost gross, bag-cheeked, potbellied Lancashire man" who was appointed by society to the calling of a barber. He had several difficulties to overcome: his wife burned his model of a spinning wheel and when he perfected the spinning jenny, his townspeople mobbed him for putting spinners out of work. But Arkwright was no ordinary man, continues Carlyle: "O reader, what a Historical Phenomenon is that bag-cheeked, potbellied, much-enduring, much inventing barber! French Revolutions were a-brewing: to resist the same in any measure, imperial Kaisers were impotent without the cotton and cloth of England; and it was this man that had to give England the power of cotton."[29]

But Arkwright's class-conscious contemporaries were not inclined to cover the entrepreneur with glory. The upper classes were reluctant to grant him social recognition because he lacked a pedigree: "a great *mill-monger*," writes one disdainful contemporary, "is newly created a knight, though he was not born a gentleman."[30] Upon his death Arkwright received scant praise, attention being centered upon his crude manner; his detractor conceded his practical usefulness but would not acknowledge his greatness.[31]

Carlyle was as warm in his praise for James Watt as he was for Arkwright. While the gods were at play, Prometheus-Vulcan was at work:

Neither had Watt of the Steamengine a heroic origin, any kindred

with the princes of this world . . . [who] were shooting their par-
tridges; noisily, in Parliament or elsewhere, solving the question, Head
or tail? while this man with blackened fingers, with grim brow, was
searching out, in his workshop, the Fire-secret; or having found it, was
painfully wending to and fro in quest of a "moneyed man," as indispensable man-midwife of the same.[32]

Arrogance, however, rather than praise or sympathy, was the attitude
of the gentry encountered by the inventor of the steam engine. Writing
as a manufacturer in 1787 to a correspondent in France, Watt notes the
hostility of the upper orders toward his class: "Our landed gentlemen . . .
reckon us poor mechanics no better than the slaves who cultivate their
vineyards."[33] Another manufacturer echoed Watt when he wrote of the
"gentlemen of landed property" as "the proud and bigoted landowners
[who] look down with contempt on the merchant or manufacturer."[34] T.
Gisborne, author of *Enquiry into the Duties of Men in the Higher and
Middle Classes of Society in Great Britain* (1794), a popular work on
morality, deplored the "aristocratic prejudices and the envious contempt
of neighboring peers and country gentlemen, proud of their rank and
ancient family, who even in these days occasionally disgrace themselves
by looking down on the man raised by merit and industry from obscurity
to eminence."[35]

In Manchester, the scorn with which the aristocracy met the aspirations
of the manufacturing class was returned in equal measure in the poem-
epistles of the Manchester clergyman, Thomas Bancroft, writing to a
friend at Cambridge in 1777. In praise of Manchester manufacturers who
were looked upon as "servants" Bancroft wrote:

Such are England's true patriots, her prop and her pride;
They draw wealth from each state while its wants are supply'd;
To mankind all at large they are factors and friends,
And their praise with their wares reach the world's farthest ends. . . .
Is it then, ye vain lordlings! ye treat us with scorn,
Because titles and birth your own fortunes adorn?

What worth to yourselves from high birth can accrue?
Are your ancestors' glories entailed upon you?
And is your lazy pomp of much use to a nation?
Are not parks and wide lawns a refined devastation?
But peace—'tis presumption,—too much would demean 'em
To hold converse with upstarts, a *vulgus profanem.*
Their blood in pure currents thro' ages conveyed
It were impious to taint with the contact of trade.[36]

The antagonism between hereditary wealth and the new industrial affluence cannot be dismissed on the superficial grounds that the new class was composed of rough, coarse upstarts who would not pass as gentlemen in an old aristocratic society. The issue involved more than an absence of pedigree. The resentment underlying the attitude of the aristocracy toward the new class of industrialists is perhaps partly explained by Emerson in his discussion of Napoleon as symbol of the spirit of commerce and industrial enterprise:

> I call Napoleon the agent or attorney of the middle class of modern society; of the throng who fill the markets, shops, countinghouses, manufactories, ships, of the modern world, aiming to be rich. He was the agitator, the destroyer of prescription, the internal improver, the liberal, the radical, the inventor of means, the opener of doors and markets, the subverter of monopoly and abuse. Of course, the rich and the aristocratic did not like him.[37]

If the old order did not consider industrial achievement as meriting notice, the manufacturing classes might have been moved to seek social prestige by working for a seat on the as yet unreformed Parliament. Many an Englishman thought of such service as highly praiseworthy. Yet the early industrialists were largely indifferent to politics even if the opportunity were open to them. "It was not by the arts of lobbying or propaganda," observes T. S. Ashton, "but by unremitting attention to their own concerns and their specialized trade organizations, that, after the end of our period [1830], they became a power—perhaps the greatest power—in the State."[38]

"The discovery of the steam-engine," wrote J. A. Froude in his biography of Disraeli, "had revolutionized the relations of mankind. . . ."[39] With the coming of the factory system a new class of potential leaders of English society came into existence. In this chapter which was intended to assess the newness of this class, we have attempted to demonstrate that, whether or not they were the old yeomanry transformed, the captains of industry stood in a new relation to both the upper and lower orders of English society after the successful application of mechanical invention to machine production had changed their workshops into factories. Despite their affluence, the old order was reluctant to extend social recognition to the "great yeomen of the Yarn," "the lords of the Loom," as Cobbett derisively addressed them, and the "iron gentlemen."[40] With this historical background in mind, we shall, in the next chapter, examine the characterization of the early industrialist in fiction.

TWO

The Early
Industrialists
in Fiction

"Well, well, 'duke'," cried the Sheriff, "you will
find it no easy matter to make a gentleman of him.
The old proverb says, 'that it takes three generations to make a gentleman.' "

Cooper, *The Pioneers*

T. S. ASHTON'S OBSERVATION THAT INDUSTRI-
alists came from every social class is somewhat misleading, for it does not
take into account the statistical matter of frequency.[1] Ashton's method
for arriving at this conclusion is to cite remarkable individuals. For every
Duke of Bridegwater, however, and every outstanding barber, innkeeper,
or school teacher, there were many ordinary men who had risen from the
ranks of the yeomanry, the petty manufacturers, the operatives, and the
merchant manufacturers. Although, as we have seen, the early industrialists who were successful shared certain qualities which enabled them to
survive in the highly demanding business of industrial enterprise, their
various social backgrounds redeemed them as individual social types. By
the time, generations later, that the novelist treated the first generation of
manufacturers in fiction, they had become stereotypes. As such, the novel
reading public's expectations were fulfilled by characters conceived according to simple and popular but fundamentally correct notions that
had become traditionally associated with the early industrialists.

What were some of these crystallizations that a reader would find readily
recognizable? For an answer to this question, we must consider four representative types of early manufacturers—the yeoman, the Puritan, the
parvenu, and the self-made man—as they appear in historical novels.[2] As

a starting point for the study of the aristocratization of the industrialist in fiction, an examination of these four types is intended to demonstrate that their social origins and the circumstances of their accession to wealth give them an identity distinct from that of the "aristocracy of lineage, land, and learning."[3] As a consequence, the first generation of industrialists is not oriented toward the aristocratic way of life, but tends to adhere to its own sphere of interests.

Before proceeding with an analysis of early types as viewed by novelists writing long after the period of their initial historical emergence, it is necessary to account for the anomalous position of John Galt, an early chronicler of the social changes brought on by the Industrial Revolution and almost a contemporary of the first generation of industrialists. Galt's work brings up a literary problem that cannot be ignored in a study of the representation of a new class in fiction: how does a writer who works in an established tradition of character delineation accommodate a new social type into the world of his fiction? The following discussion of Galt will attempt to answer that question and at the same time account for Galt's isolation from the majority of industrial novelists.

I

Annals of the Parish

As a novel dealing with industrial history, Galt's Annals of the Parish (1821) is unique for reasons of its genre, its date of composition, its method of portraying an early industrialist, and lastly its account of his social origins.

With respect to genre, there are two factors to consider: for one, the problematical status of the Annals as a novel, and for another, its place in the tradition of works of its kind. In spite of being conceived as "a kind of treatise on the history of society in the West of Scotland during the reign of King George the Third," the Annals was received as a novel.[4] Galt himself considered it at most a fable of progress and expressed his surprise at the judgment of the public. According to its author, the Annals is not a novel or romance but a "theoretical history" without a plot, "for the only link of cohesion which joins the incidents together, is the mere remembrance of the supposed author and nothing makes the work complete within itself but the biographical recurrence upon the scene of the same individuals."[5] Sir Walter Scott was one of the readers who considered Galt's work a novel, though with some resesrvation. In a letter to Joanna Baillie written in 1821, Scott added the following postscript: "Pray read, or have read to you . . . the Annals of the Parish. Mr. Galt wrote the worst tragedies ever seen, and has now written a most excellent novel, if it can be called so."[6] A modern interpreter, Lionel Stevenson, has synthesized the elements of social history and the novel in the *Annals* by calling the work "the first English novel that takes a whole community as its subject rather than an individual or a single family."[7]

Despite Galt's emphasis upon social history, the *Annals* remains the most literary of the novels dealing with industrialists because Galt followed an established literary tradition easily recognized by his contemporaries. Revealing the source of his inspiration, Galt wrote: "When very young, I wished to write a book that would be for Scotland what the Vicar of Wakefield is for England, and early began to observe and conjecture in what respects the minister of a rural parish differed from the general inhabitants of the country."[8] To one reviewer the *Annals* suggested not only Goldsmith's work, but also *The Memoir of P. P. Parish Clerk*, Pope's and Arbuthnot's parody of Burnet's *History of My Own Time*.[9] Francis Jeffrey noted in the *Annals* traces of "the humorous and less dignified parts of [Scott]" and suggestions of Sir Roger De Coverley and Sterne's Uncle Toby.[10] Unlike many of the later writers of industrial novels and their reviewers, John Galt and his critics were largely interested in the literary associations of the *Annals*. When the industrial novel came forward in the early 1830s, it was polemical; and writers and reviewers both were more concerned with the moral issue of an employer's social responsibility than the literary aspects of a work.[11]

Galt's era, however, was free of that kind of social and economic controversy in fiction, and this is the point of our second reason for calling the *Annals* a unique work; namely, the early date of its composition. As we have seen, Galt (1779-1839) from early youth had planned to write a register of a village. The projected work, however, was postponed until 1813. When nearly completed it was sent to the bookseller Constable, who told Galt that Scottish novels would not succeed. After Scott established a vogue for Scottish novels with *Waverley* (1814), Galt subsequently published the *Annals* in 1821.[12] The early conception and composition of this work is significant. If the work can be said to have been outlined in Galt's mind about the year 1800, or even earlier, the *Annals* would then antedate by at least a generation the social and economic controversy which introduced the industrialist into English fiction. Since industrialists were coming forward in the 1790s, becoming rich during the wartime boom, Galt was virtually their contemporary. What is most important for our purposes is that the question of whether the new class and its source of economic power, the factory system, were a blessing or a curse had not reached in fiction, or in actuality for that matter, the stature of a social problem. As a result, Mr. Cayenne,

Galt's cotton lord, exists in the golden age of manufacturing, a time in which he does not meet with the kind of resistance that was to come a generation later from both the working classes and the landed interest. In the heyday of Cayenne, workmen's efforts to organize were prohibited by a wartime government which regarded combinations as a form of conspiracy. And, moreover, an enterprising industrialist could make a fortune importing grain, a move not so easy to make after the landed interest instituted the Corn Laws of 1815.

Since the age did not demand that the novelist account for the virtues or failings of the new class, it is not unnatural that Galt's method of portraying the industrialist according to eighteenth century conventions was still viable. Mr. Cayenne is a combination of the choleric humor character and the man of benevolence. As such, he has an affinity to that well-known figure in the eighteenth-century novel, the country squire. For irascibility, he is a match for Squire Western; but for magnanimity, he is the equal of Squire Allworthy and to a lesser extent, Smollett's Matthew Bramble.

Examples of the effects of Cayenne's ungovernable temper are numerous.[13] But one incident, wherein irascibility leads to blasphemy, strikingly displays Galt's conception of this early industrialist as a choleric character. During the year 1793, the Reverend Balwhidder records that two "democratic" weavers were brought on a suspicion of high treason before Cayenne, newly appointed as justice of the peace:

> [Cayenne] began to ask them how they dared think of dividing, with their liberty and equality of principles, his and every other man's property in the country. The men . . . told him they sought no man's property, but only their own natural rights: upon which he called them traitors and reformers. They denied they were traitors, but confessed they were reformers, and said they knew not how that should be imputed to them as a fault, for that the greatest men of all times had been reformers.
> "Was not," they said, "our Lord Jesus Christ a reformer?"—"And what the devil did he make of it?" cried Mr. Cayenne, bursting with passion. "Was he not crucified?"[14]

Although Balwhidder could not consider Cayenne a Christian after such an utterance, the minister acknowledged him as a benefactor to the parish by virtue of his timely purchase of wheat in expectation of a bad crop, and his aid to Irish refugees. Mixing benevolence with business, Cayenne bought all the wheat he could from America and the Baltic countries. The harvest fell short as anticipated and Cayenne made a great deal of money. His honesty and patriotism prevented him from making even more by buying up some of the home crop. "In short," records Balwhidder, "we all reckoned him another Joseph when he opened his garnels at the cotton-mill, and, after distributing a liberal portion to the poor and needy, sold the remainder at an easy rate to the generality of the people."[15] In the same year, 1798, Cayenne performed another act of benevolence, this time without mixed motives. During that year many Irish refugees of rebellion came to Scotland. Cayenne, remembering his own experience in America, succored these people. Although some had rebel sympathies, that fact was of no consequence to Cayenne. The Scottish lairds were puzzled by this apparent turn of mind, for Cayenne was known as the most strict government-man in the countryside. But Cayenne's political principles applied to the "camp and council" only. "To the hospital and the prison," said he, "I take those of a man."[16] Cayenne's choleric temper and his magnanimity come together in an incident in which he strikes and dismisses Trowel, a builder, after a disagreement over building plans, generously recompenses him for the injury, and later employs him again to build his house.[17]

If, because his portrayal belongs to an established mode of characterization, Galt's Cayenne is unlike other industrialists in this study, his social origin, when considered in the light of the background of historical figures, is no less unusual. Cayenne is an American loyalist, exiled to Scotland after being dispossessed of his Virginia plantation by American revolutionaries. He is thus all the while a member of the landed gentry, a factor which accounts for his Tory, government-man sympathies.

In summing up the uniqueness of Galt's industrialist, it is evident that a combination of factors is at work. Galt wrote the *Annals* during a historical period when the economic assumptions of the new class of industrialists were as yet unchallenged by novelists. Moreover, he was consciously following the literary conventions of the eighteenth century. As a consequence, he has created a rare type of early manufacturer who is indistinguishable from the country squire of both literary and historical tradition.

II

Scarsdale: Life on the Lancashire and Yorkshire Border Thirty Years Ago

The four types of manufacturer who are the primary subject of this chapter conform more to historical expectations than does Galt's unique creation. The first of these is the quasi-mythical yeoman-turned-manufacturer who appears in Sir James Kay-Shuttleworth's novel, *Scarsdale: Life on the Lancashire and Yorkshire Border Thirty Years Ago* (1860).

Since Kay-Shuttleworth was an eminent Victorian by virtue of his non-literary accomplishments, and what Gordon N. Ray would term only an "occasional novelist,"[18] a review of his background and life's work might explain in part his qualifications for writing a historical novel depicting members of the new class.

James Phillips Kay (1804-77), who took the additional surname Shuttleworth upon his marriage in 1842, was a member of the old Lancashire family of Kay and the son of a cotton manufacturer.[19] After qualifying as a physician in 1827, he went to Manchester to work in a dispensary and also to study the effects of the inhalation of cotton fluff, an occupational hazard of textile workers. Out of this experience came a widely read pamphlet, *The Moral and Physical Condition of the Working Class Employed in the Cotton Manufacture in Manchester* (1832). This was a work which Engels later used as one of the sources for his *Condition of the Working Class in England* (1845) and which was also one of the titles that Lord Shaftesbury recommended to Mrs. Trollope before she visited Manchester to gather material for her factory novel, *Michael Armstrong* (1839-1840).

In his pamphlet Kay-Shuttleworth treated the questions of sanitation and excessive hours of labor, concluding that moral and physical evils must be dealt with as one. Among the causes of social unrest were the increased living costs brought about by the Corn Laws and bad fiscal legislation. Moreover, the working classes, without schools, were ignorant and barbaric. In 1833 he helped found the Manchester Statistical Society, whose aim was to study social problems more methodically. Leaving Manchester in 1835, he became an Assistant Poor Law Commissioner. In 1839 he was made the first state official for English elementary education and devoted the rest of his life to creating a national, public-supported system of education which did not materialize until the Education Act of 1870.[20] It is for this last public service that he is best remembered, his efforts having earned him the esteem of Matthew Arnold, who paid him the following tribute: "When at last the system of that education comes to stand full and fairly formed, Kay-Shuttleworth will have a statue."[21]

Having such a busy career as a public man, Kay-Shuttleworth, as his son attests, wrote novels as a form of recreation.[22] That he was singularly well equipped to reconstruct a bygone era in *Scarsdale* is evidenced by his faculty of total recall and the testimony of Mrs. Elizabeth Gaskell. His biographer records examples of his ability to remember in detail people and incidents of his childhood. Of his early acquaintance with the industrial regions, Kay-Shuttleworth has written: "I had, from my early youth been familiar with the rapid growth of the handloom-weaving hamlets, the manufacturing villages and towns of the cotton districts."[23] In connection with *Scarsdale*, Mrs. Gaskell describes Kay-Shuttleworth in a letter written to the publisher, George Smith, in 1860: "He is a clever, painstaking man, and has really laboured hard to make this novel a good picture of Lancashire country society. . . ."[24]

Though not primarily a man of letters, Kay-Shuttleworth was not without literary relations; and it is through his friendships with writers that the literary aspirations of the man come to light. Among the people he sought to cultivate were Mrs. Gaskell and Charlotte Brontë, who were brought together for the first time in 1850 at Kay-Shuttleworth's home. Following Charlotte Brontë's death in 1855, Mrs. Gaskell went with Kay-Shuttleworth to Haworth in order to obtain material for her biography. Mr. Nicholls, Charlotte's husband, was reluctant to have her portrait photographed and to have *The Professor* published. Kay-Shuttleworth, however, believed that he deserved a voice in the matter of handling Charlotte Brontë's literary effects because he had helped her begin her literary career. His aim was to edit and publish *The Professor*. His preemptory manner toward Mr. Brontë and Mr. Nicholls lost him the respect of his fellow visitor, Mrs. Gaskell, who recorded the incident in a letter to George Smith, noting that Kay-Shuttleworth "over-rides all wishes, feelings, and delicacy."[25] With respect to his literary aspirations, Charlotte Brontë in her assessment of the balance of his utilitarian and artistic qualities, has left a picture of Kay-Shuttleworth as the artist manqué:

> Nine points out of ten in him are utilitarian—the tenth is artistic. This tithe of his nature seems to me at war with the rest—it is just enough to incline him restlessly towards the artist class, and far too little to make him one of them. The consequent inability to do things which he admires, embitters him, I think—it makes him doubt perfections and dwell on faults.[26]

Kay-Shuttleworth's *Scarsdale* is an expression of that artistic "tithe" that Charlotte Brontë saw. As Galt's *Annals* was a novel whose subject was a parish, so *Scarsdale* treats early nineteenth-century Lancashire. In addition to portraits of the machine-breaking weaver, the manufacturer, and the aristocrat, the novel contains digressions on old superstitions and customs, topography and dialect. Nor is the state of society and its future slighted. Unlike Galt's *Annals*, however, *Scarsdale* has a thread of plot. Distressed weavers attempt to destroy a mill. They are checked by the force of Sir Guy Scarsdale, and later pacified by both the evangelicalism of the "Methodee" weaver, Barnabas, and by the free trade panacea proposed by Oliver Holte, the manufacturer's son. Only a poacher and a

psychopath, hardly the usual "outside agitators" found in other industrial novels, fail to be converted. The rest of the plot concerns the devious
attempts of the deranged Ascroft to gain entrance through secret passages
into Scarsdale Hall in order to assassinate Sir Guy.

In *Scarsdale*, it is Mr. Holte who is represented as the yeoman-turned-
manufacturer, his family being described as "the link between the old
yeomanry of the county with their not infrequent puritan faith, and the
classes growing into wealth and power by manufacturing enterprise."[27]
Mr. Holte remains distinct from the aristocratic Scarsdales because of his
humble yeoman origin, his subordinate position as part-time steward of
the Scarsdale estate, his thrift, his religion, and stemming from the latter
his lack of a feeling of social responsibility. Moreover, the disparity is mag-
nified by the author's manipulation of literary convention, the effect of
which is to keep the manufacturing class at a further distance.

It is evident that to Kay-Shuttleworth the early manufacturers were not
the social equals of the Scarsdales who dominate this novel. When Sir Guy
Scarsdale seeks to create a relief fund for unemployed weavers, he invites
only a few of the "highest and most intellectual" manufacturers to dine
with him in order to discuss contributions. Even at that, he is patronizing
toward them and is implicitly apologetic to his aristocratic houseguests
from France for their presence. Sir Guy avoids the general run of manufacturers who are "men risen from the ranks, illiterate, of a coarse mold, con-
tracted ideas, and selfish habits" (3:47).[28] Their progenitors, we are told,
"had been either small yeomen, or tenant farmers, with a few looms at
work in their homesteads; or even industrious, thrifty, handloom weavers,
who had gradually increased the number of journeymen in their *loom-
shops*" (3:127). The Holtes, however, were among the "highest and
most intellectual" of their kind and "had risen to opulence from the condition of humble yeomen, under the sheltering wing of the Scarsdale
house" (1:36).

As representatives of the new class at a stage between the yeoman and
the more modern millowner, in this case semi-independent of the landed
interest, the Holtes are portrayed as protégés of the aristocracy. On the
occasion of Sir Guy's homecoming, Kay-Shuttleworth outlines Mr. Holte's
status as a dependent and exhibits his deference to his social superior. As
the squire of Scarsdale Manor approached with his daughter Mabel, and
the Holte's son Oliver, who has been serving as physician to Sir Guy,

> There was an increase of bustle in the hall. The family thus returning
> to their ancestral home were to be received with due honour. For, even
> in those parts of England in which a new society has been created by
> the growth of manufacturing enterprise and wealth, the traditions of

families who have held their estates since the Conquest, or since the
Wars of the Roses, still shed a halo round their name, and attract a
homage which is paid to the representative of whatever flatters the
national feeling, that our Constitution has solved the difficult problem
of reconciling progress with stability. Therefore Mr. Holte, the principal
tenant of the estate, in whose charge the hall, the home farm, and the
management of the estate had been left, and who was, moreover, one
of the chief manufacturers of the district, assembled his family from
the distant wing inhabited by them, and stood in the great entrance
hall, with his servants in the background. When the coach drew up at
the porch of the courtyard, Mr. Holte advanced with a quiet confidence,
but with marked deference, and without hurry, waited till the family
party emerged from the carriage. He met them in the entrance, bowing respectfully. Behind, his wife, Mistress Hannah, also stood and
curtsied. (1:18-19)

Sir Guy, fulfilling the traditional role of the aristocrat as military man,
has like Chaucer's knight spent a number of years soldiering on the continent "in the wars of the revolution" (1:145). In his absence Mr. Holte
has been profitably supervising both the work of the landowner's plow
and his own looms. Wealth, however, has not altered the simple life of
the Holtes. Their "cautious, thoughtful, and provident career had been
crowned with much wealth; but both Mr. and Mrs. Holte preserved habits
of yeomanlike simplicity, and were as diligent and punctual in the daily
business of life as when their fortunes were humble" (1:146). In the face
of their numerous duties—Mrs. Holte's responsibility for the dairy and the
farm servants and Mr. Holte's task of cultivating the home farm, conduct-
ing his manufacturing enterprise, and caring for the Scarsdale forest and
estate—the couple continued to live in the manner of a latter day Baucis
and Philemon, deriving their pleasures from "the common incidents of
daily life, the successes of their honest endeavours" (1:146).

In addition to the qualities of simplicity and attention to duty, the
Holtes exhibit traits that are at odds with traditions that were a matter of
course on country estates:

One thing which jarred painfully on the thrift of Mistress Hannah,
and brought her often into collision with the old and privileged servants
of the hall, left in charge of hounds, game and horses, in the absence of
Sir Guy, was their wasteful outlay on such profitless objects. Her
vigilance restrained such expenses within the limits of absolute necessity while the family were absent, but on their return the reign of
prodigality was restored by the daring with which the demands of these
dependents were reiterated with significant hints of an appeal to the
squire. Knowing how generous Sir Guy was to all who had won his

confidence, Mistress Hannah evaded such an appeal as far as possible, and preferred a petty warfare against what she deemed abuses—an effort which fretted her life with constant skirmishes. (1:146-47)

Sir Guy's arrival is timely: unemployed handloom weavers are bent upon destroying the machines in Mr. Holte's mill. This incident brings out another of Holte's traits that differentiates him from the squire of the manor. When Sir Guy asks him what he has done in the way of preparation for the defense of the mill, the manufacturer answers: "Nothing as yet. We are men of peace. You know, Sir Guy, we are little disposed to resort to the arm of the flesh. Our times are in the lord's hands, and we could ill answer our own consciences if blood were shed" (1:27). By emphasizing Holte's scruples, Kay-Shuttleworth is able to exhibit the functions of the landed interest as the bulwark for safeguarding property and the preserver of law and order, the role assigned (together with the responsibility for the protection of the poor) to the knight by Langland, when his knight asks Piers Plowman if he may be of assistance to him. (B Text, Passus 6:11, 24ff.) Sir Guy knows his duty:

> Tush, tush, my friend—that doctrine comparts little with my duties as a magistrate, or my habits as a soldier; and I must see . . . what means of defence I have for your mill in the clough—and for our neighbours. We seem to have come in the nick of time to show you what sort of training your son has had; in our wanderings over Spanish Sierras, and African Deserts, and ouadis, I have done all I could to make him a man in the style of David, rather than one of your modern puritans; the men of the Commonwealth had fighting blood in them. (1:27-28)[29]

Sir Guy organizes the defense of the mill with brisk efficiency, but he demonstrates that superior power is not inconsistent with kindness (an attitude that G. K. Chesterton affirms is "the one thing that England as England has to say"[30]): "Order must be restored . . . the violence of despair, though it spring from want, must be restrained. This must be done as gently as may be . . . the arm that is swift to rebuke can also be merciful, not to say beneficent" (1:32). To his daughter Mabel's ascription of cowardice to Holte for shrinking from violence, Sir Guy explains, "You will discover a very strong leaven of the non-resistance doctrine even among the old puritans of this county" (1:33).

In portraying the relationship of aristocrat and manufacturer to the lower orders, Kay-Shuttleworth suggests that it was the landed gentry with their sense of duty toward inferiors who sought to make the transition from hand to power loom easier. Implied in the author's depiction of Sir Guy as the primum mobile in relieving unemployed weavers is that the manufacturer was not concerned about the fate of those who stood in the way of material progress:

> Mr. Holte had substituted the power-loom for hand weaving in his manufacturing arrangements, but as soon as Sir Guy found the condition of the cottage weavers on his estate, he had requested Mr. Holte [in his capacity as Sir Guy's steward] to supply about fifty cottagers, scattered over the property, with constant work, as Sir Guy's own private enterprise until trade should revive, or other plans could be formed. (2:256)

If the gulf between the older generations of plebeian manufacturer and patrician landowner can be explained on historical grounds, the separation between the son of the former and the daughter of the latter might be accounted for by the author's manipulation of literary convention. In the first volume of *Scarsdale*, we are led to believe that Kay-Shuttleworth will make the symbolic gesture of uniting the younger generation of the two classes, Sir Guy's daughter Mabel with Oliver Holte. The genteel grooming and chivalry of the manufacturer's son make him an eligible young man, but he is not destined to marry Mabel because the predominantly aristocratic traditions in the novel take precedence over the conventions of classless romantic love.

Oliver Holte, as has been mentioned before, has served as Sir Guy's personal physician, secretary, and companion in travel during his Continental military exploits. He has acted the part of squire to the knight, and we are told that "the constant friction of rank with rank in English life educates and refines" (1:136). This process, then, accounts for "the chivalrous daring of Oliver, his delicacy of feeling, his accomplishments, and high principles of action," and these qualities are not, as Mabel had unknowingly assumed, "a rare result of his early training" at home (1:136). Acquired from his association with Sir Guy, these genteel characteristics qualify Oliver for the hand of Mabel. Oliver, moreover, has found himself, not once but twice, in an archetypal situation that usually leads to marriage in novels—the position of having rescued Mabel from mortal peril, once from the hands of Spanish brigands, and once from the indiscriminate fury of a mob of machine breakers. Desiring to reward Oliver for his personal services and for rescuing his daughter, Sir Guy proposes to help Oliver set up as a manufacturer on his own; but Oliver does not wish to be elevated, insisting as a consequence of hastily introduced religious convictions, upon going away to Manchester as a medical missionary. When Mabel asks Mrs. Holte about the temptation to a higher sphere that Oliver fears, Mrs. Holte answers, "He says he fears a worldly ambition, or an unrighteous and selfish presumption" (3:243). Turning a third opportunity of saving Mabel (this time an attack of typhus) over to another physician lest he find himself presuming to make his declaration of love, Oliver departs for Manchester.

It is not surprising that a novel dominated by an aristocratic family should contain elements of those two arch-aristocratic literary traditions, the silver-fork novel with its sprinkling of French dialogue (3:185) and the Gothic novel with its standard prop, the castle honeycombed with secret passages. The presence of these two traditions gives rise to the expectation that a high born heroine will adhere to class lines and not marry below her station. Though not without an initial conflict with others, these expectations are fulfilled: a Lord Pendleborough is introduced in the middle of the novel, and at the end Mabel becomes the Countess of Pendleborough.

Judging from the roles assigned to the principal characters in Scarsdale, one surmises that the aristocracy is portrayed as a class that the early captains of industry would have done well to emulate, in order to preserve for a nascent industrial society the best that had gone before. England's role as an industrial power depended on the manufacturing classes, but the landed gentry still had an important function. Sir Guy was not merely a policeman who defended the property of the existing order, but as a representative of the finest in the aristocratic tradition his actions served as an object lesson to the industrialist. He was bound by his sense of social responsibility, by the duties and obligations of the upper ranks to the lower, to provide for the wants of his cottagers at the time when domestic industry was rendered obsolescent. The spirit that pervades Scarsdale in the idealized figure of Sir Guy is a tribute to what should have been, as the new class of industrialists, in this case, left the "small, old stone mansions" of the yeomanry to engage in manufacturing.

III

Ribblesdale or Lancashire Sixty Years Ago

In Chapter One we have noted the existence of a body of historical opinion viewing the new class of industrialists as descendants of the disappearing yeomanry. We have, moreover, seen this opinion reflected in the novel, Scarsdale. In a second novel, Ribblesdale or Lancashire Sixty Years Ago (1874), Kay-Shuttleworth portrays another representative type of early manufacturer, the Puritan, some qualities of whom have been seen in the characterization of Mr. Holte in Scarsdale.[31]

By way of introduction to Ribblesdale, it is appropriate to account for the Puritan manufacturer as a type of Lancashire industrialist by examining the assumptions which underlie the relationship of "godly Geneva and industrious Manchester."[32] In Charles Kingsley's novel, *Yeast* (1848), Lancelot Smith, a young gentleman given to raising questions about the status quo (which in one instance earn him the label of "communist") vociferates over Stock Exchange activities and railway manias, calling them part of the "frantic Mammon-hunting which has been for the last fifty years the peculiar pursuit of the majority of Quakers, Dissenters, and Religious Churchmen." In the next breath, however, Lancelot vindicates their worldliness, stating that the tenets of their religion have left Nonconformists with little else to do in this world: "I don't complain of them, though; Puritanism has interdicted to them all art, all excitement, all amusement—except money making; It is their *dernier ressort*, poor souls!"[33]

It remained, however, for twentieth-century scholars to prove Kingsley's generalization. In *Die Protestantische Ethik und der Geist des Kapitalismus* (1904), Max Weber made a celebrated attempt to link Calvinism and Capitalism. Montesquieu, he noted, had observed that the English "had progressed furthest of all people in three important things: piety, commerce, and freedom." The debt of freedom to piety had been recognized, but Weber posed the question of whether commerce might also have been in debt to piety. He affirmed a connection between the two through the agency of the religious movement of Calvinism.[34] The circumstances which led to Tawney's work in the same area of study are out of place here, but some of his conclusions will serve to outline the link between Puritanism and Capitalism.

Unlike its predecessor, medieval Christianity, Calvinism did not regard economic motives as incompatible with spiritual endeavor, nor did it regard the capitalist as one who grew rich solely at the expense of his neighbors. Instead, Calvinism was perhaps the first religious system to acknowledge and accommodate the economic virtues. Provided that he not be extortionate, the money lender, that pariah of the medieval English community, was useful to a society that had seen new commercial possibilities following the age of discovery. The enemy of Calvinism was "not the accumulation of riches, but their misuse for purposes of self-indulgence or ostentation. Its ideal [was] a society which seeks wealth with the sober gravity of men who are conscious at once of disciplining their own characters by patient labor, and of devoting themselves to a service acceptable to God."[35] Viewed in these terms, "the good Christian was not wholly dissimilar from the economic man,"[36] the gospel of the Puritan divine Richard Baxter, not unlike the gospel of Samuel Smiles. Thus the seventeenth-century Puritan ideal of economic man anticipates the "new type of economic character" that accompanied economic reorganization after 1760.[37] This later stage of Lancashire Puritanism, "an almost Utilitarian individualism,"[38] is described by Louis Cazamian as obtaining in the early nineteenth century. Cazamian, whose work, *Le Roman Social en Angleterre: 1830-1850*, still remains the major study of the early Victorian social problem novel, deserves to be quoted in full (my translation):

> Puritanism was concentrated among the manufacturing population of the North. Until the day when they, because of their riches, aspired to social elegance and the Established Church, employers remained faithful to the austere worship of the dissident sects. At the time of the Oxford Movement . . . the stronghold of a religion that was sober and introspective was the factory. By a natural affinity in harmony with a rigid will, a grasping energy, and a strongly hardened character, this belief sustained the strict and harsh individualism of the industrial bourgeoisie with a divine nourishment. Strengthened by his intimate contact with God, by his severe and narrow-minded morality, basing his robust instinct of personal property upon the Decalogue ["Thou shalt not covet thy neighbor's goods."], the millowner was able to reconcile with his conscience the merciless pursuit of gain. Closed to all perception without utility, braced against all dangerous emotion, he proceeded without hearing or perceiving the appeals or the mute entreaties which men and the state of things addressed to his heart. It is an absence of sympathy, a radical lack of feeling, which alone explains the hostility of these natures, in other respects so upright, toward the first efforts at legislative intervention.[39]

The image of the Puritan as economic man that Kingsley, Tawney, and Cazamian project is considerably toned down in Kay-Shuttleworth's *Ribblesdale*. This, for the most part, is due to the love story element and the use of a romantic heroine as the representative of the Puritan point of view. Before considering the effect of the author's choice of story line upon the kind of Puritanism that figures forth, it might be well to examine the characteristics that made the Puritan successful in business and in war, traits found in a minor character, the heroine's cousin and rejected suitor, Robert Hindle. Having come from a race of Puritan yeomen who had owned farms for several generations, Robert was at the time of the story engaged in the manufacture of textiles. During the years he attended the local school, he showed himself dogged in effort and tenacious of purpose in his unsuccessful attempts to outdo, in competition for scholarly prizes, the representative of the local aristocracy and hero of the novel, Rufus Noel.[40] School days over, Robert Hindle now found himself competing with Rufus Noel for the hand of his cousin Alice. Robert's ruminations over this new challenge to try his capacities against the aristocratic race of the Noels echo the struggle of Roundhead against Cavalier, though couched in the rhetoric of the aspiring lover and the metaphor of genetics. In the course of his monologue, Robert asks himself,

> Was there anything in [the Noel's] blood, like that of the horse or hound, which gave them the force of a higher and purer breeding? Or could their force—whatever it were—be combatted by a Saxon strength of will, and powers of enduring the exhaustion of constant application? He would test to the utmost the relative strength of the two capacities. He had a consciousness that he was possessed of a somewhat coarser nature. His perceptions were less quick—his sensibility less keen—his facility for action far less active and rapid. There were subtle powers possessed by Rufus with which his ruder intellect was not endowed. But might art, the latent force of mass, impelled by an indomitable will contend with these qualities? His notions were summed up in the comparison familiar to the borders of Yorkshire and Lancashire. "Over heavy ground, in a long race, strength may beat breed—bone and muscle may run against blood. (1:121)

But the singlemindedness and doggedness that have made Robert a successful manufacturer are at a discount in a love story. His cousin Alice is repelled by his aggressiveness, and after being rejected, he drops out of the mainstream of the story through the necessity of going to Australia in order to acquire a new source of raw materials. One is reminded of the aversion that Isabel Archer, a much more sophisticated heroine than Alice Hindle, feels toward Caspar Goodwood whose business virtue of aggressiveness, though restrained in comparison with Robert Hindle's, stands him in no good stead. It is evident that, by his disposal of Robert Hindle, Kay-Shuttleworth has little interest in the economic virtues of the successful Puritan manufacturer.

In the preface to *Ribblesdale*, Kay-Shuttleworth, drawing upon his knowledge of the homes of Puritan manufacturers of sixty years before, states his intention of depicting the rivalry between the new class of independent industrialists and the old aristocratic families of Lancashire at the turn of the century (1:vii). Contrary to what one might expect, the rivalry is not a matter of parvenus vying with peers, but a drama of conflicting class temperaments. Kay-Shuttleworth's principal concern is with the problem of whether Alice Hindle, daughter of a Puritan manufacturer, brought up in the Calvinistic faith and having conceived of her duty to consist of undertaking works of piety and charity among the humble, can reconcile her mode of life with that of Rufus Noel, an aristocrat who believes that it is his duty to himself and his family to pursue a worldly ambition, guiding the destinies of nations in diplomatic circles.

Ribblesdale may be called a novel of character because its principal action consists of the inner conflict of values in the minds of hero and heroine regarding the possibility of compromising their natures and bridging the psychological gap which divides their classes. By observing the stated basis for the separation of classes, by examining the psychological disposition of Alice, and by tracing the process of self-scrutiny that Rufus and Alice undergo before they marry, it is possible to understand the significance of the Dissenter's religion as a factor dissuading the early industrialists from aspiring to the condition of the landed gentry, regardless of the reluctance of the old order to consider them as social equals. Not only in its early years but also throughout most of the nineteenth century, one of the greatest obstacles to the assimilation of the industrialists of the North was their Nonconformist religious persuasion.

In one volume of *Ribblesdale*, Kay-Shuttleworth compares class relations at the time of the writing of the novel with the state of affairs prevailing sixty years before, the time when the story takes place. The following interjection of social history, tending to emphasize the aristocratic viewpoint, explains the bases for class antipathy as the pride of race, the disdain for industrial economic independence, and an aversion to industrial Nonconformity:

> The man of landed estate was entrenched in pride and prejudice. He was himself often much less enlightened than those of his own class now are. He was unwilling to yield anything of the prestige of his caste. He arrogated to his class the administration of rural justice, the representation of the county and most of its boroughs in Parliament, and the distribution of all county patronage. Any marriage between the hereditary landed gentry and the classes enriched by trade was certain to be followed by the exclusion of the degraded person from the privileged circles of the county aristocracy. The trading classes were in every sense humbler than they now are, less wealthy, less intelligent, less influential. They had not emancipated themselves from the domination of the landlords, who had been accustomed to govern all below them. In the olden times, when the yeoman and clothier accepted their inferior position, they were treated with the bluff, hearty goodwill which a generous superior shows to a loyal dependent [cf. *Scarsdale*]. But when the trading classes became first independent, then more or less rivals, and then antagonistic, a new form of separation occurred, which was at its height about the beginning of this century. (2:40-41)

In addition to economic and social rivalry, religion confirmed class divisions:

> If to these distinctions were added Puritanic nonconformity, either in the form of Presbyterianism or Independency, the causes of repugnancy were complete between a family of humble origin engaged in

trade, and one like that of Sir Hubert Noel, proud of its long line of ancestry, enriched by ample landed property, and allied immediately with the peerage. Even the growth of the wealth of such a family would not then, in one or two generations, render possible a marriage of the heir of the Noels to the daughter of a man whose ancestors had been simple Puritan yeomen and who was himself a dissenting manufacturer. (2:42)

As had been stated earlier, Alice Hindle possesses the characteristics of the romantic heroine. She has a "highly wrought sensibility" and the "highest degree" of beauty of "form, feature, and figure" (1:97, 101). Although inexperienced beyond the pale of family as a result of her "life of religious contemplation and charitable self-devotion," Alice has been trained in several accomplishments suggestive of both the genteel heroine and the devout Puritan: "She sang sacred music with power, she sketched with great skill, she was a good botanist, she was well acquainted with English and Italian literature, above all she was well read in the history of the Reformation, of the religious struggles of the Commonwealth, and in the works of their divines" (1:101-2). Despite Alice's interest in literature, her sensibility, unlike that of many a romantic heroine, is not the product of reading polite literature, but of her religious training:

> that which had displaced the balance of her high-wrought intelligence on the side of imagination and sentiment, was the peculiar form of flesh, and anticipates immortality by purity and prayer. (1:102)
> insight as keen and far-reaching as that of Alice Hindle, revealed the awful claims of an ever-present spiritual world, on which she gazed with the eye of an unshrinking faith. She accepted absolutely the alternative of the future, eternal doom or blessedness. Her spirit strove to realize the spiritual life which, even here, disrobes itself of the garment of flesh, and anticipates immortality by purity and prayer. (1:102)

In the course of realizing her ideal of "purity and prayer," however, Alice avoided what Tawney calls the "shadow" of the lofty teaching of Puritanism: "To urge that the Christian life must be lived in a zealous discharge of private duties—how necessary! Yet how readily perverted to the suggestion that there are no vital social obligations beyond and above them!"[41] Alice, together with her father, a retiring and unworldly manufacturer of woolens, devoted themselves to the sick of the church, the Sunday school and the orphans and widows (1:103). One particular activity of theirs reveals that they were not rigid Calvinists. Once a week they met with itinerant preachers who were pious weavers themselves and provided them with Bibles and religious works to be sold among "a scattered population of weavers as coarse, as unlearned, and as heathenish as the serfs of the Saxon thanes at the time of the Conquest" (2:238). Mr. Hindle supported these preachers and Alice instructed them at these weekly meetings with the result that,

> They were thus led by her from the Judaic view of their message— too common among the Presbyterian and Independent congregations— to a gospel of infinite mercy, hope, and charity to the penitent who had faith to lay hold of its promises by prayer and amendment of life. She instructed them to avoid the rigid schemes in which Calvin and the scholastic divines sought to express in a logical formula of words a plan which they conceived solved the mysteries of the Divine Love, and rather to follow the simplicity of expression of the evangelists. (2:239)

In the absence of Rufus Noel, who is serving his apprenticeship to statecraft as secretary to Lord Castlereagh during the Napoleonic Wars, Alice experiences the world of the courtier in order to see if, as the wife of Rufus, she could function in such an atmosphere. At a fashionable gathering in London, she is shown various personages, among them a bubble company king and his aristocratic sycophants (2:274-75). She discovers both that the way of the fashionable world runs counter to her education and convictions and that she could not discharge the duties of that world (2:299-300). She is convinced that such a society is,

> the Vanity Fair of Bunyan, in which the great realities were forgotten in the maze of bewildering phantasmagoria, or in the excesses of a festival of the senses. Then the great pageant of power, the ceremonial of supreme rank, the luxury of wealth, the "pomp and circumstance" of military force, even the intellectual gladiatorship of Parliament, and intercourse with literary and scientific celebrities, while they astonished her by their novelty, awed her by their revelation of a world vaster and more energetic than that which she ever conceived. . . . She felt wearied and oppressed. . . . (2:302-3)

It would be a mistake, she believed, for her to enter a society of rank, distinction, and fashion: "The punishment for such an error would certainly be personal unhappiness from a want of preparation for new duties, and from a discordance between her own life and that about her" (2:314). Moreover, because of her humble origin and simple duties she could not, in such a position, expect to exert a beneficial influence upon such celebrities and people of rank (2:315). She then resolves to give up all thought of such a life, but her decision is complicated by the discovery that Rufus had not forgotten her in spite of his involvement in affairs of state. Yet the rank of Rufus as an heir to an earldom still remains an obstacle. Alice would prefer him as a country gentleman (2:316-19).

From the day that he rescued her from a crowd of brawlers at a local fair, Rufus Noel, ambitious, proud of his race, and destined for a career "dominating the destinies of empire" (1:181), has remained constant in his love for Alice. But he too has subjected himself to self-questioning over the feasibility of marrying a young woman whose conception of duty is so totally different from his:

> He had certainly, from time to time, reflected whether one bred in the middle-class view of life, as a state of labour and self-control—to whom the pomp of wealth seemed prodigal waste, the pride of race unreal, and the love of power a temptation, and especially one in whom these feelings were strengthened by religion—could fill a station in which ambition would make even its pageantry and splendour instruments of self-aggrandisement, and devote every energy of mind to this first great aim in life. (2:122)

At one point he consults the Vicar for advice. This clergyman outlines to him the difference between a woman of his rank and a woman of the manufacturing classes as choices for a wife:

> The life of a statesman, to be consistent with domestic happiness should be sustained by a wife with a spirit like his own. The women of the aristocratic classes are bred to think their husbands may be long separate from them in extreme perils in their country's service; in command of regiments or ships of war; in winter campaigns, exposed to famine and disease; in the fiercest heats of the tropics; in battles, sieges, or even disastrous retreats. In all, they are taught to endure and to encourage. So, too, they inspire them in the struggles of statesmanship, in Parliament, in the Cabinet, and on distant missions. (3:36-37)

On the other hand, women of Alice Hindle's background are accustomed to a domestic life as normal: "The merchants and manufacturers of this country are singularly home-loving. The day is spent in the work of trade, but the evenings are almost invariably occupied in the family circle" (3:37). In order to find happiness with Alice, the Vicar advises, Rufus must bring his life into harmony with hers, for Alice's religiosity would exert a beneficial influence upon him by keeping in check his worldly ambition (3:38-39). Rufus, however, is not quite his own man. The worst sort of pride of race belongs to Rufus's grandmother, an Italianate Corsican and the very devil in disguise, whose ambition is to keep her family's lineage pure at any cost.

By a stroke of fate Rufus loses his heirship to an earldom, after which his prospects are those of a country gentleman. Robert Hindle comes back from Australia in time to offer his opinion that Rufus's rank in life is now one which Alice could adorn. Rufus accommodates himself to Alice's sense of duty both by joining the Dole committee in a time of famine and by volunteering to help the sick during an outbreak of typhus (3:308-11). The result of this experience is that Rufus submits to Alice's guidance of his moral and spiritual life. He also renounces a statesman's career for the less worldly goal of curing social ills (3:316). As at the end of *Emma*, when the accepted suitor decides what is to be done with his beloved's father, the reader is assured that a marriage will take place.

We have seen that the choice of an irreproachably religious romantic heroine has tended to put into prominence only the gentler, more spiritual, not to say feminine, qualities of Puritanism and that the aggressive Puritan economic man has been put into the background. Kay-Shuttleworth, of course, was not committed to emphasizing the latter, who he may have thought, along with some moderns, was merely the product of a dark conspiracy to "confound Calvinism and Capitalism . . . in a common ruin."[42] It is perhaps unprofitable to speculate upon how much Kay-Shuttleworth knew or was willing to admit about the "shadow" of Puritanism. That a novelist is free to write his own story goes without saying. There are, however, two factors that might explain the absence of the less savory aspects of business life in both *Scarsdale* and *Ribblesdale*: Kay-Shuttleworth's melioristic social philosophy and his regionalism. Regarding the first, although he was the author of a popular pamphlet describing the moral and physical sufferings of Manchester's working population in 1832, a work that supplied grist for the mill of early Victorian social problem novelists and commentators such as Engels, Kay-Shuttleworth's novels are free of that kind of social criticism. This is because he believed education and a higher Christian civilization would eradicate topical evils, and for a meliorist it was fruitless to conjure up again the horrors of the early factory system, most of which had disappeared by 1860 and 1874, the years in which he wrote his novels. Secondly, as a regional novelist Kay-Shuttleworth exhibits a characteristic love of the land and all classes of its people. In *Scarsdale*, he shows his fondness for the topography of Lancashire, and for the aristocrat, the manufacturer, and the working man. The villains in that novel are either outsiders such as Silas Whitaker, an emigrant from Ireland, or an anti-social type such as Ascroft, a descendant of a family of murderers. In *Ribblesdale* the villainess is not a Lancastrian but a Corsican. It would seem, then, that as an "occasional novelist" Kay-Shuttleworth believed that fiction had its domain, not to be transgressed by social criticism that rightly belonged to the occasional pamphlet. The villain in the novel should not be a representative of a particular social class, lest class antagonism result. Instead he should be depicted either as classless or as the traditional Machiavel of Renaissance drama or the Gothic novel. For Kay-Shuttleworth, complacent Victorian that he was in his later years, fiction was not so much a criticism of life as a mirror of manners.

IV

Plebeians and Patricians

The parvenu, the next type of early industrialist under consideration, needs little introduction as a fictional type. The acquisition of sudden wealth which propels an individual from a lower station to a higher is not a phenomenon peculiar to the emergent industrialist alone. During the late eighteenth century, new wealth from sources other than industrial enterprise was moving up the social scale, much to the consternation of a member of the landed classes such as Matthew Bramble, who complained about the company at Bath:

> Every upstart of fortune, harnessed in the trappings of the mode, presents himself at Bath. . . . Clerks and factors from the East Indies, loaded with the spoil of plundered provinces; planters, negro-drivers, and hucksters, from our American plantations, enriched they know not how; agents, commissaries, and contractors, who have fattened, in two successive wars, on the blood of the nation; usurers, brokers, and jobbers of every kind; men of low birth, and no breeding, have found themselves suddenly translated into a state of affluence, unknown to former ages; and no wonder their brains should be intoxicated with pride, vanity, and presumption. Knowing no other criterion of greatness, but the ostentation of wealth, they discharge their affluence without taste or conduct, through every channel of the most absurd extravagance. . . . Such is the composition of the company at Bath; where a very inconsiderable proportion of genteel people are lost in a mob of impudent plebeians, who have neither understanding nor judgment, nor the least idea of propriety and decorum. . . .[43]

The omission of the industrialist from Bramble's list of the newly-arrived is not an oversight. Because of the circumstances peculiar to their career and class, the early industrialists were not likely to be interested in the fashionable society of Bath. That celebrated watering place is mentioned only once in the novels under consideration and that is in Geraldine Jewsbury's *Marian Withers* when John Withers forbids his daughter Marian a trip to Bath because he does not want her to visit out of her station in life. Nor did London, the political as well as fashionable center, seem to hold an attraction for the first generation of manufacturers. We have noted Ashton's observation that the emergent class avoided politics and paid unceasing attention to their business affairs.[44] They had little occasion to go to London for political reasons before 1832, except to testify before Parliamentary committees investigating the causes of popular disturbances; namely, rioting handloom weavers, in the industrial North. Moreover, since a start in cotton manufacturing required only a modest capital, those who began with only a few looms had no need of the resources of London as the capital of finance. To economic independence and noninvolvement in politics as factors isolating the early industrialist from London may be added the Quaker or Puritan religious persuasion, which was inimical to the life of idleness characteristic of fashionable society. Since London was also the center of the literary world, the majority of novelists knew little about the industrial magnate. Hence, the parvenu that appears in fiction, found in London or in places such as Bath, is more likely one of the varieties of newly-enriched described by Bramble. For the industrialists, on the other hand, Manchester and its environs, Birmingham, and Leeds were the center of activity, and Liverpool their seaport. For the reasons conjectured above, it would seem that the subject of the industrialist as parvenu (which one might expect to loom large in a study of the emergence of a new wealthy class) did not attract writers of fiction.

The novel which best represents the industrialist in this light is the anonymous *Plebeians and Patricians* (1836).[45] Like *Scarsdale*, this work describes a yeoman-turned-manufacturer but unlike Kay-Shuttleworth's book, it also judges him as a social being by the standards of the aristocratic class. If we observe the manufacturer's vulgarity, absurdity, and ignorance, qualities which set him apart from the aristocratic element in the novel, and if we consider the landed gentleman's attitude toward the qualities needed for success in business, we can account in some degree for the unwillingness of the old order to admit such an early industrial entrepreneur as Richard Arkwright as a social equal. That former barber, we may remember, though praised for his usefulness was faulted for his coarseness. Moreover, since a historical source exists for this novel, we might briefly examine how the author, in order to accommodate polite readers, softens the historical portrait which, though perhaps questionable in itself, undoubtedly passed for current among many contemporaries.

John Manford, the "plebeian" industrialist in this novel, was the descendant of yeomen who had once possessed several small estates. His father had come to ruin after having spent money entrusted to him as a kind of banker at a time when there were no county banks. The cost of maintaining the proverbial hospitality of the yeoman was high. Having lost all but a small piece of property, the Manfords, with John now at their head, were reduced almost to the level of cotters. Their fortunes changed, however, with the introduction of cotton manufacturing. John

Manford sold some of his remaining land to a neighbor who wanted to build a cotton mill. By watching its construction, John gathered the general principles of the process. At first he cleared out the old hall and installed machinery and with the aid of industry, economy, and good profits, he afterwards built his own mill and a new home, splendidly furnished and decorated.[46]

Having made the transition to large scale industry, John Manford still retained the coarseness of manner that characterized the yeoman. But his adoption of a foundling factory apprentice, Anne Talbot, who has "nobility stamped legibly upon her brow" (1:65), does much to bring out the kindlier part of his nature, thus revealing that he is not incapable of some of the noble feelings embodied in Sir John Scarsbrook, who represents the gentlemanly ideal of the novel's patricians. It is at the female Manfords, however, that the charge of absurdity and coarseness of mind as well as manner is at this point leveled. Taught by his large acquaintance in the business world, Manford is not unaware of the discrepancy between the manners of his mother and sisters and their splendid residence, an incongruity which leaves them open to ridicule. The lack of a community of taste between plebeian and patrician shows itself during the Manfords' visit to Scarsbrook Hall, particularly when Sir John's sister, Lady Lucy, tries to entertain the women:

> The most beautiful articles of bijouterie, splendid specimens from burines of the most famous artists, books of drawings and of illustrated costumes, portfolios of scraps, sketches and caricatures were laid before them, and all failed in exciting their pleased attention,—they looked first at the rare collection and then at each other, and were vastly uncomfortable; the gems, pictures and books, were gems, pictures and books, and nothing more, and they knew as much about them as a Hottentot.
>
> Everything she did being in vain, the good-natured countess began to feel an uneasy restraint; there was, she saw, no topic in common between them no community of feeling, no point of similarity or taste, no open ground in fact, on which both could speak. (1:55-56)

Lady Lucy and Sir John can forgive this kind of ignorance, but they have another reason for disliking the Manford women; namely, their spiteful treatment of Manford's protegée Anne Talbot. Jealous of her lest Manford make her his heiress, the women fill his ears with malicious gossip about Anne. Finally, he is "powerless to resist the battery of four female tongues, all within point-blank range" (1:74). He agrees to send Anne back to the mill and marries a woman of his mother's choice. Without Anne to bring out his better nature, Manford, under the influence of his female relatives and now a wife, becomes as vulgar as they:

"He became proud, coarsely proud, fond of his vulgarism, because being backed by his wealth, it passed current among his contemporaries for wit" (1:110). Moreover, in his treatment of rioting weavers he is unduly severe and unjust, using military power to disperse them and pressuring magistrates to convict the workers' leaders without adequate proof. Sir John Scarsbrook, serving as an example of responsible power, thwarts Manford's illegal proceedings, and once more, as in Kay-Shuttleworth's novel, the aristocracy is depicted as the protector of distressed workers, the responsibility for whom lies rightly with their own employers (1:104-8). A summons to London to appear before a Parliamentary board of inquiry in the matter of workers' distress offers an opportunity for Manford's absurdity to be exhibited further. John's fondness for "animal enjoyments" leads him to get drunk and his habit of boasting about his wealth results in his being gulled out of a sizeable amount of money (2:36). The Manford women visit Westminster Abbey but find it dismal because of all the dead buried there. Ignorant of history or of the traditional associations of the Abbey, the women are drawn, in this episode, as country boobies. And in keeping with their lack of feminine delicacy, the women show themselves perfectly capable of protecting themselves from the unwanted attentions of a stranger by kicking him in the stomach (2:49).

After making the Manfords sufficiently ridiculous, the anonymous author reveals himself more charitable than hostile to the parvenus. When Anne Talbot is married to Sir John, the Manford women apologize to him for their ungracious treatment of the factory girl. Because of Sir John's civility in the matter, the Manfords begin to realize that wealth is not the only criterion which makes one worthy of respect, that there are certain personal qualities and social amenities which are the foundation of respectability (2:137-39). The patricians, no less, begin to see sterling traits under the coarse and gross natures of the plebeians (2:186). As another instance of his lack of ill feeling toward the plebeians, for all their vulgarity, the author excuses the peculiar social behavior of these early industrialists as the result of their isolation from both the lower orders and the genteel classes:

> Their license and debauchery seem to have been the natural consequence of rapid accumulation of money, unaccompanied by mental culture and social elevation—they formed a little republic of their own, shut out for a time from their more wealthy and respectable neighbours, and separated from the rank from which they had arisen by the simple barrier of master and man, unrelieved by any of the ornaments bestowed on that barrier by birth or long established respectability. They thus aped the style of building and dress of the higher class, and

retained the personal habits of the lower, and this accounts for many of the anomalies which marked the early career of the wealthy plebeians. (2:186-87)

It would seem, then, from the plot line that the parvenu industrialist remained distinct from the old order largely for lack of *savoir faire*. Toward the end of his story, however, the author assures us, and rightly so, that this is no problem. Good manners can be acquired; frequent contact between plebeian and patrician will civilize the former. This final, tidy optimism notwithstanding, a still more fundamental and more permanent reason for the existence of a gulf between the two classes is raised in the novel; and that is whether the industrialist's quality of single-mindedness in pursuing his business affairs is not antithetical to the liberality ascribed to Sir John Scarsbrook as the gentlemanly ideal. Or as Hazlitt has stated the matter in his essay, "On Thought and Action:"

> a question may be started, whether, as thought relates to the whole circumference of things and interests, and business is confined to a very small part of them, viz, to a knowledge of a man's own affairs and the making of his fortune, whether a talent for the latter will not generally exist in proportion to the narrowness and grossness of his ideas, nothing drawing his attention out of his own sphere, or giving him an interest except in those things which he can realize and bring home to himself in the most undoubted shape?[47]

Upon meeting John Manford for the first time, we learn not only that he has inherited from his mother a degree of "intellectual imbecility," but also that this shortcoming will be no detriment to his later business success:

> Little Johnny . . . although showing unequivocally his mental defect, in his speech and countenance, was, in many things singularly shrewd and penetrating. He soon learned the value of money, which he hoarded with the care and secrecy of an experienced miser. He was also oddly persevering, and had a quickness in discovering character rather remarkable. . . . His ideas of decency in manners were also very slight; and had it not been for the kindness and attention incessantly paid to him, he would have sunk into absolute idiotism. (1:6)

This seemingly unpromising combination of personal traits is still in evidence after Manford becomes a prosperous manufacturer. When Sir John and his sister Lucy return from a visit to Manford's mill, Lucy is puzzled by the incongruity between Manford's physiognomy and his entrepreneurial success: "What surprised me the most amongst the many curious things we were shown . . . was the man; apparently, when first looked at, so unfit, so inadequate to be the conductor of an establishment, which must certainly require much mental acuteness to keep in judicious order" (1:38). According to the physiognomy of ordinary observation, continues Lucy, no faces "could offer less prospect of mind" (1:39). Upon his introduction to the manufacturer, Sir John was equally astonished at the discrepancy between an inauspicious countenance and achievement:

> It then appeared to me an absurdity to enter upon important business [a sale of land], with a man having a countenance so strikingly indicative of mental imbecility. This impression, too, was much heightened at the moment, by his uncouth manners and coarse speech. But I erred in my estimation of the man; without a single idea beyond the sphere of his own employment, he has acuteness and quickness of apprehension, and a readiness for seizing upon minute improvements joined to persevering industry. (1:39)

One of the party of patrician conversationalists, an earl who is later discovered to be the die with which nobility was stamped upon the foundling Anne's brow, consoles his pride of rank with the reflection that the "very inferiority" of Manford is the cause of his success (1:39). Sir John obligingly dilates upon this genteel sentiment:

> It may be questioned . . . whether a man of more extended views, or of a higher order of intellect, would have been equally successful with Manford. Great men . . . are born for particular epochs; it would, perhaps, be more correct to say, that particular trains of events, which pave the way for such epochs, call into activity, men with qualities and capacities fitted for their direction; though such men, under ordinary circumstances, would remain "unsung by fame." Mr. Manford, though not a great man, is yet a man admirably fitted for encouraging and pushing forward manufacture by steam power. Destitute of imagination, he applies himself to mathematic details, and mechanical contrivances with unwearying perseverance, without swerving to the right or to the left, and never looking for any thing beyond what may prove accessories to these. (1:40)

Following Sir John's charitable evaluation of Manford, the earl enlarges upon his belief that the successful businessman is a man of inferior talents:

> It is indeed very likely . . . that a man of greater talent, of more discursive mind, and of more expanded views, would have done less for the advancement of this branch of industry, than Mr. Manford. Experience . . . proves this. Since the manufacture has made a decided progress, several gentlemen of fortune and education have embarked in it, and they have, I believe, hitherto, uniformly failed. Look around

you, and notice the many extensive mills, large and splendid houses, and vast collieries—these are, without exception, the property of men, the majority of whom are totally illiterate, and sprung from the lower, if not the lowest class of society—and yet these very men or their immediate descendants will, from the mere force of wealth, in a very few years, tread upon the heels of our hereditary nobles, and establish for themselves, a new order of aristocracy. (1:40-41)

The earl then returns to the more superficial concerns of the novel as a picture of the early industrialist's manners and concludes with an uneasy hope for improvement: "I have ridiculed and condemned their manners with but an imperfect knowledge of their character. . . . But I do most sincerely trust that mere wealth without social refinement, will never 'kibe our heels' " (1:41).

The opinions of Sir John and the earl seem to be an expression of aristocratic self-satisfaction. But akin to their rationale is the general attitude of the artist toward the businessman, and behind this bias may lie the explanation for the minor role and unsympathetic treatment offered to industrialists in fiction. Unless he speaks for a state-controlled society which uses fiction to propagandize the heroic efforts of production managers to meet quotas, the artist is by nature not in sympathy with the cast of mind that makes for success in business; his notion of reality, as Hazlitt observes, makes the businessman the enemy of metaphor and symbol:

> To the man of business all the world is a fable but the Stock Exchange: to the money getter nothing has a real existence that he cannot convert into a tangible feeling, that he does not recognize as property, that he cannot "measure with a two-foot rule or count upon ten fingers." The want of thought, of imagination, drives the practical man upon immediate realities: to the poet or philosopher, all is real and interesting that is true or possible, that can reach in its consequences to others, or be made a subject of curious speculation to himself.[48]

In spite of his gentle handling of the industrialist as nouveau riche, it is unlikely that the unknown author of *Plebeians and Patricians* had the kind of connection with manufacturing, (that of the sympathetic or even myopic regional novelist) which would lead him to minimize the less attractive side of the first generation of cotton lords. Instead, this darker element seems to have been suppressed in order that the work, which might be described as a fashionable novel gone slumming, be acceptable as polite fiction. A more unwholesome picture of the "mushrump" plebeian can be found in Peter Gaskell's *The Manufacturing Population of England* (1833), which suggests itself as a source for *Plebeians and Patricians*. This conjecture as to source is based upon two ideas that appear to have been derived from Gaskell's history: one, the notion that, their virtue of hospitality traditionally associated with the wives of the early manufacturers aside, the female was the more vulgar of the species; and two, the assumption that in the early days the refined man of means was not successful in manufacturing.[49]

In the interest of propriety, the author of *Plebeians* has restricted the "animal enjoyments" of the new men to excessive drinking, and has omitted Gaskell's additional discussion of the "lascivious indulgence afforded them by the number of females brought under their immediate control,"[50] an aspect of behavior that, as we shall see in a later chapter, formed the staple of radical popular fiction. As a consequence, Manford's act of taking Anne out of his factory and setting her up in a cottage of her own as his protégée is used to exhibit his response to Anne's noble characteristics, rather than to suggest the absence of moral discipline that Gaskell declares marked the conduct of the early manufacturers.[51] The use of the convention of the foundling who turns out to be of gentle if illegitimate blood, in turn, provided the author with an agent who, through her marriage to Sir John, was employed in such a manner as to symbolize the affinity of both plebeian and patrician for noble impulses. Thus, the structure of the novel reinforces direct statement, and we are reassured that, shorn of his vulgarities, the parvenu promises to acquit himself with honor in the station of life to which his wealth has brought him.

v

Marian Withers

The last type of early industrialist to be considered is the self-made man of whom the best account is the story of John Withers in Geraldine Jewsbury's *Marian Withers* (1851). Contrary to what one might expect, most of the industrialists who appear in the novels we are considering are introduced as already established. The circumstances of their way to wealth are not made part of the narrative. In this novel, on the other hand, the rags to riches pattern through which a pauper child eventually becomes a prosperous millowner is narrated at length. Because his success was the result of hard work accompanied by near starvation, Withers has little use for the get-rich-quick aspect of joint stock company operations, and much less for the speculator. The scorn of Withers and his fellow manufacturers for the counterfeit captain of industry, that "parasite fastened on the labour of business men,"[52] is expressive of the Victorian attitude which equated honest industry with hard work. Moreover, Withers's inventor's dedication to perfecting his machinery, even at the expense of business profits, leaves him with little personal inclination for the kind of social aspiration toward gentility that characterized the subsequent generations of industrialists.

Geraldine Jewsbury is in many ways singularly qualified to depict in detail the rise of a self-made man and to record the attitudes which grow out of that experience. A native of Lancashire who grew up in Manchester, she came from a family connected with the new industry. Her grandfather had been an engineer of canal navigation and a colliery manager. Her father, Thomas Jewsbury, had learned the process of cotton manufacturing from Robert Peel, the father of the Prime Minister, and later set up a small mill next to his house at Measham.[53] Several of the novelists in this study, Disraeli, Charlotte Elizabeth, and the author of *Plebeians and Patricians* take the reader on a tour of a cotton mill; but none of them would have been able to serve as an actual guide nor did they possess the interest in and knowledge of things mechanical which make the detailed description of the manufacturing process in John Withers' mill the only one of its kind in this fiction. Attributing Geraldine's curiosity about machinery to a masculine mind, her biographer records the "unquenchable enthusiasm with which she piloted distinguished visitors to Manchester [Carlyle for one] . . . through machine shops and factories until they must have been ready to drop from exhaustion."[54] Coming from a family who had risen to a small eminence by their own labor, Geraldine was particularly receptive to the gospel of work. That John Withers was largely indifferent to rank might be explained in part by Virginia Woolf's judgment of his creator: "Geraldine was a clever, witty woman who thought for herself and hated what she called 'respectability' as much as Mrs. Carlyle [her confidant] hated what she called 'humbug.' "[55] Unlike her fellow Lancastrian Kay-Shuttleworth who, having acquired a landowning wife, was inclined in his fiction to patronize the manufacturing class from which he had sprung, Geraldine Jewsbury was as much a product of Manchester as its textiles.

The story of John Withers begins in 1794, when he was a child whose parents subsisted on a parish dole supplemented by John's scanty income as a beggar. Learning about his brutal stepfather, a Miss Fenwich helps him escape the vicious circle of pauperism and sordid family life by having him placed in the workhouse from which he could be sent off as a pauper factory apprentice. As Sir Samuel Romilly records, it was, for better or for worse, the established practice of parish authorities to send children whose parents were on the parish rolls to be apprenticed in factories.[56] John was a model child at the workhouse. There, he learned to read, and "having once picked up a copy of 'Whittington and his Cat,' it had made a deep impression upon him, and he burned with the idea of 'going to seek his fortune,' and becoming a great man."[57] His first and

only possible step forward, he thought, was through a factory apprenticeship. T. S. Ashton declares that the story of the pauper factory apprentices
was in many places, "a tale . . . of neglect, promiscuity, and degradation," but that some employers, such as Arkwright, the Gregs, Samuel
Oldknow, and Robert Owen acknowledged a responsibility for pauper
apprentices and made it possible, in some cases, for them to rise to the
position of spinners.[58] It was John Withers's good fortune, unlike that of
Frances Trollope's Michael Armstrong, to fall into such "Christian
hands":

> When the little band arrived at [the Union Mills in Staffordshire],
> they were boarded, along with many others in a large building erected
> for the purpose: it was both clean and airy, and in a healthy situation.
> Parish apprentices and children working in factories were not always
> victims of ill-treatment. The apprentice system had many faults—too
> much was in the power of the masters, who were irresponsible; it is
> well abolished. But these children were in Christian hands; and though
> they worked long hours, they were well lodged, well fed, and well treated
> and had no cause for complaint. (1:22)

In the midst of an epidemic that broke out among the apprentices, John
Withers made himself useful and agreeable, and his employer desired to
reward him. John expressed a wish to be taught to write, and the millowner obligingly sent him to the clerk of his counting house in the
evenings (1:23-25).

After John had served his apprenticeship, he went to work in Lancashire. His plans for making his fortune, however, were balked by the
necessity of his having to work at a monotonous task that offered no prospect of advancement. While he was working overtime one day, his machine broke down; and when he rigged it in order that it would work for
the rest of his shift, he discovered a mechanical aptitude of which he was
not aware: "Henceforth, all his labour was in a new spirit. The machine
had become to him a living creature; he had obtained an insight into the
power which moved it" (1:27). The idea of making a simpler and more
efficient machine than the "mule" possessed him, and more time and
money than he could spare went into this project. In order to deaden
the pangs of hunger and also to fight off sleep, it was his practice to bind
a rope tightly about his waist. Knowing far too little about the principles
of mechanics, he experienced failure after failure. His exertions brought
him to the pass of having to choose between his factory work and his
models. At that point the idea for his invention was hardly realized, "but
with that sublime undoubting faith which according to its success, stamps
men either as heroes or visionaries, he determined to sacrifice the factory

to the models" (1:29). After having given up his only source of income, Withers, hating the begging experience of his childhood days, managed to survive by eating vegetables that had been thrown away in the market-place. He worked on the verge of madness, slowly learning from his failures, until he completed a successful model. The effort had proved too much for him and one day he collapsed in the street. When he came home from the hospital, he found children playing with his delicate wheels and parts of his model. Recovering these, he found the rest in the possession of a lodger whom he had befriended (1:30-41). His model proved successful and he sold his patent for a thousand pounds to one of the creditors of his old master who had failed in business. Reverencing the old man for teaching him to write, John, out of gratitude, bought up some of his former employer's effects at an auction; and, out of pity, married the latter's now destitute daughter (1:41-55). The story of Marian Withers, their only child, begins in 1825, the year of the specula-tive mania in which joint-stock companies sold shares in steam ovens, steam laundries, milk and egg companies, life insurance, brewing, coal-portage, and wool growing enterprises, not to mention Mexican mining companies and foreign loans to the new republics in South America.[59]

At a dinner given by a Mr. Wilcox who is a millowner of very much the same mind as John Withers, the conversation turns to the subject of joint-stock companies. Withers expresses the self-made man's lack of faith in getting something for nothing:

> they are all just schemes for making everybody rich without work-ing; they have taken the place of lotteries, where everybody hoped by putting a bit of paper into the wheel to see it come out the ten thou-sand-pound prize at least; It is a bad look-out for a country when the people of it take the notion of getting rich in a hurry; it is trying to cheat nature into working miracles, and getting things without paying the price for them. . . . There is nothing but hard work that does not deceive a man; if he sticks to that, he finds the good of it in the end, though his back may be half-broken before it comes. (2:15-16)

A fellow millowner, Mr. Higginbottom, who adds that the individual consciences of company directors are lost when they act in concert, ex-hibits the reluctance of the economic individualist to engage in corporate activity:

> The worst thing in these joint-stock companies is that the share-holders lose all thought of working for themselves, but trust to the directors juggling with their money, so as to make two and two into five, whilst the directors, though perhaps they may none of them be rascals on their own account, yet when they all come to act together,

their conscience evaporates, for one gives in to another; one is squeamish in this, while the other is squeamish in that, so that any kind of rascality gets done amongst them; and if they are called to account, there's the "Board" to come upon, which is, just like trying to catch "Nobody,"—who, along with the Cat, had done all the mischief since the world began. I, for my part, can see no good in going partners with the whole world; I am just for a fair stand-up fight in business, each of us to fend for ourselves: "a fair field and no favour"; this is my motto. (2:16-17)

Mr. Sykes, another manufacturer, adds that a millowner risks not only his own livelihood by gambling in shares, but also that of all his employees. Never does the employer go bankrupt without a general groan: "I remember the time that followed the canal mania; the master my father worked with, failed along of his canal shares . . . the mill stopped and two hundred hands were thrown out of employ in a minute" (2:18). The consequences to his family were the workhouse for his parents and a factory apprenticeship for him, fortunately under the elder Peel. Following the usual pattern of the self-made man, Sykes rose to eminence by dint of overwork and living on scanty means in order to amass capital. Experience and capital qualified him for a partnership and in time a mill of his own (2:18-22). Sykes concludes with an assertion of the gospel of work: "But I never tried no way to get rich all of a sudden, and I never will try; for them schemes only take the work out of a man, and make him a coward like. I have been in straits since I was a master and when I was a man, and its the work that has kept my heart up . . ." (2:22).

If John Withers dislikes joint-stock operations in principle, he soon has a personal basis for his prejudice. Milbank, director of a joint-stock bank and partner in a Manchester commercial house with which Withers had dealt, absconds to America with all available funds. As a result, Withers stands a chance of losing his credit on the Exchange. Credit meant to the cotton manufacturer what the idea of honor did to the aristocrat: "No old Castilian noble ever felt more jealous of the honour of his house than did John Withers of his commercial credit" (2:81). With the help of Wilcox, however, he survives the financial crisis.

Withers and his fellow manufacturers were not alone in their condemnation of shareholding. Throughout the half century covered in this study, their viewpoint is reiterated on the pages of fiction and nonfiction alike.[60] Harriet Martineau was emphatic about the "hardship on the sober man of business of being involved in the destruction which overtook the speculator" in 1825-26.[61] Her father, a Norwich manufacturer, never quite recovered from his business setbacks at that time. Disraeli playfully satirized the follies of foreign investment in the imaginary voyage of *Popanilla* (1827). In Chapter Two of *Nicholas Nickleby* (1838-39), Dickens ridiculed the joint-stock "United Metropolitan Improved Hot Muffin and Crumpet Baking and Punctual Delivery Company"; and in *Martin Chuzzlewit* (1843-44), the bogus life insurance company of Jonah Chuzzlewit and Montague Tigg, operating with no capital. Thackeray lampooned the scoundrel company director seen through the eyes of a trusting, Candide of a clerk in *The History of Samuel Titmarsh and the Great Hoggarty Diamond* (1841).

Following the railway mania of 1845-46, another barrage of criticism was leveled at the company director and the principle of shareholding. Treating both speculative manias, a writer in *Chamber's Miscellany* defined joint-stock speculation as dishonest industry or the acquisition of riches without useful service and without contributing to the resources of the country. Share speculation, continued this writer, was immoral and could be likened to cheating at cards or other games of chance. Honest fortunes were built up slowly by steady industry.[62] Charles Kingsley called shareholding "the devil's selfish counterfeit of God's order of mutual love and trust."[63] Commenting on a bronze statue of George Hudson the Railway King, Carlyle called it a "brazen image" that deserves a deep coal shaft instead of a high column. This speculator, vociferated Carlyle, was a member of the "new aristocracy" elected by the populace in a most positive way: by buying shares in his ventures.[64] Following this second rage for speculation, the denunciations of novelists were no longer in the vein of light satire found in the fiction dealing with the crash of 1825-26. In *Little Dorrit* (1855-57), the characterization of Merdle, a combination of George Hudson and John Sadleir, the suicide Irish banker-speculator, belongs to the tradition of the ironic panegyric. The technique befits the temper of the times when many Englishmen were prepared to accept the vehicle of Dickens's encomium of Merdle's greatness without recognizing its ironic tenor, an era in which the unscrupulous man who was successful was considered clever.

Charles Lever, in *Davenport Dunn* (1859), depicted the rise of a company promoter to a position from which he could demand a peerage. Lever excoriated the nation that, "intending to honour Industry . . . had paid its homage to Money!"[65] And toward the end of our period, it is Dickens who most bitterly denounces the company director as a cipher, devoid of human attributes but commanding the highest respect of his fellow countrymen by virtue of his possession of stock:

> Have no antecedents, no established character, no cultivation, no ideas, no manners; have Shares. Have Shares enough to be on Boards of Direction in capital letters, oscillate on mysterious business between

London and Paris, and be great. Where does he come from? Shares. Where is he going? Shares. Has he any principles? Shares. What squeezes him into Parliament? Shares. Perhaps he never of himself achieved success in anything, never originated anything, never produced anything! Sufficient answer to all; Shares.[66]

Despite arguments for the joint-stock company as in keeping with the principle of association which might end class antagonism, the notion of shareholding was slow to take hold. Joint-stock companies were often tainted with dishonest speculation because of the failure of legal machinery to keep pace with the economic reorganization which accompanied the Industrial Revolution. Large scale ventures, such as canal building and later railways, required an amount of capital that no one man could raise, except perhaps the Duke of Bridgewater who led the canal building movement with the cutting of the Worsley Canal in 1758-61.[67] Joint-stock ventures, then, were useful and necessary. But commercial expansion gave rise to numbers of unchartered companies (charters were to be had from Parliament for special purposes, not for general trading) which illegally assumed the privileges of chartered companies.[68] Because unchartered companies were outside the law, they lent themselves to great abuses. Moreover, there was no legal redress for investors cheated by brokers. The failures of the law to protect all investors from fraud encouraged the rascality which gave joint-stock undertakings a bad reputation generally.[69]

F. Cobbe's generalization about the social aspirations of the first generation of the nineteenth century seems to apply to John Withers: "The principle which most largely actuated men in the last generation in these matters seems to have been precisely the reverse of *l'art de parvenir*. It was the Art of Standing Still. *Noblesse oblige* meant that a man's actions, habits, modes of life, should be consistent with his birth; i.e., with a certain fact."[70] Also true of John Withers is what Robert Owen wrote about his lack of association, in his early career, with people of social standing: "Absorbed in my attention to business, I knew little of the habits, customs, and fashions of families having pretensions to some standing in society. . . ."[71] Like Owen, who relates that in these matters he "was sensitive to a painful excess, for [he] had at this time a high opinion of the attainments of the wealthy educated classes,"[72] John Withers "set an immense store upon book learning and cultivated manners" (1:81-82).

On the other hand, unlike Owen, who later became acquainted with statesmen and foreign royalty, John Withers moved in the same circle throughout his life. He expected his daughter Marian, by going to the best schools, to acquire the social refinements that he lacked. Still, Withers did not believe in a life of fashionable idleness for his daughter. Despite all of her schooling he did not want her to be a fine lady. It was his opinion that "women had better come and work in a factory than do nothing but sit all day with their hands before them" (1:238). It came as a surprise to a social climbing merchant's wife to discover that Marian was a girl whose father did not allow her to go to Bath because "it did girls no good to visit out of their station in life" (1:103). That the early self-made manufacturers were satisfied with their station is suggested when Mr. Cunningham, a wealthy, retired man who went into partnership with Withers in order to improve the condition of the working man, attempts to introduce ideas of taste and refinement among the masters, so that possession of wealth might cease to be their only criterion of success. Judging from Geraldine Jewsbury's equivocal account of the results of his endeavors he seems to have been only vaguely successful:

> In his travels he had collected choice books, pictures, and curiosities. The chief of these he had conveyed to his new residence; and though the rich millowners were far from understanding their value, yet they gradually became desirous of possessing similar treasures. At first, it was a species of Fetish worship: they began to buy pictures and engravings without anything higher than a vague idea that they were worth the money, and that there was a certain distinction in possessing what they persisted in calling "articles of bigotry [for bijouterie] and virtue;" and although many of the old race of spinners and mill-owners would still sit in the kitchen and smoke their pipes, leaving their drawing rooms full of beautiful things which they thought much too grand to live amongst, still a taste for art and a respect for cultivation of the intellect had begun to make itself felt. (3:239-40)

As a representative of the self-made man, John Withers himself is not typical. As has been shown, he was, like James Watt, a rare combination of the successful inventor-manufacturer. It has been said that he was modeled in part upon Sir Joseph Whitworth, the nineteenth-century inventor and industrialist whose system of wrench sizes continues at present to estrange England from the Continental metric system. Withers's characterization is, moreover, doubly unique, for out of approximately fifty novels which deal in large part or in small with the industrialist, he is the only self-made man whose early career in the factory receives attention. We may remember that the explanation for the rise of Josiah Bounderby, of whom we shall hear in connection with the *myth* of the self-made man, was limited to a sentence: "And a steady lad he was, and a kind master he had to lend him a hand, and well he worked his own way forward to be rich and thriving."[73]

Why only John Withers? A satisfactory answer might be that most novelists did not know as much as Geraldine Jewsbury did about the early career of industrialists. Another plausible answer might be that novelists were not prone to celebrate the thrift and perseverance of the early career of the self-made man. The kind of interest is better served by the nineteenth-century industrial hagiographies of Samuel Smiles.[74] What then would lead a reviewer of *Marian Withers*, Hepworth Dixon, to praise the account of John Withers's struggle as the best part of the book?[75] It is perhaps because Geraldine Jewsbury was commemorating the dedication of a creative genius to an idea, and not the accumulation of capital by thrift. She was holding up for commendation the sacrifice of a man, who even as a successful manufacturer "might have been much richer had he been less ingenious" (1:83), a man who bears out one of Hazlitt's observations about thought and action—that the innovator is less likely to succeed than he who follows custom, looking neither to the left nor to the right but keeping his eye solely on his own interests.[76]

The Eternal Order of the Bourgeoisie

But Mr. Lebeziatnikov who keeps up with modern ideas explained the other day that compassion is forbidden nowadays by science itself, and that that's what is done now in England where there is political economy.

Dostoevsky, *Crime and Punishment*

THE NEXT FOUR CHAPTERS WILL DEAL WITH the image of the industrialist in the course of the social and economic controversy of the 1830s and 1840s, the period during which the industrialist first appears in contemporary fiction. Making his entrance under these circumstances, the industrialist is made the subject of propaganda by friends and adversaries alike. Broadly speaking, the industrialist is viewed in three ways: apologists for the factory system envision him as a national benefactor; extremist critics of industrialsm consider him an enemy of the people; and a third group of novelists, rising above the polemics of partisanship, attempts to treat the captain of industry symbolically in terms of the Carlylean concept of a working aristocracy. The sharply contrasting attitudes of the bourgeois and the proletariat constitute the subject of this and the next chapter.

As an apologist for the manufacturer, Harriet Martineau stands as an advocate of the status quo. In her two tales, *The Hill and the Valley* and *A Manchester Strike*, written for her *Illustrations of Political Economy* (1832-34) she argues for the perpetuation of things as they are, by an appeal to unalterable economic laws. But an examination of her tale *The Rioters* (1827), written before she became engrossed in the subject of economics, reveals that at that time she supported the manufacturer on the grounds that the existing state of things was in accordance with the eternal laws ordained by God. This sort of argument reveals her affinity with such eighteenth-century apologists as William Paley, spokesman for the Established Church, who sought to calm political and social unrest in the 1790s by endeavoring to persuade the laboring population that the laws of property were the laws of Providence.[1] Appended to the first edition of Archbishop Paley's *Reasons for Contentment* is a dialogue in the course of which an employer convinces a factory worker that inequality is in the nature of things and that each should be contented with his station.

In her first tale of labor troubles, *The Rioters*, Harriet Martineau employs a commercial traveler to preach the sanctity of property and respect for the laws which protect it to starving handloom weavers, who seek to destroy the new power looms which have put them out of work. The point of view of the middle class property holder is given further prominence through the use of the man of commerce as first person narrator as well as teacher.

At the opening of the story the nameless narrator, having arrived in Manchester on one of his periodic business trips, is a spectator of rioting. He is deeply moved by the destitution of a weaving family, the Bretts, whose two sons were taken up for trying to get at the new machinery. While not devoid of compassion as he looks upon the melee of weavers and dragoons, the traveller is comforted by the reflection that partial evil is universal good: "When I went about from place to place, looking only on the sorrows before my eyes, I might well feel heart-sick: but when I remembered whose hand had inflicted these miseries, I remembered also that, in that hand, evil is the instrument of greater good."[2] He is nevertheless appalled at the irrationality of the weavers. On one occasion when the militia confront the mob, a magistrate assures the weavers that the millowners are ready to share their last shilling with the workers rather than that they should starve. But the millowners do not have the opportunity to make good their promise, for the mob, incensed by the presence of the soldiers, begins to fling its brickbats (pp. 44-45). During this incident the soldiers conduct themselves with "admirable temper," trying to avoid injuring the rioters, who in turn attack them "with every species of violence" (p. 46). The narrator is supremely confident, however, that if the ignorant weavers were taught to understand the existing state of economic affairs, they would readily know their duty, which is to be patient and obedient to the law. Optimistic about the civilizing effect of useful knowledge, he sets out to teach the Bretts the working man's duty with the hope that they will disseminate this knowledge among other weavers. Compared to the exhortations to obey the law, the lesson in economics is brief. By catechizing Brett with leading questions, the man of business obtains the desired answers. The briskness of trade depends on underselling foreign competitors. This cannot be done by a return to a handloom industry because English machine builders without work in England would go over to the Continent and construct machines for foreign competitors, who would then be in a position to undersell the English.[3]

After having driven home that economic principle, the narrator proceeds to convince Brett that obedience to the law and government is a very high duty. The wise men in Parliament "agree that private property of every kind must be protected; everybody knows that laws exist for this purpose . . . it is the duty of every man to submit" or be justly punished (pp. 79-80). Brett promises to teach his baby to fear the laws. For the present, however, the narrator suggests that Brett proselytize some misguided neighbor by demonstrating to him that the evils of rioting reverberate through the hierarchy of society to the cosmos:

> Tell him, that, by rioting he sins against himself, by endangering his life and liberty; he sins against his family, by exposing them to misery and disgrace; he sins against society by violating public order, and invading the security of property; he sins against the state, by despising its laws; he sins against his king, by denying his authority and disobeying his commands; he sins against God, by breaking his solemn oath of allegiance to his sovereign, and by neglecting the sacred precepts, *Be subject* to them that are in authority. Submit yourselves to every ordinance of man, for the Lord's sake; whether it be to the king as supreme, or unto governors as unto them that are sent by him. Fear God; honour the king. (pp. 81-82)

Having persuaded the weaver that the laws made to protect property are also the laws that protect the propertyless, the narrator then dramatizes the punishment of the violators of those laws. In order to impress the weavers with the gravity of their crime, a magistrate records a sentence of death against all the rioters; but it is commuted to a three-year prison term.

As a work of fiction *The Rioters* is a heavy-handed piece of propaganda designed to intimidate the hungry working man into accepting the established order of things, however unjust it might seem. Although the narrator's attitude toward the weavers' plight is compassionate, the work is so structured as to exalt the manufacturer at the expense of the weaver. It is, as we have observed, the mob's fault that the millowners are not permitted to share their last shilling; and it is Brett, who even after having conned his lesson, is not spared the disgrace of hearing a magistrate pass sentence on his sons. As a work of propaganda and in spite of the narrator's protestations that he is "not one of those who think 'the

poor have nothing to do with the laws but obey them' " (p. 59), the tale,
as it stands, clearly suggests a prevalent attitude about how much the
poor ought to know. The essence of this conservative middle and upper
class point of view is expressed by the millowner Higginbottom, as a
contrast to John Withers's enlightened opinion that the laboring population needs schools that will teach them more than mere submission to
what the wealthy consider is the duty of the poor. For Higginbottom, to
teach the worker more than his duty was to put a torch in the hand of a
firebrand:

> Educate them! Teach 'em reading and writing that they may turn
> radicals, politicians, and trades' union demagogues! . . . they will not
> be content with reading their Bibles; they will read newspapers—low,
> radical, seditious immorality. If they want to learn their duty, they
> may go to Church; don't we pay the parsons wages to teach them? But
> I would throw any man out of the window, pretty sharply, who came
> canting to me about educating the people.[4]

Not very long after having written *The Rioters*, Harriet Martineau obtained from a neighbor a copy of Jane Marcet's *Conversations on Political
Economy* (1816).[5] "I took up the book," she records in her autobiography, "chiefly to see what Political Economy precisely was; and great
was my surprise to find that I had been teaching it unawares, in my stories
about Machinery [*The Rioters*] and Wages [*The Turn-Out*]. It struck me
at once that the principles of the whole science might be advantageously
conveyed in the same way. . . ."[6] That the science needed teaching had
been expressed in 1825 by the *Quarterly*. In that Tory organ's view of the
matter, the apologetics of Paley and the principles of political economy
are offered together as a palliative for working class dissatisfaction with
the established order of things. The writer in the *Quarterly* stated both
that the laws of political economy would explain that inequality was
natural to society and that he would be "grateful for any measures which
may tend to diffuse such knowledge."[7] In 1832 Harriet Martineau em-
barked upon the ambitious project of popularizing "the whole science."
Her *Illustrations of Political Economy*, comprising twenty-four tales, appeared monthly from 1832 to 1834. Her method of composition involved
reading the standard works on the subject and summarizing the principles. And then "the next step was to embody each leading principle in
a character; and the mutual operation of these embodied principles supplied the action of the story."[8]

Only two of the *Illustrations* deal with industrial problems: *The Hill
and the Valley* (1832) and *A Manchester Strike* (1833). The two tales
differ from *The Rioters* chiefly by the secularization of the argument for

contentment; the "wiser Being," in whose hands the economic problems posed by The Rioters ultimately rested, is now replaced by the trinity of Adam Smith, Malthus, and Ricardo. Moreover, since each industrialist embodies a principle of political economy, he appears as economic man and even his social obligations are viewed in economic terms.

In The Hill and the Valley Harriet Martineau enlarges upon the question of labor-saving machinery that was the subordinate theme of The Rioters. Her purpose is to illustrate the following principles:

> "Since Capital is derived from Labour, whatever economizes Labour assists in the growth of Capital.
> Machinery economizes Labour, and therefore assists the growth of Capital.
> The growth of Capital increases the demand for Labour.
> Machinery, by assisting the growth of Capital, therefore increases the demand for Labour."[9]

The setting of the story in which these principles are embodied into characters is in South Wales. There an iron works is being set up in a valley by Capital which takes the form of Mr. Wallace. The works are being constructed near a hill on which is the abode of capital's foil, John Armstrong, who has retired prematurely from business after having been cheated by a partner. He is now living with his housekeeper away from the world and close to nature. As a man of capital, Wallace is an incarnation of the principle of thrift as a means of accumulation. His experience serves as an object lesson to the working classes. His grandfather had been a laborer who by industry and saving rose to a modest position with a firm of linen drapers. He left a small amount of capital to Wallace's father who became a shopman, and who by living frugally, managed to accumulate a few thousand pounds, which he gave to his son to invest in his iron works. Wallace never forgot that his capital was the product of the thrift and industry of his forebears: "He was accustomed to say . . . that it arose out of labour and grew by means of saving; and that if it was henceforth to increase, it must be in the same way" (p. 20).

The crisis of the tale approaches when there is a glut on the iron market, a consequence of the flourishing of rival competitors in Europe and America (pp. 84-85). Wallace and his partner agree that fixed capital cannot be reduced, but savings can be effected in the area of reproduceable capital or wages. They plan to substitute machinery or "hoarded labor" for the labor of men whose wages have to be paid regularly, and whose work can be done more efficiently by machinery (pp. 88-89). The partners' intention is to dismiss the least industrious and with the aid of new machinery, keep the works going for the benefit of the remaining employees (pp. 90-91). The discontented group who are dismissed taunt the employed workers and seek to convince them that machinery was the cause of unemployment, not the consequence of changing times (pp. 91-92). The crisis comes to a head when a boy through his own carelessness is killed by some part of the machinery which is then made to bear the blame. The boy's mother vows revenge; the discontented workers are bent on destroying the machinery, but in the process the entire works are set on fire and gutted before the soldiers arrive (pp. 97-122).

After the burning of the works, Wallace lectures his workers on the folly and crime of the course they have followed, so that they can train their children not to do likewise. He reminds them of the original agreement between capital and labor to produce iron for their mutual benefit. Here he reiterates the principle of mutual interest: capital is dependent upon labor for its accumulation, and labor is dependent upon the profits of capital for its wages. Because of fluctuations in the state of trade, however, no agreement was made about the length of time that capital and labor were to work together. A prosperous trade brought high wages, and a glut, reductions in pay. The workers who were fired were unable to see that the partial evil of creating permanent unemployment for some, through automation, contributed to the general good of the concern and the remaining employees (pp. 128-129). If capital grows by saving, labor in the abstract grows by improving its total efficiency through the economy of automation. "Machinery," affirms Wallace, "is a saving of labour; and as all saving of labour is a good thing, our machinery was a good thing" (p. 130).

The lesson of the rights of property to protection and the consequences of the violation of those rights are driven home to the workers with inexorable logic. Those responsible for the conflagration have, by breaking its laws, forfeited the right to protection extended to all its citizens by a social state; and they must take their chances before the magistrate. The innocent are jobless. The masters suffer least because their works can be repaired through the public fund, but they choose not to rebuild because "the confidence being so completely destroyed between the two parties to the original contract, there is little encouragement to enter upon a new one" (p. 131). Wallace will close the works and "then this place, lately so busy and so fruitful of the necessities and comforts of life to so many hundreds of persons, will present a melancholy picture of desertion and ruin" (p. 131).

We have observed the industrialist guiding his destiny and that of his workers by economic principles. But what is the social status of the capitalist? And what are his social obligations? A seemingly inconsequential incident provides the first answer and leads us to the second. At the beginning of the tale Wallace pays a visit to Armstrong in the latter's absence. Upon Armstrong's return, his housekeeper notifies him that a "gentleman" had called. When asked to define what is meant by a gentleman, the housekeeper is initially at a loss for words; but when she finds her tongue, her idea of a gentleman is limited to economic qualifications: a gentleman is he who is dependent upon no one for his living (pp. 11-12). Although this remark might appear a trifle in another work of fiction, or at most the answer one would expect of a servant, nevertheless, it gains significance in this tale when considered in the light of the economic man's social obligations. In the context of this tale, society's benefactor is the capitalist who contributes to its welfare by using his capital to put people to work. According to this definition, it is Armstrong, the recluse, who is antisocial—once more for economic reasons. We are told that he wastes resources and performs no service to society; his offense is his inclination to keep two hundred guineas in a chest instead of putting them out in the three percents (pp. 21-22). If there is a villain in this tale, he lives with his housekeeper on a hill. In order to receive grace, he must bring his cashbox down to the valley.

If the workers in *The Hill and the Valley* had perceived the inevitable workings of the laws of political economy with the clearsightedness of their employers, they would have understood that their free will was circumscribed by those laws. There was no alternative but to submit to the forces that worked so well to their employers' advantage. In *A Manchester Strike* the industrialist appears once more as an advocate for the status quo, as Harriet Martineau recounts the futile efforts of strikers to amend the iron law of wages. In her summary of the wages fund theory, she puts two principles in uppercase letters: "THE PROPORTION OF THIS FUND RECEIVED BY INDIVIDUALS MUST MAINLY DEPEND ON THE NUMBER AMONG WHOM THE FUND IS DIVIDED." The condition of laborers may be improved by inventions that create capital for additional investment, by putting money into savings instead of supporting strikes, and "BY ADJUSTING THE PROPORTION OF POPULATION TO CAPITAL."[10] In order to exhibit these principles at work in fiction, the writer begins appropriately by having a trades union challenge them with a demand to three manufacturers for an equalization of wages. A deputation from the union approaches Mortimer, the manufacturer who pays the lowest wages, with their proposal. As might be expected, Mortimer will not give the deputation a moment's attention. His sentiments are that the masters were already much too tolerant of the union's grievances and that "it was high time the lower orders were taught their proper place" (pp. 27-28). Without success at Mortimer's, the deputation approaches Elliott, who pays the highest wages but who is indifferent to this distinction. He is more interested in his favorite hunter and calls the workers' petition "a piece of insolence" (pp. 29-30).

A third manufacturer visited by the deputation pays a rate of wages midway between that of Mortimer and Elliott and is the mouthpiece for the wages fund theory. Clack, a stereotype of the union delegate as parasite, expresses the union's desire that Parliament fix wage rates by statute. To this notion of interfering with the law of supply and demand, Wentworth replies: "Parliament has no more choice in the matter than we masters. . . . If ever Parliament passes a bill to regulate wages, we must have a rider put to it to decree how much rain must fall before harvest" (p. 34). The millowner then turns the question of who controls wages back upon the workers, stating that the power to regulate wages lies in their hands alone: "If you choose to bring a thousand labourers to live upon the capital which was once divided among a hundred, it is your fault and not mine that you are badly off" (p. 38). A master cannot be blamed, argues Wentworth, for employing three men out of a thousand for the same sum that he once paid just one man out of a hundred. The evil is clearly an overstocked labor market. Strikes are useless, for without reducing their numbers workers cannot alter the wage rate by combining. Moreover, strikes make matters worse by decreasing the capital with which labor is paid: the wages fund is wasted, during a strike, on the maintenance of an idle establishment (pp. 38-60).

After the failure of their attempts to obtain a uniform wage rate, the union, in spite of Wentworth's advice, calls a strike (p. 61). During the strike the real culprits make matters still worse, for young factory workers use the period of idleness to make improvident marriages. In order to repeat and reinforce the principle of the wages fund, Wentworth makes periodic visits to the workers. On one occasion, he paints them a grim picture of the working classes underselling each other on the labor market (pp. 97-101). What can be done when the demand for labor increases, as it were, arithmetically, while the supply increases geometrically? Little for the better, and much for the worse is Wentworth's reply:

> It is not with the view of giving present comfort . . . that I represent what appears to me to be the truth; for alas! there is little comfort in the case anyway. My object is to prevent your making a bad case worse; and, if it were possible, to persuade you not to prepare for your descendants a repetition of the evils under which you are yourselves suffering. All that you can now do, is to live as you best may upon such wages as the masters can give, keeping up your ambition to improve your state when better times shall come. You must watch every opportunity of making some little provision against the fluctuations of

our trade, contributing your money rather for your mutual relief in hard times than for the support of strikes. You must place your children out to different occupations, choosing those which are least likely to be overstocked; and above all, you must discourage in them the imprudent early marriages to which are mainly owing the distresses which afflict yourselves and those which will for some time, I fear, oppress your children. You ask me what you must do. These things are all I can suggest. (pp. 102-3)

When the strike is settled only two-thirds of the work force is taken back, since one-third of the fixed sum set aside for wages had been, as Wentworth warned, expended for the upkeep of an idle plant. As an admonition to those who would organize a strike, Allen, an honest and respectable man, is proscribed by employers; and his sole recourse is to sweep streets for the rest of his life. We are reminded that the last strike leader was forced to become a strolling player (pp. 131-132). There is no prospect of meliorism in this "gloomy world of Parson Malthus"[11] and Ricardian wages fund theory.

It is evident that in spite of her dislike for "the practice of making use of narrative as a trap to catch idle readers,"[12] the fiction of Harriet Martineau is unquestionably didactic. Throughout the tales the industrialist expounds natural laws to the irrational working man, who refuses to acknowledge the capitalist's principle of mutual interests. The industrialist's doctrine is fully supported by plots constructed to follow the working out of economic laws. Refractory characters are ultimately dealt with, as plot reveals the inevitable consequences of disobedience to those who resist. It is perhaps this relentless dogging of characters who will not accept the fixed order of divine and economic law which has led to Humphry House's judgment that Harriet Martineau "mercilessly used fiction in her teaching."[13]

Judging from the three tales discussed above, it would seem that Harriet Martineau's attitude toward capital is that of an upholder of the vested interests of the bourgeois industrial class. She was after all the daughter of a Norwich manufacturer of bombazine. Even as late as 1855 she wrote a pamphlet, *The Factory Controversy: A Warning against Meddling Legislation*, which was her response to the agitation for laws against unfenced machinery; given impetus, no doubt, by a series of articles in *Houshold Words*, pointing out the dangers of being "ground in the mill." But even though her fiction leaves her open to this charge, it would be a gross oversimplification to judge her as merely a special pleader for selfish class interests which were served by the existing order of things. The philosophical basis of her attitude lay in the doctrine of Necessarianism, which held that the individual had to conform to certain natural laws which governed the universe, or otherwise be punished by the operation of those laws. Therefore, it behooved every man to learn those principles, for improvidence and poor calculation would bring ruin. Man's happiness was possible only within the framework of obedience to those laws.[14] Because of her belief in Necessarianism, Harriet Martineau was temperamentally suited to a rationalistic commitment to laws protecting property rights, and to fixed economic laws governing the relations of capital and labor. In her autobiography she does not discuss at length the ideology of Necessarianism, but she makes some useful generalizations: "All human action proceeds on the assumption that all the workings of the universe are governed by laws which cannot be broken by human will." She has lived her life confident that there existed "eternal and irreversible laws, working in every department of the universe, without any interference from any random will human or divine." She rejects the main objection to the doctrine; namely, "that it is good for endurance but bad for action," and cites her own case as one in which "the invariable action of fixed laws has certainly been the mainspring of my activity."[15] Herein lies the explanation for her prescription of patience and obedience for the working classes. It is then in the nature of things that improvident working men who disobey eternal laws must face all the consequences of their actions at the end of her stories, while her clearsighted industrialists are able to put fate into their own hands through their knowledge of causes.

FOUR

Radical Fiction

"Here's a book written by a friend o' mine, and if
yo'll read it yo'll see how wages find their own
level, without either masters or men having ought
to do with them; except the men cut their own
throats wi' striking, like the confounded noodles
they are." So I took th' book and tugged at it; but,
Lord bless yo', it went on about capital and labour,
and labour and capital, till it fair sent me off to
sleep. I ne'er could rightly fix i' my mind which
was which; and it spoke on 'em as if they was
vartues or vices; and what I wanted for to know
were the rights o' men, whether they be rich or
poor—so be they only were men.

Mrs. Gaskell, *North and South*

Harriet Martineau's image of the indus-
trialist as national benefactor was sharply challenged by representatives
of the Radical proletarian point of view.[1] Although the political economist might bemoan the improvidence of the generality of the working
class, he acknowledged that there were "good" workmen who were thrifty
and industrious. On the other hand, it is the refusal to acknowledge the
most trivial good in the opposition that is the distinguishing characteristic of the radical attitude in both nonfiction and fiction alike. Thackeray's
definition of the "outrageous Radical Snob" best illustrates the Radical
penchant for wholesale denunciation of the upper classes. This type of
Snob is "a man [who] preaches to you that all noblemen are tyrants, that
all clergymen are hypocrites and liars, that all capitalists are scoundrels
banded together in an infamous conspiracy to deprive the people of their
rights."[2] Serving as a rebuttal to the bourgeois notions of Harriet Martineau, the pronouncements of Marx and Engels exhibit the tendency of
the Radical to stereotype the industrialist as an enemy of the people.
Moreover, one of their accusations, it will be seen, becomes a motif in

Radical fiction. To the lesson in obedience to the law protecting property rights that is taught to the weaver in *The Rioters*, the Radical replies:

> The middle classes certainly are all in favour of the sanctity of the law. That is not surprising. They have made the law; they approve of it; they are protected by it; and they gain advantages from it. The bourgeoisie appreciate that, even though some particular enactment may injure their interests, the whole body of laws protects their interests. The middle classes know full well how firmly their position in the social order is buttressed by this principle of the sanctity of the law—a principle established by an act of will on the part of one section of society and accepted by the other section. The middle classes hold fast to the sanctity of the law because they believe that the law has been made, like their God, in their own image. That is why the policeman's truncheon is such a reassuring symbol of authority.[3]

Law, morality, and religion then are to the proletariat merely bourgeois prejudices behind which are concealed bourgeois interests. As for the principles of political economy, they are only the rationalization of bourgeois interests into eternal laws for their own benefit:

> Your very ideas are but the outgrowth of the conditions of your bourgeois production and bourgeois property, just as your jurisprudence is but the will of your class made into a law for all, a will whose essential character and direction are determined by the economic conditions of existence of your class.
>
> The selfish misconception that induces you to transform into eternal laws of nature and of reason the social forms springing from your present mode of production and form of property—historical relations that rise and disappear in the progress of production—this misconception you share with every ruling class that has preceded you. What you see clearly in the case of ancient property, what you admit in the case of feudal property, you are of course forbidden to admit in the case of your own bourgeois form of property.[4]

The bourgeoisie had enslaved the proletariat by making laws to their own advantage and punishing him for breaking them. They also sought to inculcate in him a morality that would lead him to obey those laws, and to espouse a religion which upheld those laws and that morality, by emphasizing that it was God's will that there should be the propertied and the propertyless and that it was the duty of a good Christian workingman to submit to God's ordinances. What sort of charitable opinion, therefore, could the industrialist expect from his slaves in the factory? What was the use in making distinctions between good, not so bad, and bad manufacturers in an industrial system in which the proletariat had no freedom, no equality? As in all conflicts of moment, the enemy has only one face.

Such was the cast of mind of Engels which would not permit him to view any of the industrialist's actions other than as detrimental to the welfare of his employees. The editors of Engels's *Condition of the Working Class in England* have aptly summarized his inflexible enmity toward the manufacturer and their account is worth quoting in full:

> If a job demanded heavy physical labour then Engels declared that the employer was ruining the health of his hands. If only light repetitive work was required then Engels denounced the factory owner for reducing his workers to nervous wrecks by making them perform excessively tedious and boring tasks. If the manufacturer provided no amenities for his workers then Engels exhausted his extensive vocabulary of vituperation to denounce him as a creature devoid of all common humanity. But if a millowner built cottages for his artisans Engels promptly accused him of being a greedy and tyrannous landlord. If a manufacturer built a school for the operatives' children Engels attacked him for trying to train a new generation of workers to be obedient slaves to the wicked capitalists. If a factory owner erected a reading room Engels complained because no copies of the *Northern Star* were displayed. As far as Engels was concerned no employer was ever in the right and the factory owner was always the villain of the piece.[5]

Nor did Engels's detestation of the millowner cease with his condemnation of him as an economic oppressor. He also turned his polemic into an argument ad hominem by accusing the factory owner of exercising a droit de seigneur. This kind of attack is significant to fiction because it is taken up by the Radical popular weekly:

> It will, of course, be appreciated that the girls who work in a factory, even more than girls working in other occupations find that they have to grant to their employers the *ius primae noctis*. In this respect, too, the factory owner wields complete power over the persons and charms of the girls working for him. Nine times out of ten, nay, in ninety-nine cases out of a hundred, the threat of dismissal is sufficient to break down the resistance of girls who at the best of times, have no strong inclination to chastity. If the factory owner is sufficiently debased— and the Report of the Factories Enquiry Commission recounts several such cases—his factory is also his harem.[6]

Then there follows chop-logic which, offering another instance of Engels's refusal to acknowledge virtue in a factory owner, betrays the fact that his impressions of present conditions are most likely derived from obsolete evidence: "As far as the girls are concerned, the situation is not altered by the fact that not all manufacturers take advantage of their opportunities in this matter. In the early days of the factory system most of the manufacturers were uneducated upstarts and quite uninhibited by social hypocrisies from denying themselves the exercise of their vested rights."[7]

The unmitigated hostility toward the industrialist that is ubiquitous in Engels's writings found literary expression in the cheap periodical fiction of G. W. M. Reynolds. Because the emergence of the popular press is contemporaneous with that of the factory employee, a brief review of the history of the penny press might account both for the Radical strain in such a class-oriented penny weekly as *Reynolds's Miscellany* and for the literary interests of the working class to whom it was addressed.

The parents of the new spirit that came to Galt's parish with the construction of the first cotton mill in 1790 were the French and Industrial Revolutions. That new spirit was reflected in the challenge to the old agrarian order represented by the democratic opinions of the new class of factory workers, whose Radical views were garnered from the London newspapers to which they subscribed. Thus from the beginning of his long struggle for equality, the working man was supported and encouraged by the popular press. After the Napoleonic Wars, inventions made possible the growth of cheap publications. By 1820 the paper-making machine came into use after overcoming the resistance of the trade. The paper thus made was of better quality and of a larger size, two conditions necessary for printing with a rotary steam press. "The combination of cheap paper and mechanical printing," writes Louis James, "was the greatest step forward in book production since Caxton."[8] One of the possible uses of the inexpensive periodical which resulted from the combination of those two publishing processes was the dissemination of Radical opinion, by which working class movements could be guided. That this was an actuality is evident in the Government's efforts to check the news periodical in the early 1830s by invoking the Seditious Publications Act of 1820, which required that periodicals printing anything like news be taxed four-pence in the hopes of pricing them too high for the working man's pocket. This Whig tax was known as "the Tax on Knowledge": reading and self-improvement were looked upon by reactionaries as weapons in the class struggle. The 1840s saw an increase in periodical fiction. In 1840 there were eighty cheap periodicals in existence around London; twenty-two of these contained tales and romances only. Throughout the decade, however, a larger proportion of periodicals were exclusively devoted to fiction.[9]

In order to exist, the penny press had to sell. In order to sell, it had to stimulate. The mass literature of the 1840s intended to please the tired and bored mind of the working man. Thus such a periodical as *The Dodger*, which became *The Sunday Chronicle* in 1841, published the following advertisement about its fiction: "Tales of the most Absorbing Interest, and which absolutely engage the attention of the reader with a species of galvanic force. These Tales are replete with MYSTERY, HORROR, LOVE AND SEDUCTION!"[10] The poor needed to escape into a world of excitement—crime, vice, suffering, love—and the popular press catered to this need. The publisher Lloyd once wrote, in a letter to the wood engraver who made the blocks with which the penny dreadfuls were illustrated, that, "The eyes . . . must be larger, and there must be more blood—much more blood!"[11] And judging from the opinion of Mayhew's costermongers in his London Labour and the London Poor, the first parts of which appeared in 1851, the poor did not want to read about their own class but about the wealthy, the "haristocrats."[12]

G. W. M. Reynolds[13] seems to have known exactly what the poor wanted to read. As Lionel Stevenson has observed, the best-selling novelist of the mid-century was not Dickens but Reynolds.[14] Toward the end of his career, the Bookseller claimed that Reynolds had written more and sold more copies than Dickens; and in an obituary notice of 1879, that same periodical called Reynolds "the most popular writer of our time."[15] Mayhew recorded that Reynolds was considered "a trump" by the people of the streets.[16] Thackeray, having noted the tendency of lower class literature to paint a poor but virtuous hero pitted against a wicked aristocrat, attributed the great popularity of Reynolds' Mysteries of the Court of London to his radicalism. A bookseller at the Brighton station told Thackeray that "this book was by many, many times the most popular of all periodical tales then published, because . . . it lashes the aristocracy."[17] The secret of Reynolds's popularity among the poor, moreover, lay not only in his belligerence toward the rich but also in his attack on all kinds of lawful authority. Government, for example, conspired with the rich against the poor. In The Mysteries a new magistrate is advised by the Home Secretary: "You must always shield the upper classes as much as possible; and . . . bring out the misdeeds of the lower orders in the boldest relief."[18] In the class hostility expressed in that novel one critic sees "the pale ghost of the radicalism of the Chartist press."[19]

While Reynolds took as his province the misdeeds of the aristocracy in London, one of his partners in class antagonism, Paul Pimlico, assailed the manufacturing classes of Yorkshire in two serialized tales, "The Manufacturer" and "The Factory Girl," which were published in the Miscellany in 1849.[20] Appealing to the tired minds of his readers by offering them the sensational, Pimlico dwells upon Engels's frequent accusation that the factory owner's establishment is no better than a harem. In addition to sexual misconduct, the manufacturer is also guilty of the often-voiced Radical charge of using the law as an instrument of the rich against the poor, for whom justice is not to be had.

I

"The Manufacturer"

The setting of "The Manufacturer" is Bradford, the center of the worsted trade. As is the case in both tales, the working class heroine's background is not originally proletarian: her father, a well-educated, former wool merchant of Norwich, had suffered business reverses and had to fall back on work as a factory hand. Under these circumstances Pimlico can display Sarah Belford, the factory girl, as possessing the attributes of a heroine from a higher station and can cater in some degree to his readers' tastes for stories about "haristocrats":

> She was rather above the average stature of women; and her exquisitely intellectual countenance united the rose and the lily in fair proportions. Her figure, at once symmetrical and commanding, combined gracefulness of movement with ease and modest lightness of carriage; and when she cast upon you her full azure eyes, beaming with thoughtful expression, but now languid with care, it were vain to seem insensible to her charms, or deny the natural superiority of her endowments, fitted either to adorn the most brilliant circles, or command admiration and respect in whatever sphere she moved. (June 23, pp. 793-94)

At the beginning of the tale, Sarah Belford is pregnant after having been seduced by her employer, Ramsley, for whom Sarah is but one among many victims. Her indignant father goes down to the mill to confront Ramsley with his crime. The manufacturer suggests that the blame may be transferred to someone else, or the affair kept quiet because his character is at stake. But Sarah will not agree to father her unborn child upon anyone else; she will not "perjure herself that her seducer may continue, in the eyes of the world, free from the plague-spot of his iniquities" (June 16, p. 778). Ramsley, resentful of being bearded in his own den, is angered at Belford's appeal for justice, glossing it as the "scurrilous abuse" of a Radical. "I suppose," taunts the millowner, "you are or have been a hot-headed democrat, and have learnt the abusive oratorical slang of revolutionists and levellers . . ." (June 16, p. 778). Reproached for his political beliefs where he has pleaded as an injured father, Belford then answers with the rhetoric of a Radical:

> Yes—I am a democrat, it is true, and I glory in it; but I also am a father to an injured and suffering daughter, to a daughter wronged by a debauchee who ruins and despises,—who deflowers and laughs, and boasts of his crime. Yes—I am a democrat, and glory in it. But what first created democratic opinions, and yet supports them, as they gather

friends in thousands, but such heartless profligacy and oppression among the upper and middle classes which I now condemn in you? When you and such as you trample upon the poor and mock their feelings, and insult their wives and ruin their fair daughters, think you not that they will turn upon you, and in time humble you to your proper level?" (June 16, pp. 778-79)

But for now, the poor have little choice but to brook insult as well as injury from the rich. The unemployed Belford accepts both of Ramsley's measures of atonement: employment for the youngest Belford girl, Dinah, and woolen materials with which her father can work at home. Belford, however, has misgivings about being employed by his daughter's seducer and is not without a fear that the manufacturer has designs on his youngest daughter (June 16, p. 779).

In a digression upon manufacturers as a class, Pimlico, unlike Engels, admits that there are a few good men among that class; "but there are more, on the other hand, cast in a far different and deeply degrading mould,—men at once sensual and selfish—epicureans in body and sordid in mind . . ." (June 23, p. 793). Given such masters, what more can be expected of the factory system than that it be a breeding ground for vice:

> The fact that the spinning of yarns and manufacture of pieces are conducted chiefly by the female sex, pent up in hundreds in the vast prison-like mills under the direction of foremen or overlookers, throws no small degree of temptation in the way of those under the unruly dominion of the sensual appetites;—and the many cases continually occurring of infamous seduction and ruin to the young inexperienced girls who there earn their livelihood, by both masters and overlookers, is one of the melancholy effects, inseparable we fear, from the *present* factory system. While the proprietors of such establishments are themselves loose in morals, those immediately under them, down to the lowest in the scale, become their imitators. Modesty of demeanour and purity of feelings are soon lost; and the whole factory speedily becomes little else but a nursery of vice. (June 23, p. 793)

The underscoring of "*present*" in this attack on the factory system is, however, not the ominous note of the Socialist leveler; nor is it expressive of the nostalgia for a pre-industrial state that is both one aspect of Radical and a good part of Tory sentiment. Pimlico asks for neither revolution nor regression, but as Dickens did before him, he expresses the notion that all would be well if the English would emulate the American factory system found at Lowell, Massachusetts (June 23, p. 793).[21]

Not only does the manufacturer prey upon his dependent female employees, but with utter disregard for the market, he is also guilty of criminal business dealings. Sarah overhears Ramsley and three other manufacturers plan to cast large bills of accommodation upon the market for three months' additional credit. In the interval they can turn all their assets into gold and flee the country (June 23, pp. 794-95).

In addition to these charges, the manufacturer is adept at wrongfully using the law to gain his ends. Ramsley's offer of work to George Belford had been a subterfuge. In order to get Belford out of the way so that he might be free to seduce Dinah Belford, Ramsley arranged to have his over-looker, Gandy, plant three pieces of finished cloth among the materials Belford had taken home to work up. Belford is then charged with theft under the Worsted Act. When asked whether he will prefer a charge of embezzlement or felony, Ramsley replies that out of respect for the family he will be lenient and call the trumped-up theft, embezzlement (June 30, pp. 809-10). At this juncture Paul Pimlico's sustained attack on factory owners is undercut by a convention of fiction. Pimlico wants to have it both ways: to indict the legal tyranny of the manufacturing classes, yet to show the virtuous working class hero in some way triumphant over that tyranny. He effects a compromise by having the millowners who serve as magistrates grant Belford sympathy but not justice:

> Strange as it may appear, magistrates connected with manufactures are permitted to adjudicate in cases in hearing which they must natural-ly be prejudiced, and in carrying out a statute passed for their special benefit and protection, called the Worsted Act. In this the strict ends of justice are often in danger of being set aside by the minds of the judges being warped against the evidence. . . ." (June 30, p. 810)[22]

But, we are assured, "at present this was not the case." Belford tells the magistrates that Ramsley came to him on the night before the trial, offer-ing to drop the false charges if Belford would induce his daughter Dinah to surrender her virtue. The magistrates are "morally convinced" of Bel-ford's innocence, but calling themselves "law-dispensers . . . and not law-makers," they feel compelled to convict Belford, though promising to raise a fund for his family. Belford, calling the Worsted Act tyrannous and arbitrary, thanks the magistrates for their kindness and goes to prison (June 30, p. 811).

Still another of the malevolent Ramsley's diversions is to attend Chartist meetings with a view of creating a commotion which will incite working men into a breach of the peace. At one of these meetings Henry Belford, having heard from his sister Sarah of Ramsley's plot to cheat the market, determines to expose Ramsley. He addresses the crowd, catalogu-ing the qualities which have earned the manufacturer the hatred of the working man. His address also serves to put the Chartists in the light of peaceful protesters following parliamentary procedure, rather than the firebrands that many of the middle classes considered them.

> Working-men! A person has come more than once among us to ridicule our addresses, and watch whether any of his workmen support our cause. The name of this individual is Joshua Ramsley. . . . Have you seen him before? Aye, I know you are aware of him. Remember his many seductions. Consider his grinding despotism over his combers and how frequently he turns them adrift because they are democrats. Is not the monstrous case of George Belford fresh in your memory? Aye, I know you remember it, and hope in common with myself to see vengeance overtake the oppressor. Do you know the general character of the man? Is he not a robber of the market? You are surprised! But ask him in what peculiar way he intends to dupe his creditors, and he cannot deny that I am right in calling him a robber *at least prospectively* so. Shall such a man, then, who gloats over female ruin, and whose many base actions, yet partly hid, pronounce him a candidate for penal chains and slavery at Norfolk Island,—shall such a man remain among us to be a spy of our conduct, and endeavour to make us break the law that his malice may be gratified? I say no, and propose that he be immediately expelled from this meeting. (July 7, p. 825)

Ramsley has used factory girls for his pleasure and the law for his protection, all with impunity in a bourgeois society which excuses social crimes against the lower orders. There is one law for the rich and another for the poor. If, however, the manufacturer remains outside the law as a social criminal, he speedily becomes an outlaw when he commits an economic crime against a commercial society. News of Ramsley's plan of embezzlement gets abroad. One of his creditors, determined to be paid before Ramsley breaks, demands at gunpoint what amounts to all of Ramsley's portable property as his due (July 7, pp. 841-43). Taking what little money remains, the manufacturer seeks to escape. Surrounded by police after having retreated to the spectacular heights of a rock on a riverbank, Ramsley shoots himself and in an alliterative exit, "the corpse of the suicide MANUFACTURER, bounding from rock to rock in its bloody descent, found a bed in the bubbling brook below" (July 21, p. 859).

The pregnant Sarah Belford dies of "the canker of sin." Upon his release from prison, her father emigrates to the United States with a Parthian shot at the rich: "the honest working man declaring up to the moment of his departure, that England, oppressed by pauperizing laws, and overridden with a rapacious aristocracy was no longer a home for the sons of toil" (July 21, p. 859).

II

"The Factory Girl"

Paul Pimlico's second tale, "The Factory Girl," serialized in *Reynolds's Miscellany* from October through November, 1849, resembles "The Manufacturer" in many ways but differs from it by virtue of an increased stridency of tone. In all probability this is due to Pimlico's having learned the lesson of the master, that of lashing the wealthy classes as a whole, using the manufacturer and his associates as a starting point.

William and Esther Mansfield are twins who live in an idyllic rural village in the West Riding of Yorkshire, removed from the smoke and din of factories and dye-works. The brother and sister are descended from yeomen farmers whose property has been in the family for generations. The description of William exhibits both the demands of the conventions of romance—a hero with an aristocratic countenance—and the requirement of radical sentiment appropriate to a people's champion:

> William's appearance was at once majestic and imposing—yet he knew nothing of the artificial buffoonery of courts, or the mock majesty of a servile aristocracy; and that he possessed an innate consciousness of the intellectual power which sat enthroned upon his lofty wide-arched forehead, and beamed from his manly well-moulded countenance and speaking eyes, struck the beholder at the first glance. But his heart was full of the milk of human kindness; in man he saw a brother, and esteemed him as such; in many of the conventionalisms of society, he thought he beheld a forced barrier to the full development of the affections of the heart; and in the legal statutes of the realm, and the constitutional form and nature of our government, he thought he saw the germs of that injustice and misery which crush the people and repress their elevation. (Oct. 20, p. 201)

Esther, his twin, was William's counterpart as was appropriate to her sex. In comparison with her brother, who was like the "noble tree" of the forest,

> She, like the beautiful domestic plant, or garden tree, blooming in more sheltered loveliness, yet possessed a mind equally as active, an industry as untiring, a resolution, when once formed, as strong and indomitable, and a humility and virtue based on religion as deep, as high, and as lasting as her brother. Her manner, like her engaging person, was at once easy and graceful, free from the exhibition of any consciousness of superior charms, and attractive from the absence of all coquettish pride or pretension to the homage of the other sex or those whom she, perhaps, might be expected to consider her inferior in the artificial grade of rank in society. (Oct. 20, p. 201)

Respected and honored by the rural community in which they lived, the pair were esteemed "nature's true nobility." Pimlico continues his catalog of their virtues, a description which suggests that the author might have at one time written, as Reynolds did for the *London Journal*, articles on etiquette: "they bore their honours meekly, without arrogance or pretension; both modest and humble, but not timid; retiring, but not reserved; cheerful, without being vulgar or ostentatiously thrusting their thoughts or opinions upon the world of their sequestered village." (Oct. 20, p. 201)

Thus formidably armed with the qualifications of the high-born hero and heroine of romance, the two are prepared to encounter with dignity the misfortunes for which they are destined. Their mother dies suddenly and their father loses his farm, fattening "nefarious projectors" during the speculative frenzy of the railway mania (Oct. 20, p. 202). The two prepare to go to Bradford, William to work in a warehouse and Esther, in the "dungeon-like mills." Mrs. Unwin, a neighbor, forewarns Esther that she will need the help of Providence in making her way as a mill girl. Factory workers are well known for their profligacy and "as the proprietor of the mill may be in which you work, so will in most cases be those employed" (Oct. 20, p. 202). Above all, continues Mrs. Unwin, one should be on guard against the overlookers who "in such places have their favourites, and they are either open or sacred in their proceedings with the women, as they know it will suit the master. And those females who indulge them most with favours, are in turn, favoured with the best work" (Oct. 20, p. 202).

Mrs. Unwin's fears turn out to be well grounded, for things turn out badly for Esther at Mr. Alston's mill, where she obtains employment. The overlooker Judas Bromley, "was notorious for his attempts at seduction, and, in truth, only followed the bent and secret example of his master" (Oct. 20, p. 203). After working hours one day, Bromley bestows his attentions upon Esther, who promptly strikes him and threatens to report him to his master. Bromley laughs derisively, telling Esther that Alston has the same intentions as he (Oct. 20, p. 203). By way of revenge, the overlooker gives Esther a bad warp which no one had previously been able to weave. According to "*the Manufacturer's Law*," the Worsted Act, "an arbitrary and unconstitutional law for crushing the poor," a weaver who begins a warp must finish it or be "drawn like a felon before the bench of the unpaid magistracy of the locality" (Oct. 27, p. 218). Unaware of the law, Esther leaves her warp and remains at home the following day, only to receive a summons to appear before the magistrates. Here Paul Pimlico, with an echo of Engels, interjects an attack on the manufacturers, for having laws passed to protect their class interests:

But on this point, and interfering between servant and master where no legal bond is broken, no bound of honesty overstepped, and where on both sides the agreement was merely voluntary and verbal, the law is turned into an engine of oppression,—the dispensers of *law*, not *justice*, into atrocious tyrants;—and the victims of its ruthless despotism but sacrifices at the shrine of *monopoly* and *protection*, which the manufacturers of this country still profess to disdain with external signs of manifest horror and alarm. Let manufacturers talk of hypocrisy after being the promoters of, and benefited by the operations of such an unjust law as this,—a law passed by the legislature of this country for their especial protection—to subserve their own class interests, and be a check and a screw upon the rights and liberties of the industrious poor! (Oct. 27, p. 218)

Rather than go back to the bad warp, Esther decides to go before the magistrates to vindicate herself. The introduction of magistrates offers Pimlico an opportunity to discourse once more upon the partiality and injustice of legal administration. (Once again he is faced with the same problem that came up in a similar situation in "The Manufacturer": how to convey the impression that the real English working man is powerless under the evil he is attacking but at the same time demonstrate how his fictional paragon of a factory worker is triumphant over a legal force which is indomitable in actuality. In this case he resorts to the deus ex machina, an unexpected witness.) It seems that the sole recommendations of those "guardians of the law," is their inclination to "denounce democrats and radical reform" and their willingness to "hurry from the earth,—as a scion of Royalty wished to do at Leeds,—at one fell swoop whole streets of those sticklers for political justice, with cannonballs and bayonets!" (Oct. 27, p. 218). The unpaid magistrates of the factory districts are almost all manufacturers or connected with manufacturing in some way. Morally, argues Pimlico, such judges are unfit to preside over disputes between master and weaver. Moreover, the police officials (whose truncheons, according to Engels, were so reassuring to the middle classes) are represented as the tools of authority, "civil or arrogant, servile and cringing in proportion as the parties entering court were well or ill-dressed, or low or elevated in station" (Oct. 27, p. 218). But Esther has nothing to fear, for the court is favorably impressed by her genteel bearing which augurs innocence. What is most important, however, is that with the aid of a surprise witness, Maria Edgecomb, a girl seduced by Bromley and made confidante to his plan, Esther's lawyer unmasks Bromley as the oppressor bent upon revenging himself upon Esther for repelling his advances. The case is disposed in favor of Esther, and her persecutor is jeered out of court (Oct. 27, p. 219).

After the trial the millowner Alston is concerned about the effect of his man Bromley's notoriety upon the reputation of his establishment: "He wished it, apparently, to *reflect* what he wished his own character to *seem* before the world—virtuous, pure, and regular in every respect" (Nov. 3, p. 233). Alston therefore decides to fire Bromley; the millowner is confident that whatever Bromley might afterwards reveal about the secret intrigues he had engaged in for his master would be taken as the word of a known slanderer. At first it seems that Bromley will create no difficulties about parting; in his reply to Alston he catalogs his private duties as an overlooker: "I can get another place, aye, two of them . . . where I will not have secrets to keep, intrigues to put in order, procuresses to bribe, and girls to seduce in mind for my master to seduce in person. No, no, I'll keep secrets no longer; I'll split, that's certain" (Nov. 3, p. 233). But Bromley has no intention of leaving, and after he informs the millowner of his possession of a document that would blast Alston's character and expose his hypocrisy, Alston urges him to stay. At that moment Julius Arnheim, a German warehouse owner and employer of Esther's brother William, enters. Having attended Esther's trial and having been smitten by her beauty, Arnheim has just come from a visit to her, the purpose of which was to induce her to become his mistress under the double threat of slandering her and dismissing her brother from his employ. Despite his threats, Esther spurned his proposal (Nov. 3, pp. 234-35).

Now Alston, Bromley, and Arnheim are all interested in seducing Esther. Who shall have her remains to be decided. Arnheim's claim takes precedence for the following reasons: "The master cannot be expected to yield to the claims or pretensions of the servant;—the merchant customer will not give up precedency to the sensual manufacturer; and thus in discussing their diabolical purpose, Bromley throws up all in favour of Alston; and Alston, acting upon the principle of mercantile expediency, yields to the urgent wish of his friend and obliging customer, Mr. Arnheim" (Nov. 10, p. 249). The trio plan to lure Esther to a house of assignation and there Arnheim is to forcibly ruin her. Though lustfully attracted to Esther, Alston has momentary qualms about rape; but he placates his conscience on the grounds of self-interest. In his analysis of Alston's motives, Paul Pimlico interjects a commentary on expediency as the basis for business and also government ethics:

> At this stage of [Alston's] reasoning, expediency, affrighted by the shadow of stern honesty, rushed to his aid,—expediency as opposed to right and honesty, the ground of modern legislation,—the pretext for government, monopoly, and oppression,—the hinge of tyranny . . . expediency came to his aid and whispered, "It is a matter of business. Mr. Arnheim came and consulted you,—you tacitly agreed to let Bromley [arrange the seduction], but refrain from acting yourself. You know

of it, and only act negatively by refraining from interfering at all;—besides, you sold a thousand pieces by it, and at a shilling per piece higher than you otherwise would have done." (Nov. 10, p. 250)

With this excuse, the manufacturer sets his mind at rest and drops out of the tale.

Pimlico assures the reader that this kind of villainy is not an isolated instance, the attempt against Esther being but one of a thousand like cases. There follows a diatribe against the wealthy in general: such diabolical scheming is not confined to millowners and factory girls, but is to be found under the surface life of the aristocracy, the "wine-bibbing, poor-oppressing rich," who gloss over their iniquities by making contributions to charity (Nov. 17, pp. 265-66).

With the timely help of her fiance, Esther is rescued from Arnheim, but the German merchant turns the tables by making a flimsy charge of theft and attempted murder, a melodramatic turn of plot which gets the principals back into the courtroom, where Esther, once again on display, is acquitted by the device of another surprise witness. Though guilty of conspiracy, Esther's enemies are not charged with that crime. Here Pimlico again expatiates upon the power of money to shield the guilty rich. Arnheim reinstates himself with the public through philanthropic acts; and a box of German sausages sent to the magistrate who presided at Esther's second appearance in court gains the German merchant an invitation to the magistrate's ball. A final attempt on Esther results in the drowning of Bromley, and this time Arnheim decides to leave the country for good (Nov. 24, pp. 281-83).

In spite of the vehement attacks against the manufacturing classes in these two tales, the degree of genuine social consciousness reflected in Paul Pimlico's Radical attitude is open to question. This judgment is based largely upon the way in which he uses the conventions of romantic fiction. His working class protagonists, as we have seen, are aristocratic types. By virtue of his appearance and feeling for the people, William Mansfield readily resembles Disraeli's Chartist leader, "that very aristocratic-looking" Walter Gerard of *Sybil*, who turns out to have had gentle blood all along. Esther Mansfield and Sarah Belford are described as goddesses. The overriding concern of the Radical for exposing the laws' injustice seems to be subservient to the melodramatic possibilities that a courtroom affords, judging by the number of times such a scene is employed. Moreover, having, as in "The Factory Girl," created a voluptuous paragon of beauty and virtue, Pimlico uses the courtroom to exploit what amounts to voyeuristic tendencies in the reader, an effect which is suggested by the way in which Esther Mansfield awes the courtroom audience and rouses at least one, Julius Arnheim, to declare his infatuation. As a writer of sensational Radical fiction, Paul Pimlico sought to "galvanize" his readers, more, however, for the purpose of titillating them than, with the Chartist movement dead in 1848, to arouse them into political activism.[23]

III

Mary Barton

Elizabeth Gaskell, the wife of a Unitarian minister, is perhaps best remembered for the reconciliation motif in her industrial novels, a reflection of her Christian sentimentalism which urges that employer-employee relationships can be improved by a better understanding between master and man. As such, it is difficult to think of her as a Radical; and though sympathetic toward the working man in *Mary Barton* (1848), the first novel to depict realistically the life of the industrial poor in Manchester, Mrs. Gaskell was no Radical. With proper qualifying statements of her own, what she set out to do in *Mary Barton* was to dramatize what some working men of her acquaintance were thinking. In spite of making her position clear in the novel, she was accused of promoting the misconception that employers were unresponsive to the suffering of workers in periods of distress. In his review of *Mary Barton*, W. R. Greg stated that Mrs. Gaskell, by ignoring or being ignorant of the kindness felt and done for workers by employers, has done an injustice to a whole class. She "has most inconsiderately fostered the ill-opinion of [manufacturers] known to exist in certain quarters—and has, unintentionally no doubt, but most unfortunately flattered both the prejudices of the aristocracy and the passions of the populace."[24] Her intention misunderstood, Mrs. Gaskell sought to restate her position in a letter to a Miss Ewart, daughter of a Liberal M. P.: "That some of the [working] men do view the subject in the way I have tried to represent, I have personal evidence. . . . No one can feel more deeply than I how *wicked* it is to do anything to excite class against class; and it has been most unconscious if I have done so . . . no praise could compensate me for the self-reproach I shall feel if I have written unjustly."[25] In writing the novel from the Chartist working man's point of view, however, Mrs. Gaskell inevitably, if unwittingly, pictured the manufacturer and his family as Radical opinion saw them.

In order to read *Mary Barton* as a work of Radical fiction, it is necessary to examine three Radical assumptions about the manufacturer and then show how these notions are presented in toto, or modified by Mrs. Gaskell. Stated in simplest terms, these Radical attitudes toward the industrialist appear in *Mary Barton* in the themes of injustice, sexuality, and pride.

We have seen that the new class of working men emerged with democratic opinions. Since the Revolution of 1789 they had struggled for political, social, and economic justice. In England the Chartist movement of the 1830s and 1840s was what Marx and Engels termed the first revolutionary impulse of the proletariat.[26] In their first petition (1839), the Chartists displayed their feelings of injustice. The few had governed too long, to the neglect of the many, and the Reform Bill of 1832 had merely "effected a transfer of power from one domineering faction to another and left the people as helpless as before."[27] By means of the six points of "the People's Charter," the Chartists had hoped, through political reform, to put an end to the degradations of inequality. If universal suffrage, the most important of the six points to the working man, would not eliminate the people's distress, argued the writers of the Charter, "it will at least remove their repining."[28] In his essay *Chartism* (1839), Carlyle sympathetically analyzed the cause of the peoples's "repining" as the gnawing feeling of injustice which animated such Chartists as Mary Barton's father:

> It is not what a man outwardly has or wants that constitutes the happiness or misery of him. Nakedness, hunger, distress of all kinds, death itself, have been cheerfully suffered, when the heart was right. It is the feeling of *injustice* that is insupportable to all men. . . . No man can bear it or ought to bear it. A deeper law than any parchment-law whatsoever, a law written direct by the hand of God in the inmost being of man, incessantly protests against it. What is injustice? Another name for *disorder*, for unveracity, unreality. . . . It is not the outward pain of injustice; that, were it even the flaying of the back with knotted scourges, . . . is a comparatively small matter. The real smart is the soul's pain and stigma, the hurt inflicted on the moral self. The rudest clown must draw himself up into attitude of battle, and resistance to the death if such be offered him. He cannot live under it; his own soul aloud, and all the Universe with silent continual beckonings, says, It cannot be. He must revenge himself; *revancher* himself, make himself good again,—that so *meum* may be mine, *tuum* thine, and each party standing clear on his own basis, order be restored. There is something in—finitely respectable in this, and we may say universally respected; it is the common stamp of manhood vindicating itself in all of us. . . .[29]

The particular form of injustice that is treated in *Mary Barton* relates to the principle of political economy which states that capital and labor have a mutual interest and are dependent upon one another. Engels makes distinct the degree of dependency, a point ignored by the employer but one that becomes an idée fixe for John Barton: "Although, in a general sense, the middle classes depend upon the workers, this does not mean the middle classes depend upon the workers for their daily needs. After all, at a pinch, the middle classes can live on their accumulated capital."[30]

A second Radical assumption involves the oft-repeated accusation of sexual indecency on the part of employers. We have observed Engels's part in advancing this notion and Paul Pimlico's use of it as a dominant theme in his fiction. It also appears in *Mary Barton*, where a scion of a manufacturer's family is bent upon seducing Mary. By way of accounting for the prevalence of this kind of smear tactic, we might examine what seems to be its origin. Writing in 1833 Peter Gaskell sought to explain the immorality that was associated, in some quarters, with the factory workers of his day. It was his contention that the early manufacturers were to blame for the "almost entire extinction of sexual decency" which he believed characterized the factory population of the 1830s.[31] First of all, he proceeded on a common assumption that the crowding together of both sexes in the factory produced an unwholesome contact. The stimulation of the high temperature (Cobbett had said 84 degrees.) under which they worked, as in tropical climates, brought puberty to females at an early age. These conditions, together with the lascivious nature of the masters, who without refinement or education had the "animal passions" of working men, "conspired to produce a very-early development of the sexual appetencies."[32] Given the example of their fathers, together with their introduction into the factory as mill superintendents at an early age, the sons of the early manufacturers were notoriously debauched:

> Boys, at an age when they should have been sedulously kept apart from opportunities of indulging their nascent sexual propensities, were thrust into a very hot bed of lust, and exposed to vicious example, in addition to other causes, irresistibly tending to make them a prey to licentiousness. The consequences of these criminal and unadvised proceedings were, that long after the masters freed themselves from the vices incident to their first advancement, they had the shame and mortification of seeing their errors propagated through a series of ramifications, every move seeming to become more and more depraved in its character.[33]

Thus prematurely exposed to sex, it was the adolescent sons of the first generation of manufacturers who spread immorality throughout the working population on a grand scale:

> The organized system of immorality which was pursued by these

younger men and boys was extremely fatal to the best interests of the labouring community. Chastity became a laughing stock and byeword. Victim after victim was successively taken from the mill—the selection being, in the generality of cases, the prettiest and the most modest-looking girl to be found among the hundreds assembled there. One after another they yielded, if yielding it deserves to be called.

. . . .

Houses were established in some localities by parties of younger men purposely for the prosecution of their illicit pleasures, and to which their victims repaired—nothing loth it is true—to share the disgraceful orgies of their paramours; and in which scenes were enacted that even put to the blush the lascivious Saturnalia of the Romans, the rites of the Pagoda girls of India, and the Harem life of the most voluptuous Ottoman.[34]

Such notions about the early manufacturers found ready acceptance among Radicals who believed, or wanted their working class followers to believe, the worst about their employers. As for Peter Gaskell, judging from his glorification of the country squire, he seems to have been a Tory who longed for pre-industrial, patriarchal rural society, but working class polemic made use of the writings of whoever would advance its cause. That Peter Gaskell is describing an earlier generation of manufacturers is a shade of gray to which the Radicals were color blind.[35]

The third Radical assumption—that the newly-rich employer was full of arrogant pride—was also voiced by a Tory known paradoxically for his reactionary Radicalism—William Cobbett. Like Peter Gaskell, Cobbett longed for an idyllic agrarian social order, and many of his sarcastic attacks on the manufacturing classes seem to have been instigated by the knowledge that merry old England was gone forever.[36] That Cobbett's writings were popular with workmen in the first quarter of the nineteenth century is suggested in Scarsdale, set in the 1820s, where the wadding of a bullet used by a member of a working men's secret society in an attempt on the life of a manufacturer's son is found to be a piece from Cobbett's Political Register. Cobbett's account of the nouveau riche as a type, though extreme in its animosity, helps to account for the unyielding pride of Mrs. Gaskell's manufacturer, Mr. Carson. In "An Address to the Men of Bristol," which appeared in his Political Register in 1827, Cobbett comments upon the tendency of the propertied classes to endeavor to intimidate those of their workmen who attend meetings of protest, and continues with an analysis of the mind of the newly rich:

But this hatred of the cause of public liberty is, I am sorry to say it, but too common amongst merchants, great manufacturers, and great farmers; especially those who have risen suddenly from the dunghill to a chariot. If we look a little more closely into the influence of riches, in such a state of things as this, we shall be less surprised at this apparently unnatural feeling in men who were, but the other day, merely journey-men and labourers themselves.—As soon as a foolish and unfeeling man gets rich, he becomes desirous of making the world believe that *he never* was poor. He knows that he has neither *birth* nor *education* to recommend him to the respect of those who have been less fortunate than himself. Though they pull their hats off to him, he always suspects that they are looking back to his mean origin; and instead of adopting that kindness towards them, and that affability which would make them cheerfully acknowledge his superiority, he endeavours by a distant and rigid deportment, to extort from their fears that which he wants the sense to obtain from their love. So that at last, he verifies the old maxim: *"Set a beggar on horseback, and he'll ride to the Devil."*[37]

This is the worst kind of aristocracy, continues Cobbett, for it exhibits all the pride of the nobility and gentry without any of their liberal feel-ings. The manufacturer is at greater fault than the merchant in this respect, since the merchant has a more extensive acquaintance with the world, and such experience is "a great corrector of insolent and stupid pride. . . ."[38] Moreover, the nouveaux riches continuously attempt to draw the veil of oblivion over their origins: "They would with their hands pull down their superiors and with their feet trample down their in-feriors; but . . . their chief aim is to trample into the very ground all who are beneath them in point of pecuniary circumstances, in order that they may have as few equals as possible, and that there may be *as wide a distance as possible between them and their labourers."*[39]

In *Mary Barton* each of the three Radical assumptions discussed above is embodied in a character. The interaction of these characters and the connection between the motifs they represent give the novel a thematic structure that is organic. Reconciliation is Mrs. Gaskell's stated theme, her "message," lying on the surface of the narrative. The following discus-sion purposes to suggest that her structural theme is the sin of pride and its ramifications.

John Barton, whose name served as the original title for the novel be-fore the author had second thoughts about an assassin in the title role,[40] has an uncomplicated passion for justice. A second generation factory worker, Barton is a genuine specimen of the Manchester working man with Chartist sympathies. Generally speaking, working men in the fiction of middle-class writers are stereotyped as either good or bad. The "good" working man is patient, is willing to wait for better times, and puts his trust in God, sometimes a "Methodee" God. As his name suggests, Job Legh, in *Mary Barton*, personifies the enduring workman. The "Methodee" is best exemplified by Barnabas the preacher-worker in *Scarsdale*. The "bad" working man is the trouble maker who, inept at his work, is the first to be fired in slack times and usually ends up as a parasitic trades union official. Such is the case with Clack in A *Manchester Strike* and Orator Sampson in *Plebeians and Patricians*. John Barton does not belong in either category. Like Job Legh, Barton is highly skillful and steady but his religious notions are not consolatory. He clings rather to the point of view of medieval Christianity voiced by St. Thomas; namely, that the rich have an obligation to relieve the poor. Nor does John Barton resemble in any way the time-serving union delegate. On the contrary, the first glimpse of Barton reveals the countenance of the idealistic working man, the true believer who would pledge his heart and soul to the working class movement for unselfish purposes: "His features were strongly marked, though not irregular, and their expression was extreme earnestness; resolute either for good or evil, a sort of latent stern enthusiasm."[41] The description hints at a temperament that is potentially capable of carrying idealism to tragic extremes. Nor does Barton possess the traditional attitude of respect for his social superiors that a member of the lower orders in middle-class fiction often displays, with, so to speak, cap held humbly in hand. He identifies himself entirely with his class, and expresses no desire to rise above it. These sentiments are evident in Barton's vehement reaction to a friend's remark that he "could never abide gentlefolk."

> "And what good have they ever done me that I should like them?" asked Barton, the latent fire lighting up his eye; and bursting forth, he continued, . . . "If I am out of work for weeks in the bad times and winter comes with black frost and keen east wind, and there is no coal for the grate, and no clothes for the bed, and the thin bare bones are seen through the bed clothes, does the rich man share his plenty with me as he ought to do if his religion wasn't a humbug? . . . No, I tell you, it's the poor, and the poor only, as does such things for the poor. Don't think to come over me with th' old tale, that the rich know nothing of the trials of the poor; I say, if they don't know, they ought to know. We're their slaves as long as we can work; we pile up their fortunes with the sweat of our brows, and yet we are to live as separate as if we were in two worlds; ay, as separate as Dives and Lazarus, with a great gulf betwixt us . . ." and he wound up his speech with a low chuckle that had no mirth in it. (pp. 6-7)

Becoming even more gloomy and stern after the death of his wife, Barton also became increasingly involved in workmen's clubs and the trade union. Even in good times he never forgot the disparity between the condition of the employer and employed when times were bad. Mrs.

Gaskell describes what the workman "feels and thinks" about this injustice:

> At all times it is a bewildering thing to the poor weaver to see his employer removing from house to house, each one grander than the last, till he ends in building one more magnificent than all, or withdraws his money from the concern, or sells his mill, to buy an estate in the country, while all the time the weaver, who thinks he and his fellows are the real makers of this wealth, is struggling on for bread for his children, through the vicissitudes of lowered wages, short hours, fewer hands employed, &c. And when he knows trade is bad, and could understand (at least partially) that there are not buyers enough in the market to purchase the goods already made, and consequently that there is no demand for more; when he would bear and endure much without complaining, could he also see that his employers were bearing their share; he is, I say, bewildered and (to use his own words) "aggravated" to see that all goes on just as usual with the mill-owners. Large houses are still occupied, while spinners' and weavers' cottages stand empty, because the families that once filled them are obliged to live in rooms or cellars. Carriages still roll along the streets, concerts are still crowded by subscribers, the shops for expensive luxuries still find daily customers, while the working man loiters away his unemployed time in watching these things and thinking of the pale, uncomplaining wife at home, and the wailing children asking in vain for enough food,—of the sinking health, of the dying life of those near and dear to him. The contrast is too great. Why should he alone suffer from bad times? (pp. 19-20)

These feelings and thoughts were not hypothetical for John Barton. He was an earnest man who had endured a similar experience without forgiving and forgetting. At an earlier date in his life his employer, a Mr. Hunter, failed; and because of a depression in trade, John could get no employment in any other mill. At the same time his son fell ill with scarlet fever. Without money and having exhausted his credit, Barton was not able to supply the nourishment that his son needed. Hungry himself to an extreme, he stood one day outside a gourmet shop eyeing the edibles. Out of the shop came the wife of his bankrupt employer with a shopman who proceeded to load her carriage with party goods. When Barton returned home, his boy was dead. (pp. 20-21). "You can fancy, now," writes Mrs. Gaskell, "the hoards of vengeance in his heart against the employers" (p. 21). The injustice of a state of things in which such an inequality of wealth is allowed to exist and is indeed sanctioned by defenders of the industrial system became an obsession with John Barton. With the political economist's argument that capital and labor are mutually dependent and that therefore their interests are identical, Barton does not quarrel. Instead, he wants only to carry the principle to what, for the working man, would be a logical conclusion; namely, capital and labor must then be equals: "I say our labour's our capital, and we ought to draw interest on that. [Millowners] get interest on their capital somehow a' this time [a period of slack trade], while ourn is lying idle, else how could they all live as they do?" (p. 60).

The nadir of the economic depression which began in 1836 was the period, 1839-41, two years of hunger and distress to which the working classes responded with the political solution put forth in the Charter.[42] The arrival of such a time served only to aggravate the pre-existing feelings of hostility in such working men as John Barton. The "hungry forties" were an era marked by the alienation of classes. Mrs. Gaskell summarizes working class sentiment at the time of the first Chartist petition in 1839. Her account demonstrates that Marx and Engels's attack on law, morality, and religion for concealing bourgeois interests[43] was a reflection of popular feeling: "The indigence and suffering of the operatives induced a suspicion in the minds of many of them, that their legislators, their magistrates, their employers, and even the ministers of religion, were, in general, their oppressors and enemies; and were in league for their prostration and enthralment" (p. 78).

At the beginning of this period, John Barton was out of work and was forced to live upon what little his daughter Mary earned as a dressmaker's apprentice. Having refused assistance from the trade union on the principle that working men with large families were in greater need than he, Barton lived by the rule of simple justice that he expected from his employers: "With him, need was right." (p. 108). Barton was honored that his fellow working men chose him as one of the delegates to accompany the Chartist monster petition to London in order that Parliament be advised of the distress of the manufacturing population. But when Parliament refused to listen to the Chartist petitioners, Barton was deeply mortified. In addition to this disappointment, Barton was perpetually undernourished, a bodily condition to which he tried to be indifferent but which contributed to his moroseness of mind and tended to produce monomania:

> John Barton's overpowering thought, which was to work out his fate on earth, was rich and poor; why are they so separate, so distinct, when God made them all? It is not His will that their interests are so far apart. Whose doing is it?
> And so on into the problems and mysteries of life, until, bewildered and lost, unhappy and suffering, the only feeling that remained clear and undisturbed in the tumult of his heart was hatred to the one class and keen sympathy with the other. (p. 162)

Made desperate by enforced idleness and want, Barton's only outlet of activity was the trade union. To it, at least, he was useful. He had a rough Lancashire eloquence with which he could articulate the feelings of his fellow workers. Above all, he was valuable because he was moved by no selfish motives but worked rather for the rights of his class: "John Barton became a Chartist, a Communist, all that is called wild and visionary. Ay! but being visionary is something. It shows a soul, a being not altogether sensual; a creature who looks forward for others, if not for himself" (p. 163).

Such then is John Barton's state of mind on the eve of his confrontation with the pride of the Carsons. While exhibiting the intensification of the feeling of injustice in John Barton, Mrs. Gaskell has also shown the manufacturing class in a less than favorable light. What preoccupies young Harry Carson the millowner's son, while the working man is suffering mental and physical anguish in a period of economic depression? Simply the attempted seduction of the working man's daughter, the spirited but naïve Mary Barton. Young Carson flirts with Mary Barton, who is attracted to him by the possibility of becoming the wife of a rich man, a notion put into her head years before by her Aunt Esther. But Esther's departure from the Barton household in order to become a lady ended in her becoming a streetwalker. Since Mary's role as heroine does not admit of her becoming a fallen woman, her Aunt Esther serves as an object lesson in the matter of what might happen to Mary should she continue to encourage Harry Carson. Esther returns to the Barton neighborhood, and with the ubiquity of the streetwalker, quickly becomes aware of Mary's meetings and walks with young Carson. She tries to warn Barton one night in the street, but Barton, seeing that Esther had ended as he predicted, refuses to listen and casts her away. "Oh, what can I do to save [Mary]!" moans Esther in soliloquy, "How can I keep her from being such a one as I am; such a wretched loathsome creature! She was listening just as I listened, and loving just as I loved, and the end will be just like my end. How shall I save her? She won't hearken to warning, or heed it more than I did. . . ." (p. 118). But Esther's fears for the worst prove to be unfounded. Mary's childhood sweetheart Jem Wilson proposes to her. She rejects him, but in doing so, realizes that she does not love Harry Carson and resolves to tell him that she was sorry about encouraging him. "For be it remembered," interjects Mrs. Gaskell, "she had the innocence or the ignorance, to believe his intentions honourable; and he feeling that at any price he must have her, only that he would obtain her as cheaply as he could had never undeceived her" (p. 128). During their terminal interview, young Carson, who in his own eyes is "young, agreeable, rich, handsome!" (p. 129), cannot believe that Mary intends to end their relationship. In the course of their colloquy young Carson reveals his intentions, displaying at the same time the sort of egotism which later causes justice to turn to vengeance and destroy sexuality: "Listen, Mary. . . . I only want to tell you how much I love you, by what I am ready to give up for you. You know (or perhaps you are not fully aware) how little my father and mother would like me to marry you. So angry would they be, and so much ridicule should I brave, that of course I have never thought of it till now. I thought we could be happy enough without marriage" (p. 130). Mary is relieved to know that his intentions were not honorable, for then she need not be penitent about having led him on. She scorns him "for plotting to ruin a poor girl" and departs (p. 131). Carson reflects the pride of his newly rich father when discussing this turn of events with his accomplice Sally Leadbitter. Despite the fact that the elder Carson was once a factory worker, he would not have forgiven his son's marrying "one so far beneath [him] in rank" (p. 131). Though his mother too was once a factory girl, the present disparity of station between her son and Mary was too great (p. 132). Harry Carson is incapable of realizing Mary's rejection as final and is determined to continue in his pursuit of her.

The theme of vain, selfish passion represented by the younger Carson is thus developed parallel to that of injustice. Up to this point the theme of pride in the elder Carson has only been hinted at through the action of his son. Mr. Carson has remained in the background: we hear of him during the depression in trade, building a modern mill with the insurance money he received when his outmoded factory had, much to his satisfaction, burned down.

The pride of the elder Carson and the masters is displayed when the mills start to work again, and this action precipitates the crisis in the novel. In the midst of general unemployment came a large order which had to be filled cheaply and quickly. The masters knew of a duplicate order that had been sent to the Continent where production costs were not so high. In order to outdo their foreign rivals and capture the whole market for the future, the masters sought to buy cotton as cheaply as possible and to offer very low wages. To justify low pay to workmen even with the usual excuse, "undersell," was thought unnecessary: "But the masters did not choose to make all these circumstances known. They stood upon being masters, and that they had the right to order work at their own prices, and they believed that in the present depression of trade, and unemployment of hands, there would be no difficulty in getting it done" (p. 164). The working men, ignorant of the circumstances which in the long run might have benefited them, had all concerned worked to capture the market by their superior productivity, saw only the masters living at ease during the bad times and attempting to take advantage of them by offering low wages during a spurt of employment. The men refused to work. Their employers countered by advertising for power loom weavers who would act as strike-breakers. As the time for filling the order was slipping by, the masters met to encourage each other not to yield. This state of affairs brought out in the Carsons those tendencies of the new rich that the Radical Cobbett had described:

> And amongst the most energetic of the masters, the Carsons, father and son, took their places. It is well known, that there is no religionist so zealous as a convert; no master so stern and regardless of the interests of their workpeople, as those who have risen from such a station themselves. This would account for the elder Mr. Carson's determination not to be bullied into yielding; not even to be bullied into giving reasons for acting as the masters did. It was the employer's will, and that should be enough for the employed. (p. 165)

As the situation became desperate for both parties, masters and men decided on a meeting in order to negotiate a settlement. Unfortunately, the meeting was dominated by Harry Carson, the warhawk, who insisted that in the future the masters would employ no man who was a member of a trade union. In assuming this position young Carson was, as might be expected, merely bargaining for the interests of his class; but he was also guilty of an unwarranted act of arrogance: "While the [union delegates] stood grouped near the door, on their first entrance, Mr. Harry Carson had taken out his silver pencil and had drawn an admirable caricature of them—lank, ragged, dispirited and famine-stricken. Underneath he wrote a hasty quotation from the fat knight's well known speech in Henry IV. He passed it on to one of his neighbours, who acknowledged the likeness instantly, and by him it was sent round to others, who all smiled and nodded their heads" (pp. 176-77). One of the delegates observed this and retrieved the picture after the meeting. This affront was too much for Barton and his friends who then resolved that there would be no more violence against strikebreakers as poor as themselves but against the masters. Lots were drawn for an assassin's work. John Barton drew the marked paper and within a few days assassinated Harry Carson.

At this point, Mrs. Gaskell indulges the Victorian reader's love of melodrama. Jem Wilson, Mary's sweetheart, who had given John Barton his gun for target shooting and who had previously had an altercation with Harry Carson (after Aunt Esther had warned him about young Carson and Mary), is accused of the murder. Mr. Carson offers all his fortune in order to bring the murderer speedily to the gallows before he buries his son. He employs detective services, criminal attorneys and other legal advice and will brook no delay: "He would fain have been policeman, magistrate, accusing speaker, all; but most of all, the judge, rising with full sentence of death on his lips" (p. 213). The day of the trial arrives but Mary thwarts Carson's thirst for legal vengeance by managing, after a dramatic last minute search, to find Jem's cousin Will, a sailor, who provides an alibi which effects Jem's acquittal.

Upon their return to Mary's home, Jem and Mary discover Mr. Carson and John Barton who has just confessed his crime to the murdered man's father. Barton is dying from the combined effects of prolonged under-nourishment and remorse at realizing the enormity of his deed. In death, Harry Carson was no longer the obnoxious manufacturer's son who stood in the way of the rights of working men. No greater good could come for working men from this act of vengeance perpetrated in the name of justice. The elder Carson, however, still vows revenge: "Let my trespasses be unforgiven, so that I may have revenge for my son's murder." (p. 355), He departs for the police, but relenting, goes home to reconsider the forgiveness of trespasses as discussed in the Bible. He returns the next day to forgive Barton who then dies in his arms.

The pride that had kept Carson at a distance and in ignorance of the working classes has been humbled. Where sympathetic imagination was lacking, the millowner was made through suffering to feel a common humanity with his distressed workmen. But the act of suffering is only the first step to new knowledge of self. Carson's education is completed by Mrs. Gaskell's spokesman for the Christian spirit, Job Legh, who had been Barton's co-worker. The manufacturer sends for Job Legh because he is not quite certain whether to believe in John Barton's impersonal motive of revenge for the part the masters played in the strike. Job informs Carson of Barton's sense of injustice at the rich man's neglect of the poor in slack times. Carson replies that masters cannot regulate the demand for labor and that they suffer as much as the men when the market is glutted. Job Legh counters quietly with the working man's viewpoint that had obsessed Barton: "Not as much, I am sure, sir; though I'm not given to Political Economy, I know that much. . . . I never see the masters getting thin and haggard from want of food; I hardly see them making much change in their way of living, though I don't doubt they've got to do it in bad times. But it's in things for show they cut short; while for such as me, it's in the things for life we've to stint" (p. 372). Carson then exhibits the tendency of the rich to explain away the insecurity of the lot of the workers by the abstractions of political economy: improvements in machinery will of necessity bring changes in the occupations of men, and it is understood that such changes work for a greater good. But

Job Legh's eternal laws are those of St. Thomas Aquinas' God who loved the poor, not of the bourgeois god that Engels accused the middle classes of creating in their own image. Job interprets the evils of change as part of God's plan that a higher good shall come from suffering, but he reminds Carson that the rich man who benefits by such change is only a steward of wealth:

> surely it is also part of His plan that so much of the burden of suffering as can, should be lightened by those whom it is His pleasure to make happy, and content in their own circumstances. Of course it would take a deal more thought and wisdom than me, or any other man has, to settle out of hand how this should be done. But I'm clear about this, when God gives a blessing to be enjoyed, He gives it with a duty to be done; and the duty of the happy is to help the suffering to bear their woe. (p. 373)

For Carson, the representative of modern economic man, however, the teachings that characterized the medieval conception of the obligations of the rich to the poor are at odds with his notion of economic virtue.[44] He tells Job that, "Still facts have proved and are daily proving, how much better it is for every man to be independent of help and self reliant." To Carson's argument for self-help through which every man should become a capitalist in order that he may pay his own way out of his savings in periods of underemployment, Job Legh replies that the rationalism of Carson's "facts" does not take into account that,

> God has given men feelings and passions which cannot be worked into the problem, because they are forever changing and uncertain. God has also made some weak; not in any one way but in all. One is weak in body, another in mind, another in steadiness of purpose, a fourth can't tell right from wrong, and so on; or if he can tell the right, he wants strength to hold by it. Now to my way of thinking, them that is strong in any of God's gifts is meant to help the weak,—be hanged to the facts! (p. 373)

Carson is convinced, however, that he does not have the power to remedy the evils of unemployment consequent upon a slack trade; and he fears that men and masters will never come to understand each other in this matter. Job Legh, then, states the point that for Mrs. Gaskell is central to the novel; it matters not whether the masters have that power; what matters is that they lack the inclination to try to find an answer:

> If we saw the masters try for our sakes to find a remedy,—even if they were long about it,—even if they could find no help, and at the end of all could only say, "Poor fellows, our hearts are sore for ye; we've done all we could, and can't find a cure,"—we'd bear up like men through

bad times. No one knows till they have tried, what power of bearing lies in them, if once they believe that men are caring for their sorrows and will help if they can. If fellow-creatures can give nought but tears and brave words, we take our trials straight from God, and we know enough of His love to put ourselves blind into his hands. (p. 374)

Job Legh's qualification that the working man would be satisfied with the attempt at, if not the accomplishment of a remedy, is not lost upon Carson. Although the manufacturer keeps the outward sign of pride, a hard and cold manner, he changes inwardly. He who had "submitted to be taught by suffering" comes to desire,

> that a perfect understanding and complete confidence and love, might exist between master and men; that the truth might be recognized that the interests of one were the interests of all; that hence it was most desirable to have educated workers capable of judging, not mere machines of ignorant men; and to have them bound to their employers by the ties of respect and affection, not by mere money bargains alone; in short to acknowledge the Spirit of Christ as the regulating law between both parties. (pp. 375-76)

It is evident that *Mary Barton* was not the work of a Radical. Still it is the only novel that consistently criticizes the employer, according to assumptions about factory owners common among the working classes. Other novels rap the manufacturer even harder, but as we shall see in the next chapter, their authors' point of view does not reflect a working class bias. Mrs. Gaskell has used Radical accusations of injustice, sexuality, and pride as the warp of her fabric of fiction and has interwoven it with a woof of Christian feelings of reconciliation. The deadly sin of Mr. Carson's pride dominates the novel: it is the parent of the sense of injustice which drives John Barton to a tragic act, as well as that of the egotistical sexuality of Harry Carson, who seeks to rob the poverty-stricken factory girl of her last resource.

Humanitarian
and Millocrat

We have profoundly forgotten everywhere that
Cash-payment is not the sole relation of human
beings; we think, nothing doubting, that *it* ab-
solves and liquidates all engagements of man. "My
starving workers?" answers the rich mill-owner:
"Did I not hire them fairly in the market? Did I
not pay them, to the last sixpence, the sum cov-
enanted for? What have I to do with them more?"
Carlyle, *Past and Present*

ALTHOUGH THERE WERE FEW NOVELISTS
who knew enough about the biases of factory workers' opinion to be able
to write proletarian novels, nevertheless, the working man had allies who,
despite their fundamental ignorance of him and the industrial North,
espoused his cause on principle. The spirit that abhorred the a priori rationalism of political economy, whose overriding commandment, "Laissez-
faire!", was largely responsible for the evils of the factory system, was
humanitarian.

If, however, both the Radical and the humanitarian writers were sharply
critical of millowners during the third and fourth decades of the nineteenth century, the humanitarians, owing to their middle class social backgrounds, were reluctant to be identified as Chartist Radicals. The Chartist
cause both attracted but more decidedly repelled these writers as a consequence of its division into "moral force" and "physical force" factions. It
is the latter element that aroused fears of violent political upheaval in the
minds of middle-class writers who sympathized with the "lower orders"
in times of hunger and distress. Moreover, unlike the Chartists, these
writers were not interested in reforming the electoral system. Frances
Trollope clearly reflects this reluctance on the part of the humanitarian

novelists to make common cause with the Chartists. Her violent attack against the industrialists was praised solely by the Chartists who expressed their approval in *The Northern Star* (read regularly by Mrs. Gaskell's John Barton), edited by Feargus O'Connor, leader of the physical force element.[1] Mrs. Trollope's reaction to this endorsement was to cancel her plans for writing a second novel about the factories lest she be construed as encouraging Chartist agitation.[2] Another writer, Charlotte Elizabeth, attacked socialism and Chartism even more vehemently than the factory system. And Dickens, despite his broadly liberal views that critics have called Radical,[3] had a middle-class abhorrence for mob action as well as a lack of faith in political parties as instruments for the regeneration of society. For the reasons stated above, then, a separate chapter is devoted to these critics of industrial society. We shall see, moreover, that these writers, while having a community of humanitarian feeling as a group, represent middle and upper-class attitudes in their attacks upon the millocrat.

Before entering upon a discussion of humanitarian fiction, it behooves us to consider historiographical matters in order to point out the difficulty of arriving at the truth about the industrialist and the factory system in a controversial era. It has been suggested earlier that humanitarian novelists did not possess an intimate knowledge of the factory worker or the conditions of his existence. Indeed, much of their knowledge was based upon flying visits to the factory districts or the reading of monographs or reports of parliamentary committees studying factory life. The record of impressions that these novelists have left in answer to the question whether the Industrial Revolution was a benefit or a calamity stands as an indictment of industrial society. Why is this so?

The critics of the 1830s and 1840s who believed that the effects of industrialization were disastrous came to that conclusion after making inquiries into the conditions of factory work, particularly those of women and children. Novelists drew from these historical sources, and in their endeavor to alert public opinion, they appealed to the humanitarian sympathies of Englishmen. That conditions in the factories were deplorable is true; but in order to understand the fierce partisanship that characterized the controversy between the friends of the factory owner and those of the worker, we must examine some of the propaganda with which both sides sought to further their cause.

With the report of his Select Committee of 1832, Michael Sadler, the Tory humanitarian, began agitation for a bill which would limit a day's work for women and children in factories to ten hours. Sadler found conditions of cruelty, wretchedness, and disease among factory children.[4] But even so thorough-going an enemy of the factory system as Engels declared that Sadler was led astray by strong feelings and that his findings were "misleading," "erroneous," and gave "a wholly false impression."[5] Angered at Sadler's condemnation, the manufacturers obtained in 1833 another inquiry which, though closer to the truth, tended to favor the manufacturer.[6]

In addition to the conflicting findings of parliamentary committees, book length studies helped spread contradictory evidence. On the question of child labor, we can understand, from the opposing opinions of Peter Gaskell and Andrew Ure, why the government found it almost impossible to acquire correct information about working conditions, a factor which probably played no small part in delaying the passage of the Ten Hours Bill until 1847. In his study Peter Gaskell argued that the long hours of factory labor definitely had a pernicious effect upon children:

> It is beyond all question then, for it is abundantly proved by physiological and pathological considerations, that factory labour, continued for twelve or fourteen hours, is liable to produce certain distortions of the bony system, in consequence of the previous want of healthy growth; that it prevents proper and natural exercise; and that, in conjunction with a continuance of imperfect nurture, and want of domestic comforts, it keeps up an unhealthy condition of the digestive organs—leading or making the body peculiarly prone to take on a variety of chronic diseases, such as scrofula in all its protean forms, diseased joints, enlarged glands, and c.: and that it checks growth, partly by impairing the necessary supplies, and partly by positively lowering the height of the body.[7]

Gaskell derives his authority from a statistical study in which two thousand children were examined with the following results: "The children were stunted, pale, their flesh soft and flabby; many with limbs bent, in most the arch of the foot flattened; several pigeon chested, and with curvatures in the spinal column; one hundred and forty had tender eyes; in a great majority the bowels were said to be irregular; . . . and ninety showed decided marks of having survived severe rachitic affections."[8] On the other hand, the children observed by Dr. Andrew Ure, whom Engels called "the chosen lackey of the bourgeoisie," seemed to evince none of the maladies that Gaskell ascribed to factory labor. In fact, such work was sport for children:

> I have visited many factories, both in Manchester and in the surrounding districts, during a period of several months, entering the spinning rooms, unexpectedly, and often alone, at different times of the day, and I never saw a single instance of corporal chastisement inflicted on a child, nor indeed did I ever see children in ill-humour. They seemed to be always cheerful and alert, taking pleasure in the light play of their muscles,—enjoying the mobility natural to their age. . . .

It was delightful to observe the nimbleness with which they pieced the broken ends. . . . The work of these lively elves seemed to resemble a sport in which habit gave them a pleasing dexterity. . . . As to exhaustion by the day's work, they evinced no trace of it on emerging from the mill in the evening; for they immediately began to skip about any neighbouring playground, and to commence their little amusements with the same alacrity as boys issuing from a school.[9]

That the English public, however, was prepared to believe the worst about the factory system as represented by Sadler and P. Gaskell was no doubt the effect of the testimony of umpires such as Leonard Horner, who was appointed factory inspector in 1833. In his *Journal*, H. S. Tremenheere records that in 1840 Horner had told him that, over the seven years since his appointment, "he had not met six Mill Owners who expressed any sympathy with, or regard for the improvement of the labouring classes in their employ."[10]

I

Michael Armstrong

Frances Trollope most clearly exhibits the tendency of the humanitarian novelist prompted by strong feeling to depict the factory system at its worst. Espousing the cause of the Tory reformer, Sadler's successor Lord Shaftesbury, Mrs. Trollope did not ascribe the evils of factory work to the unavoidable circumstances of a primitive stage of production, nor did she accept the political economist's explanation that the prosperity of England depended upon the beneficial efforts of manufacturers to provide work for a population that created the misery of its own existence by overpopulating the labor market. Instead, she transformed those impersonal evils into the human form of the manufacturer and attributed wretched working conditions and low wages to the selfish malice and greed of the industrial employer.

With letters of introduction from Lord Shaftesbury, Mrs. Trollope and her son Thomas Adolphus visited Lancashire in 1839. She intended to gather information for a factory novel, the purpose of which was to attract the public to the need for Shaftesbury's proposed Ten Hours Bill. Before she set out, Shaftesbury had written her a letter directing her to an account of the factory system and reviews of nine books and reports favorable to his cause, which had appeared in the *Quarterly Review* of December, 1836.[11]

Michael Armstrong, the fruit of her trip to the manufacturing districts and her reading about the factory system, is characterized by an attitude of violent hostility toward the "millocracy,"[12] an antagonism grounded in exaggerated Tory prejudice. It goes without saying that Mrs. Trollope's cotton manufacturers are cruel to children: one wantonly manhandles them; another imprisons them in his mill and malevolently permits an epidemic to ravage among them unchecked; and still another harasses them on their only day of rest. But humanitarian purposes aside, the portraits of the manufacturers are of interest for what they reveal about a Tory's social, political, economic, and religious attitudes toward the new class.

Largely because he is vulgar and pretentious as well as cruel, the mill-owner, Sir Matthew Dowling, receives the burden of Mrs. Trollope's attack. With a heavy-handed irony, she presents Dowling's pretensions to gentility, wit, and gallantry in such a manner as to make him look ridiculous. By his slavish attention to the whims of an aristocratic house guest Lady Clarissa, who is neither young, nor pretty, nor particularly wealthy, but who is the descendant of earls, the newly-made industrial baronet is also depicted as desirous of obtaining at any price the good opinion of the titled landed gentry. It is Lady Clarissa who suggests that Dowling take into his home Michael Armstrong, the factory apprentice who rescued her from an old cow that she thought was a bull. In order to appease work-men who are murmuring at the death of a girl in the factory, Dowling decides to adopt Michael in an act of staged benevolence. In his treatment of the factory boy, Dowling is gross and brutal. Filled with an un-explained, physical loathing for the factory child, Dowling quickly tires of playing Michael's benefactor and ships the child off to Elgood Sharpton's secluded factory, where he is forced to remain as an apprentice until he reaches maturity. Escaping from Sharpton's factory eight years later, Michael returns to the Dowling household to find his enemy married to Lady Clarissa, bankrupt and on his deathbed, haunted by the dangling, broken limbs of all the factory children maimed and killed in his employ. It is Lady Clarissa, inconvenienced by Dowling's failure in business, who delivers a final salvo of invective at the moribund magnate: the best that the "abominable, wicked, low-born, brutal, treacherous," the "pitiful, cheating, brutal manufacturing savage" (p. 345) can do by way of atonement for his bankruptcy is to die (p. 352). To be sure, Dowling as a character is a dramatic monster, but by linking vulgarity with cruelty to dependents, Mrs. Trollope doubly denies the industrialist's aspirations toward gentility.

The portrayal of another manufacturer Elgood Sharpton reveals the political and economic antagonism of the landed classes toward the manu-facturers, fostered by the latter's agitation for repeal of the Corn Laws. Along with factory legislation, perhaps the most controversial issue of the 1830s and 1840s pertained to the Corn Laws. The landed classes had succeeded in passing this measure in 1815, the effect of which was to keep the price of cereal-grain at an artificially high level based on a war economy. But after the Napoleonic wars England's economic base was shifting to manufacturing. The high price of food tended to curtail spending on manufactured goods at home, while the prohibition of the purchase of foreign wheat (unless the price at home reached 80 shillings a quarter) limited the ability for foreign exporters to sell grain to England and to buy manufactured goods in return. The landed interest reasoned that they were justified in using this expedient to maintain a high income for agriculture because they bore the burden of the poor rate and the support of the Established Church.[13] During the economic slump of 1836-42 working men, faced with both under-employment and a high cost of food, agitated for higher wages. But their employers, confronted with the additional problem of glutted markets, pointed to the landed interest as responsible for labor's having to spend so much of what little earnings they received on foodstuffs. In the "millocratic" position of Elgood Sharpton, however, Mrs. Trollope outlines an exaggerated version, bearing the earmarks of a Tory's nightmare, of the landed gentry's view of the real motives behind the manufacturers' drive to repeal the Corn Laws.[14] Dowling explains Sharpton's economic plot to his company physician, Dr. Crockley:

> [Sharpton's] idea is, that if we could get rid of our cursed Corn Laws, the whole of the British dominions would soon be turned into one noble collection of workshops. . . . He says that if his system is carried out into full action, as I trust it will be one of these days, all of the grass left in England will be the parks and paddocks of the capitalists. Sharpton will prove to you as clearly as that two and two make four, that the best thing for the country would be to scour it from end to end of those confounded idle drones, the landed gentry. They must go sooner or later, he says, if the corn-laws are done away with. Then down goes the price of bread, and down goes the operative's wages; and what will stop us then, doctor? Don't you see? Isn't it as plain as the nose on your face that when the agricultural interest is fairly drummed out of the field, the day's our own? Who shall we have then spying after us to find out how many hours a day we choose to make our hands work? . . . If we choose to work the vitals out of them, who shall say we shan't?[15]

Matthew Dowling then expatiates upon the capitalists' use of the support of the working classes against the Corn Laws and the fate of the latter after repeal: "Our policy is, you must know, to give out that it is the operatives who are clamouring for the repeal of the corn-laws, whereas many among them, saucy rogues, are as deep as their betters, and know

perfectly well, and be hanged to 'em, that our only real reason for trying
to make 'down with the corn-laws,' the popular cry is, that we may whisper
in their ears, 'down with the wages' afterwards" (p. 118). With the Corn
Laws done away with, England will become a manufacturers' paradise,
and capitalists "shall suck in gold, gold, gold, from all sides" (pp. 118-19).
Then Dowling offers the doctor his complete confidence. He tells him
that Flemish flax will never again compete with English cotton because
the Flemings "don't know yet how many baby sinews must be dragged
and drawn out to mix as it were with the thread before the work can be
made to answer" (p. 119). The Fleming will have to go back to growing
corn, as will the Poles, and Russia will become a granary in the service of
England. Dowling continues rhapsodising about the fate of the aristocracy and the economic subservience of nations to the workshop of the
world:

> Where will your aristocratic landholder be then, Crockley? Perhaps
> you can't tell? but I suspect I can. They'll just be in the factories, sir.
> Your manors and your preserves will be covered with factories, except
> just here and there, you know, where we capitalists may have taken a
> fancy to my Lord This-thing's grounds, or the Duke of T'other-thing's
> mansion, for our own residences. And this I maintain is just as it should
> be; and the reason why is plain. We have got before all the world in
> machinery, and so all the world must be content to walk behind us. By
> Jove, if I had my way, Crockley, I'd turn France and the Rhine into a
> wine-cellar, Russia into a corn-bin, and America, glorious America,
> north, south, east, and west, into a cotton plantation. Then should we
> not flourish? Then should we not bring down the rascals to work at our
> own prices, and be thankful too? What's to stop us? Trust me, there's
> not a finer humbug going, than just making the country believe that
> the operatives are rampant for the repeal of the corn-laws. (p. 119)[16]

In addition to the manufacturer's objectionable political and economic
ambitions, his religion was also obnoxious. Unlike Carlyle, who praised
the Quaker captain of industry in Past and Present, Mrs. Trollope betrays
a Church of England prejudice against Nonconformists in her depiction
of the Sunday school of the brothers Tomlin. In her search for Michael
Armstrong, who has been spirited away to Sharpton's factory, a Miss
Brotherton is determined to visit as many mills as possible. She asks one
of the Tomlin brothers for permission for a Sunday visit to the school adjoining his mill. One of the brothers replies in a nasal tone that marks him
an evangelical as clearly as the brogue does an Irishman. Miss Brotherton
is then informed that the school convenes punctually at seven o'clock on
Sunday morning. Arriving at that time, she watches the approach of the
exhausted and sleepy children. On questioning them she discovers that

they had worked until five minutes before midnight on the previous night, stopping only to avoid working into the Sabbath. Two sleepy latecomers are reprimanded by Tomlin: "Wicked and ungrateful children! . . . Is this the way you obey your earthly master, who leaves his comfortable bed, and his breakfast untouched, to lead you to the feet of your heavenly One!" (pp. 240-41). During the service, "the sonorous voice of Mr. Joseph Tomlin was . . . heard pronouncing an exhortation, intended to show that obedience to their earthly masters was the only way of saving children from the eternal burning, prepared for those who were disobedient, in the world to come" (p. 241). The most that the Nonconformist can be charged with, however, (especially by a member of the Established Church), is that he kept his child laborers from a well-earned sleep. As we have seen, the Church of England was no less guilty of using religion to teach the working classes to know their duty of obedience.

Advanced with the view of furthering Shaftesbury's Ten Hours Bill, the Tory attitudes delineated in *Michael Armstrong* would seem to be the sectarian fancies of a party hack. But Mrs. Trollope was not Shaftesbury's dupe, for many of the attitudes expressed in her factory novel have their origin in her well-known American sojourn. In the first place, her sympathy for institutionalized pauper apprentices arose from her experience of sending her ailing son to what she thought was a boarding school at the Owenite settlement in New Harmony, Indiana. The stated purpose of this institution was work-study, but its administrators neglected the study aspect and reaped a "golden harvest" from the "thews and sinews of the youth they had collected."[17] Mrs. Trollope did not find this out until Henry had been overworked. It is probable that she associated Henry's death a few years later with his stay in that institution. Secondly, Mrs. Trollope's scorn for the would-be gentleman was nurtured by her observations of the "pretensions" of brother Jonathan who "will be a fine gentleman, but it must be in his own way."[18] Last of all, her distaste for evangelical Nonconformity does not stem entirely from an undefined fear for the Establishment but most likely from her acquaintance with American revival meetings during her three years in Cincinnati.[19]

While Mrs. Trollope's integrity was not compromised by her partisanship, the validity of her portraitures might be questioned. Anthony Trollope, who inherited his mother's ability to write under any physical circumstances along with her prolificacy, wrote the following candid evaluation of his mother as a person and as a novelist: "She was an unselfish, affectionate and most industrious woman, with great capacity for enjoyment and high physical gifts. She was endowed, too, with much creative power, with considerable humour, and a genuine feeling for romance. But she was neither clear-sighted nor accurate; and in her attempts to describe morals, manners, and even facts, was unable to avoid the pitfalls of exaggeration."[20]

II

Helen Fleetwood

While Mrs. Trollope's factory novel was being published in monthly parts by Henry Colburn during the years 1839-40, *Helen Fleetwood*, the work of Charlotte Elizabeth née Browne Phelan Tonna, hereafter referred to by her pen name of Charlotte Elizabeth, was serialized in the *Christian Lady's Magazine*. For Charlotte Elizabeth, a religious enthusiast with ultra Protestant leanings, the industrial system brought out the innate depravity of both masters and men. If Mrs. Trollope was concerned with the effects upon the body of the strap, the billy-roller, and long working hours, Charlotte Elizabeth was preoccupied with the destruction of the soul. If Mrs. Gaskell's Carsons were indifferent to the poverty of their employees, Charlotte Elizabeth's Messrs. Z. disclaimed responsibility for the moral corruption of workers that was inherent in the factory system.

Charlotte Elizabeth, a Tory Evangelical, is one of the critics of the Industrial Revolution who, possessed of a reactionary nostalgia, longed for a patriarchal, agrarian England wherein the country squire and not the cotton lord was the master of men. All that had occurred since the invention of the steam engine, this group would seem in essence to say, was "Not English!" Aware, however, that there was no turning back and looking upon the future as merely increasing the gulf between the present and the past, this backward looking element had no viable alternative to industrialization. Unable to accept the present and without a plan of action for the future, the reactionary critics of industrial society could only snap at the heels of this beast struggling to be born. Hence men like Cobbett, who through the 1820s rancorously attacked the industrial classes, are remembered more for their fulminations than for their counterproposals. And digging below the surface of the Tory humanitarian agitation of men such as Shaftesbury (whose own agricultural workers were said to have been in need of a champion), who proposed to act constructively rather than merely rage, one suspects not a little class antagonism in the attempts to curb, or even hamstring through factory legislation, the growing power of millowners.

It is perhaps Peter Gaskell and Cobbett who best formulate the attitude of this group toward industrialization. Their first assumption, made by Peter Gaskell, echoes the Wordsworth of *Michael*. It is that cities and towns where men congregate in great bodies, whether for factory work or other reasons, are responsible for the immediate moral deterioration of individuals.[21] Cobbett had earlier expressed the notion in connection with factory work, and quick to put the worst construction on the effects of congregating people in factories with a room temperature of eighty-four degrees, he interprets an employer's restrictions upon the use of men's room facilities as evidence of homosexual activity. Not only was the heat of the East artificially maintained in factory rooms, but its most abominable vices were also hatched there.[22] Secondly, the greatest evil effect of the factory system upon the social and moral condition of the working man was not poverty, not the conditions of factory labor in themselves, not inadequate opportunities for education, but "the breaking up of those family ties; the consequent abolition of the domestic circle, and the perversion of all the social obligations which should exist between parent and child on the one hand, and between children themselves on the other."[23] Though Peter Gaskell does not make the connection, parallel to the destruction of the hierachy of the patriarchal family unit that had engaged in domestic industry was a corresponding change in the structure of a squirearchal rural society when its inferior ranks had become independent of the need of the bounty and good will of the patriarchal country squire because a livelihood could be made in the factory towns.[24] In his address to the landowners, Cobbett was writing in the same spirit when he complained of the injurious effect to the land of the concentration of factories in towns, by which the "lords of the loom" were able to draw women and girls away from domestic spinning and weaving.[25]

In *Helen Fleetwood* Charlotte Elizabeth expresses the Tory nostalgia discussed above with all the religious fervor of a zealot whose sect, in danger of being overwhelmed by more powerful forces, seeks to maintain its identity through a reiteration of its fundamental tenets. And by making change itself somehow immoral, Charlotte Elizabeth takes the position that those who would pretend that the Industrial Revolution was a blessing will have to justify before God the moral deterioration which accompanied it.

The novel begins by demonstrating how poor law guardians are in league with factory owners. The widow Green and her grandchildren, together with the adopted orphan Helen Fleetwood, are presented to a recruiter of factory labor by the parish authorities who are afraid that Mrs. Green will be unable to support her young wards. Convinced of the advantages of factory work by the representations of the agent, Mrs. Green moves all of her charges but Richard from the country to a factory town, where years before her daughter had gone to work, had subsequently married, and now had a family of her own. All is not well with this family, however. The husband has lost the psychological status of head of household, because with women and children being preferred in the factories he is only intermittently employed. The girls, Sarah a cripple and Phoebe a prostitute, symbolize the only two choices that a factory girl has: ruin of body or of soul. Together with Phoebe, the son Charles is used to represent the unnatural independence of factory children grown to maturity, knowing that they may leave home for another factory town should their parents make too many demands.

The trials of Helen Fleetwood begin as soon as she gets employment. She refuses to compromise the purity of character which identifies her as the ideal of the English country maiden; her godliness and efforts to maintain her respectability are met with scorn in the factory. The low level of morality in other workers contrasts with Helen's moral superiority. But her show of self-possession serves only to irk her co-workers, and she becomes the butt of their mischievous malice.[26] If the factory system has perverted the obligations of Helen's cousins, Phoebe and Charles, toward their parents, it has done the same to the relationships between children. When Helen, using Charles as messenger, sends religious instructions on scraps of paper to Phoebe's crippled sister Sarah, she is for this made out by Phoebe, who hates her respectable ways, to be an "unprincipled character" who deserves to be exposed to the other factory workers as a hypocrite (p. 89). When Mrs. Green hears of that betrayal of kindred, she determines to appeal to the overlooker; but Helen informs her that overlookers care not about a factory girl's reputation, being worse in their attitude than the workers. Helen then accounts for the malice of the factory hands: "It is my trying to keep myself unspotted from that wicked little world, and refusing to partake in their sins, that makes them spiteful. It is not me they hate, but the holiness which I strive to follow, because without it, I shall not see the Lord" (p. 91). Factory workers, however, commit sin in ignorance; it is the millowner who knowingly violates his knowledge of good and evil:

> Oh, it is a dreadful thing to see so many poor children given up to learn all manner of wickedness, with nobody to care for their souls! I would not be a millowner, granny; no, not for the worth of all the manufacturers in England. I could have fallen on my knees in the midst of that crowded room to bless God that I was a poor despised factory-girl, and not an employer. Aye, and I would almost sooner be the worst among those wretched characters, with none to teach or guide me, than the person who, with knowledge and opportunities, and a BIBLE IN THE HOUSE, has to answer to God for letting those souls perish, while their poor bodies are worn out by hard and cruel labour to swell his unholy gains. (pp. 91-92)

Such was not the case under the squirearchy when the squire's daughters taught the children of the poor and marched them to church. But Mr. Z. would never allow his daughters to come among the mill people for an hour every day, lest they be contaminated by the contact:

> He knows too well that their health would be destroyed by staying even so long in the heat, the steam, the stench and the dust of rooms where we are pent up from early morning to late night; and he knows that they would never again be let into respectable society if they were supposed to hear the vile, filthy talk that his poor labourers use, and the men he sets over them encourage; and which he never dreams of checking, either by his own presence, or by setting any moral, not to say religious person, to watch them. (p. 92)

As for the spitefulness of Phoebe, continues Helen, it was not out of the ordinary. What is unnatural is that Phoebe's conduct is considered normal in the factory while her own fight to retain her country innocence and uprightness should be so out of place in such surroundings (p. 94).[27]

In spite of Helen's belief that an appeal to the mill authorities is futile, Mrs. Green, thinking that the mill agent and the employer are not aware of the extent of evil in the mill, resolves to inform them. Mr. M., the mill manager or agent so-called, proves to be rude. He is not unaware of the behavior of workpeople, but the mills do not exist to please the grandmothers of thousands of factory children. When the widow Green then consults the owner, Mr. Z., amidst his magnificent furnishings, she finds that he is not interested in discussing the moral condition of his employees. He refers her back to his manager with the advice that she should learn her place (pp. 95-98). Convinced that she has spoken to the wrong Mr. Z., Mrs. Green tries the elder brother of the employer. To him, she relates both the story of Helen's attempts to preserve her integrity among the persecutions of fellow workers and the oppression of those in authority. All that Mrs. Green desired "was an intimation from the superiors of the concern to the men who overlooked the common hands, that they required to have virtue protected, and industry encouraged, instead of the reverse" (p. 100). With the widow Green's speech made in the presence of his daughter, the elder Mr. Z. sees an opportunity to sidestep the real issue in a puff of anger at the widow for having brought up improper subjects before delicate ears. Ushered out by one of the servants, Mrs. Green is told by him that an appeal to the owners is useless: "If the agent [Mr. M.] isn't your friend, never reckon on any good by coming to the owners; and our agent is nobody's friend but his own" (p. 101).

Having found both millowner and manager without a sense of responsibility for the needs of factory workers' souls, Mrs. Green applies to a clergyman for advice. This worthy assures her that the depravity found in the factory cannot be checked and that her only recourse is to seek help in God (p. 103). At this point, however, the widow determines to exhaust all earthly possibilities. She asks a neighbor whether the factory inspectors, who were a means of putting teeth into the Factory Act of 1833, might help her. But according to Charlotte Elizabeth's knowledge, Shaftesbury's Act (which was hailed as the first piece of major factory legislation because of its provisions for inspectors and also for two hours a day of school for children) is a dead letter. The factory inspector has under his jurisdiction eighteen hundred mills spread over the counties of Lancashire, Northumberland, Westmoreland, Durham and part of York. This official is in charge of four superintendents who manage to visit each mill three times a year, but not without the previous consent of the owners. Moreover, the inspector has no power to interfere if a violation is not reported within fourteen days.[28] As for the other provisions of the Act, millowners circumvent the twelve hour day limit for workers under eighteen by tampering with the clock, shortening meal times, or cheating in various ways on the two hour time set aside for schooling (pp. 106-7). If, in spite of impediments to his movements, the factory inspector manages to get up a case against a manufacturer for illegal proceedings, it is no difficult task for the factory owner to thwart him by intimidating witnesses, shifting responsibility, or putting a relative on the bench to try the case (p. 137). With no hope of redress, the devout Mrs. Green can only attribute the misfortunes of herself and Helen to the will of God.

As a contrast to the asocial attitude of the manufacturer, Charlotte Elizabeth praises the squire's sense of obligation to his laborers in her account of an annual harvest celebration in the village where Mrs. Green left her grandson Richard as a gardener:

> The owner of the field was the principal landed proprietor in this place; and the spot was chosen among many, just because it had, from time immemorial been the scene of the annual celebration. This year was one of unusual abundance, and not a day of adverse weather had thwarted the harvestmen. The Squire was pleased at the diligence with which they had availed themselves of the favourable season; the men were gratified by his praises, and no less by his liberality; while the women and elder children, who had found plentiful employment, too, upon his extensive lands, had similar causes for gladness. As for the little ones, they were delighted to gambol and exhibit their activity in the presence of the Squire's family, whose daughters took no small pains in disciplining the urchins at their infant school, and marshalling them for an orderly march to the church door. Each, both old and young, enjoyed that peculiar feeling, the value of which the poor are

seldom aware until they experience its absence. "My employer knows me; I am not in his sight a mere piece of machinery, regarded only while it works in his service. There's tie between us that he, though a rich man, would not disown. If he is every thing to me, I and mine are something to him." It was this thought, unconsciously cherished, that lighted up every countenance with smiles as the Squire's family approached the happy groups; and the bow and the curtsey that respectfully welcomed them were given with greater alacrity under the sense of that individual recognition on the part of their superiors. (p. 118)

But what has happened to these idyllic patriarchal relations? The English peasantry, by leaving the land of their fathers for factory towns are fast becoming degraded creatures as a result of the cash nexus relationships of industrial society:

> The independence of an English labourer is as proverbial as his industry: and now that this is becoming, through the money-loving greediness of the few, grinding down the poverty-stricken faces of the rapidly increasing many a mere name without a reality, so also will the strength of England be. An unnatural state of things, wholly foreign to the old English character, is transforming "a bold peasantry, their country's pride," into a degraded, discontented, restless, reckless, turbulent mob. Two classes hitherto bound together by mutual interest and mutual respect, are daily becoming more opposed the one to the other. (p. 167)

For Charlotte Elizabeth, moreover, some of the by-products of the antisocial factory system are even more horrific than the immoral and abandoned conduct ensuing from the congregation of vast numbers of persons in a heated atmosphere:

> Lately a new and an almost unutterable curse had been added to those already felt in the mills. A man of whom it is hard to think otherwise than as of an actual incarnation of Satan, had been among them personally, and had circulated by his delegates a vast deal of his infernal doctrine in that and other manufacturing districts. It will suffice to say that some half dozen of the young men in that mill had become Socialists. Beyond this, it was impossible to go—Socialism is the *ne plus ultra* of six thousand years' laborious experience on the part of the great enemy of man—it is the moral Gorgon upon which whomsoever can be compelled to look must wither away: it is the doubly denounced woe upon the inhabiters of earth—the last effort of Satanic venom wrought to the madness of rage by the consciousness of his shortened time. (p. 168)

The Socialists, whose doctrines are diabolical and for whom the Bible is "the vilest book ever written," are heathen scoffers at God (p. 169).

In addition to being a stalking ground for the blasphemous "Beast of Socialism," the factory is a hotbed of sedition and false religion; "There the Chartist is taught secretly to whet his pike, and there the blight of Popery noiselessly spreads, sealing up in a false, fatal peace, such souls as may not be prepared to enter into open league with hell" (p. 170). The employers are indifferent even to these developments: "And against this host of destroyers, with what armour does the instructed, the loyal, the professedly church-going master provide his poor ignorant dependents?" (p. 170). At Judgment Day the masters, destroyers both of workers' bodies and their immortal souls, the one through overwork and the other through neglect, will be asked "WHO SLEW ALL THESE?" (p. 170).

Under the burden of all these evil influences, Helen Fleetwood struggles to maintain her purity, but the effort is fatal. Helen, "whose natural rustic reserve seemed to have given place not to the acquired boldness of a town-life, but to the expansion of a spirit about to wing its way to the company of the redeemed in heaven" (p. 176), keenly feels a sense of defilement as a result of the unwholesome moral environment in the factory. She dies, and the family returns to the pastoral setting whence they came. Charlotte Elizabeth's alternative to an intolerable situation in the manufacturing districts is not emigration, as is Mrs. Gaskell's in *Mary Barton* or Paul Pimlico's in "The Manufacturer," but a nostalgic retreat to an idyllic rural England where poverty can still be honest.

Louis Cazamian has called *Helen Fleetwood* "une dissertation, non une oeuvre d'art . . . un traité d'apologétique chrétienne, où Satan prend la forme du manufacturier."[29] Charlotte Elizabeth herself went so far as to say that she was not writing fiction but basing her story on real people and incidents, with names changed and characters grouped "with some latitude of license" and containing nothing that "has not been stated, corroborated and confirmed on oath" (p. 59). Such an attitude toward fiction on the part of the religious-minded is nothing new; it has been present since the beginnings of the novel when Defoe sought to forestall the objections of his dissenting brethren by insisting that his fiction was a true relation. *Helen Fleetwood*, then, is a sermon addressed to a nation going to the devil. The forces of light led by Lord Shaftesbury seek, within the existing structure of society, to restrain, by means of factory legislation, the sin of covetousness in the manufacturer, while other forces of darkness, unintentionally spawned by that covetousness—atheistic Socialism and "physical force" Chartism—"long to overturn all right government" and endeavor "to make our grievances a pretext for engaging in rebellious schemes" (p. 149). For the important task of alerting a nation to its perils, readers must be assured that *Helen Fleetwood* is not a work to be dismissed as a concoction of the author's fancy.

While didacticism in an author bent upon instruction might serve as an excuse for a lack of talent, with Charlotte Elizabeth the case is somewhat more complex. Her didacticism was deliberate but did not merely serve to justify her fiction to the readers of the *Christian Lady's Magazine*, which she edited from 1834 to 46 and which did not, according to its own profession, "indulge in fictitious narrative."[30] What was more important, Charlotte Elizabeth forced herself to be didactic out of a sense that she had to square her strong imaginative sensibility, which she thought an enemy to reason and an evil genius that needed exorcising, with the spiritual-mindedness that she believed proper for a Christian. She possessed a powerful faculty of imagination, but her religious upbringing crippled this tendency by construing it as diabolical. In her *Personal Recollections*, Charlotte Elizabeth records that as a child, her highly sensitive imagination occasioned her much concern, especially while she played alone in the bishop's garden:

> Seated on the grass, busying my fingers with the daisies that were permitted to spring around, I have been lost in such imaginings as I suppose not many little children indulge in, while permitting my eyes to rove over the seemingly interminable mass of old gray stone, and then to fall upon the pleasant flowers around me. I loved silence, for nothing that fell on the ear seemed in accordance with what so charmed the eye: and thus a positive evil found entrance in the midst of much enjoyment. I acquired that habit of dreamy excursiveness into imaginary scenes, and among unreal personages, which is alike inimical to rational pursuits and opposed to spiritual-mindedness. . . . I had entered betimes upon the pernicious study of nursery tales, as they then were, and without having the smallest actual belief in the existence of fairies, goblins, or any such things, I took unutterable delight in surrounding myself with hosts of them, decked out in colours of my own supplying, gorgeous or terrible beyond the conception of my classic authorities. The faculty of realizing whatever I pictured to myself was astonishingly great; and you must admit that the localities in which I was placed were but too favourable to the formation of a character, which I have no doubt the enemy was secretly constructing within me, to mislead, by wild, unholy fiction, such as should come within the range of its influence. To God be all the glory that I am not now pandering with this pen to the most grovelling or the most impious of man's perverted feelings.[31]

Her reaction to the discovery of the *Merchant of Venice* at the age of seven is another example of the power of her imagination, chained and bound by her religious belief. Upon reading this play she records, "I drank a cup of intoxication under which my brain reeled for many a year. . . . I revelled in the terrible excitement that it gave rise to . . . and during a sleepless night I feasted on the pernicious sweets thus hoarded in my brain."[32] Instead of reading a story from the Bible as a reward for docility she now wanted to read Shakespeare. A spirit "so attuned to romance" must certainly have been in the power of the devil, for, be it remembered, "the poetical taste is held in abomination with God, for it thrusts Him from men's minds and in His place enshrines a host of polluting idols."[33]

In view of Charlotte Elizabeth's negative attitude toward fiction (and her own girlish ambition to be a martyr for her religion), *Helen Fleetwood* is less a novel about a factory girl than a combination of the Old English female saint's life and such a doomsday sermon as Wulfstan's *Sermo Lupi ad Anglos*. That she chose to cast her story as a novel suggests that the resistance to fiction was abating when it was discovered that the novel could be put to a useful purpose by serving as a vehicle for social criticism.[34]

III

Nicholas Nickleby

Returning from his visit to Manchester in 1838, Dickens wrote to Edward Fitzgerald through whom Lord Shaftesbury had arranged to have the novelist visit the mills:

> I went, some weeks ago, to Manchester and saw the worst cotton mill. And then I saw the best. *Ex uno disce omnes*. There was no great difference between them. . . . With that nobleman's [Shaftesbury's] most benevolent and excellent exertions, and with the evidence which he was the means of bringing forward, I am well acquainted. So far as seeing goes, I have seen enough for my purpose, and what I have seen has disgusted me and astonished me beyond all measure. I mean to strike the heaviest blow in my power for those unfortunate creatures, but whether I shall do it in the "Nickleby," or wait some other opportunity, I have not yet determined.[35]

Two years later, in a note of acknowledgment to Shaftesbury for a copy of his speech to the Children's Employment Commission, Dickens "could not forbear . . . cursing the present system and its fatal effects in keeping down thousands upon thousands of God's images. . . ."[36]

But Dickens did not strike his hardest blow at industrialism in *Nicholas Nickleby* (1838-39). Instead, in protest against the heartlessness of the Matthew Dowlings, the Elgood Sharptons, and the Messrs. Z., he set up in *Nickleby* a positive ideal for the great employers of labor who were responsible for the happiness or misery of "thousands of God's images." A dozen years before what has been called the period of his "dark novels,"[37] Dickens was inclined to think that social questions relating to master and man might be solved if all employers followed the ideal of benevolence exemplified by his Cheeryble Brothers, London warehouse owners modeled after the Brothers Grant, Manchester calico printers.

While scanning the placards outside the Register Office in the hopes of getting employment, Nicholas Nickleby, with little money and fewer friends, makes his first acquaintance with one of the Cheerybles. Nicholas cannot take his eyes from the old man, who radiates kind-heartedness and good humor. Moreover, because "there is nothing so contagious as pure openness of heart," Nicholas cannot resist relating his misfortunes to the old man.[38] Without another word, Charles Cheeryble marches him over to his house of business, where upon their arrival, the other Cheeryble, Ned, is in the midst of arranging a liberal provision for the family of an employee who met an accidental death. For Mr. Z. in *Helen Fleetwood*, on the other hand, such a gesture "would open a door to endless imposition, extortion, and wrong if adopted as a rule" (p. 182). Certain that Nicholas's history would be confirmed, Charles Cheeryble insists that he be taken into the business as a clerk to Tim Linkinwater, forty-four years in their employ. Tim, reason the Cheerybles, might thus be able to come an hour later in the morning and take several airings in the country during the week. Hired on the spot at one hundred and twenty pounds a year, Nicholas is also offered the rental of a cottage for less than the usual sum and for rent and furnishings he is loaned money which the Cheerybles later plan to turn into a gift. In addition, the Cheerybles play at fairy elves by supplying all sorts of things for the cottage in Nicholas's absence (pp. 462-65). Their treatment of Nicholas, however, is only one instance of the presiding genius that animates them and that permeates their establishment: "Everything gave back . . . some reflection of the kindly spirit of the brothers. The warehousemen and porters were such sturdy, jolly fellows, that it was a treat to see them. Among the shipping-announcements and steam packet lists which decorated the counting-house walls, were designs for alms-houses, statements of charities, and plans for new hospitals" (p. 477). Against the possible objection to personal benevolence—that it dies with its donors, Dickens supplies a nephew Frank Cheeryble, Nicholas's contemporary, who is of much the same mind as his uncles. And lest the Cheerybles be regarded as kind hearted for the purposes of self-aggrandizement, they are shown to be politely impatient with expressions of gratitude when they are openly generous and to prefer, for the most part, to do their charitable work in secret.

If, however, the evils of the factory system can be traced back to the cash nexus relationship, the attitude of benevolent paternalism is not without its inherent danger: gratuitous benevolence runs the risk of patronizing employees. Dickens's Cheerybles suggest this strain of authoritarian benevolence. When Tim Linkinwater is informed that Nicholas is to be hired in order to lighten his duties he, without jealousy of Nicholas, resents the Cheerybles' kindly officiousness, preferring rather to die in the discharge of his duties at his post in the counting-house. Resolved against accepting their generosity, Tim stalks out; but the Cheerybles persist:

> "He must be done something with, brother Ned," said [Charles] warmly; "we must disregard his old scruples; they can't be tolerated, or borne. He must be made a partner, brother Ned; and if he won't submit to it peaceably, we must have recourse to violence."
>
> "Quite right," replied brother Ned, nodding his head as a man thoroughly determined; "quite right, my dear brother. If he won't listen to reason, we must do it against his will, and show him we are determind to exert our authority. We must quarrel with him, brother Charles." (p. 463)

Not everyone was quite as ready to succumb to the Cheeryble generosity as was Nicholas. In another episode, Nicholas himself serves as a dispenser of disguised charity for the Cheerybles, who by buying her paintings, support Madeline Bray and her sick but perversely independent father. On one of these errands, Nicholas, infatuated with Miss Bray, declines a receipt for his employers' money, stating that it is no matter. Mr. Bray remonstrates: "No matter! What do you mean, sir? . . . No matter! Do you think you bring your paltry money here as a favour or a gift; or as a matter of business, and in return for value received?" (p. 616).

In spite of the "philosophie de Noël" that envelops the philanthropy of the Cheerybles, Humphry House has expressed "horror at the utter dependence of their employees upon them" with the result that "a film of hopeless gratitude is spread upon the cash nexus between man and man."[39] But House also puts Dickens's extremes into proper perspective by showing that Dickens was reacting against the extremes of laissez-faire and Malthusianism that the "great intermediary between the theorists and the public," Harriet Martineau, "mercilessly" expounded in her fiction.[40] It might be argued that the Victorian working man had more reason to fear the hazards of unfenced machinery than the charity of the Cheerybles. Nevertheless, well-intentioned but unwarranted interference on the part of paternalistic employers was criticized by early Victorian social critics concerned with the duties of the employer to the employed.

Proceeding on the assumption that his reader, be he manufacturer, master workman, or landowner is "now thoroughly impressed with the duty of attending to the welfare of his dependents," Arthur Helps set forth one of the pitfalls into which the benevolent employer is liable to fall—paternalistic interference. Workmen are likely to resent good thus thrust upon them: "Mankind are so accustomed to the idea that government mainly consists in coercion, that they sometimes find it difficult to consider interference, even as applied to benevolent undertakings, and for social government, in any other than a bad light."[41] If the employer of labor values, as he should, independence of character and action in his employees, he must allow their own energies a place in his benevolent schemes, for he wants to produce "something vital, not something mechanical."[42]

In all your projects for the good of others, beware lest your benevolence should have too much of a spirit of interference. Consider what it is you want to produce. Not an outward, passive conformity to your wishes, but something vital which shall generate the feelings and habits you long to see manifested. You can clip a tree into any form you please, but if you wish it to bear fruit when it has been barren, you must attend to what is beneath the surface, you must feed the roots. You must furnish it with that nutriment . . . which enables it to use its own energies. . . . How slowly are those great improvements matured which our impatient nature might expect to have been effected by a single stroke. What tyrannies have been under the sun, things which we can hardly read of without longing for some direct divine interference to have taken place. . . . And can you think that it is left for you to drill men suddenly into your notions, or to produce moral ends by mere mechanical means? You will avoid much of this foolish spirit if you are really unselfish in your purposes; if, in dealing with those whom you would benefit, you refer your operations to them as the centre, and not to yourself, and the successes of your plans.[43]

In his review of *The Claims of Labour*, W. R. Greg shared Arthur Helps's regard for the necessity of avoiding patronizing benevolence. After expatiating upon the minimal duties of an employer—provision of housing, encouragement of saving, and employment of conscientious overlookers—Greg discusses extra duties that fall under the general category of benevolence about which the employer need be circumspect lest he succumb to patronage:

A wide field of usefulness still remains to him in the establishment of schools, reading-rooms, baths, washhouses, and the like. . . . But we wish strongly to urge that in all these schemes, the great employer of labour should bear in mind that his relation to his people is passing, if not passed, from the feudal into the democratic stage; and therefore that his cue should be, not so much to establish, still less to enforce, all these desirable institutions, as to encourage and facilitate them. He should cultivate every wish for them, meet every demand for them halfway and show his sense of their value; but he should not forestal the wish too much. If given, not gained, they are little esteemed. If given before wanted, half the good of them is thrown away. If bestowed upon an unprepared, unaspiring, and unappreciating body of workmen, they not only take no root, and soon wither away, but they are like pearls cast before the feet of meaner animals—creating no gratitude towards the donor, and no respect for the gift. Moreover, in this case they die out with the individual employer, having been indebted for their existence to his personal influence alone.[44]

Much that is "rich, beautiful, and useful," continues Greg, may be superimposed upon the cash nexus relationship that is customarily represented as "so meagre, so unsatisfactory and so unchristian," if the employer understands the true nature of his position,

as that, not of a patron who has legitimate right and power to guide, and who is therefore bound to govern and protect,—but of a wealthier and wiser equal, whose superiority entails upon him claims, in exact proportion as it gives him means of influence; if he have an earnest sense of the responsibility of talents, and of all the vast meaning involved in the answer to the question, "Who is my neighbour?"—he will confine himself to no formal decalogue of 'Thou shalt,' and 'Thou shalt not. . . .'[45]

Dickens, as has been shown, visited the mills under the auspices of Lord Shaftesbury, and like those of Mrs. Trollope and Charlotte Elizabeth, his impressions of the factory system were far from favorable. Yet he did not at this time attack the employer of labor as did the others. Owing to both the cynicism of Radicals who condemned the millowning class in toto and the zeal of Tory humanitarians who dwelled upon the inhumanity of the factory system, the fact that men of good will existed among the manufacturing class has been obscured. The Cheerybles represent Dickens's attempt to give good employers such as the Grants their due. But critics, Victorian and modern, persist in viewing the Cheerybles as the creation of Dickens's fancy fallen into a mood of hyper-sentimentality and as characters scarcely credible. Walter Bagehot, who knew Victorian businessmen, declared the "The Messrs. Cheeryble are among the stupidest of [Dickens's] characters."[46] A writer in *Fraser's Magazine* saw them as "unredeemed and irredeemable old idiots" and "pot-bellied Sir Charles Grandisons of the ledger and daybook."[47] Aldous Huxley has called the Cheerybles "gruesome old Peter Pans . . . old babies snugly ensconced in their mental and economic womb-substitutes and sucking, between false teeth, their thumbs," and has added that the writer who can adore such creations must be emotionally unbalanced.[48] Thomas Jackson, referring to them as "monstrosities of benevolence," has termed the Cheerybles incredible and nauseous to modern readers.[49] Finally, Edgar Johnson, aware of, but perhaps disbelieving Dickens's statement that the Cheerybles were real people, has found it impossible to believe "that the overgrown elderly babies . . . could ever have been successful in business," adding that "to most modern readers they are thoroughly tiresome in their hand-rubbing, their unctuous smiles, their childlike benevolent glee."[50]

To question the credibility of fictional characters is the prerogative of both reader and critic, but to disbelieve in the existence of people who do not conform to accepted notions of reality is another matter. Finding originals for the characters of Victorian novelists has often been a pastime of the literary antiquarian, and at times such knowledge has not been particularly illuminating. Yet, in the case of the Cheerybles, an acquaintance with their originals might serve to modify the impression of distasteful unreality that has been generated by critics. The benevolent eccentricity of the Brothers Grant, it shall be shown, equalled that of their fictional counterparts. Moreover, the Grants, though exceptional to the point of legend, demonstrate that during this period of animosity toward the new class, the industrialist as benefactor, on terms other than those of the political economist, did exist.

In the preface to *Nicholas Nickleby* Dickens, noting that readers seldom accept "a very strongly marked character" as probable in fiction, affirms that the Cheerybles were modeled after real people: "But those who take an interest in this tale, will be glad to learn that the BROTHERS CHEERYBLE live; that their liberal charity, their singleness of heart, their noble nature, and their unbounded benevolence, are no creations of the Author's brain; but are prompting every day (and oftnest by stealth) some munificent and generous deed in that town [Manchester] of which they are the pride and honour."[51] Dickens had made the acquaintance of the originals through W. H. Ainsworth, who had told him about the two brothers William and Charles Grant, thinking that their history, traits, and peculiarities made them sufficiently "Dickensian." To meet the brothers may have been part of Dickens's object in visiting Manchester in 1838. With Ainsworth supplying a letter of introduction, Dickens dined with the Grants at a party given by Ainsworth's friend Gilbert Winter.[52] Four years after the publication of *Nickleby*, one of the brothers was dead, and Dickens paid him tribute in a letter written from Niagara Falls in 1842 to C. C. Felton: "One of the noble hearts who sat for the Cheeryble brothers is dead. If I had been in England, I would certainly have gone into mourning for the loss of such a glorious life. His brother is not expected to survive him. I am told that it appears from a memorandum found among the papers of the deceased, that in his life-time he gave away in charity £ 600,000, or three million dollars!"[53]

Dickens made no further mention of the brothers, but other Victorians Samuel Smiles and Lord John Manners, have recorded parts of the Grant legend. Smiles writes that the Grants were well known for their benevolence and "various goodness" and cites an anecdote to show that Dickens "by no means exaggerated" when he delineated the character of the Cheerybles with an eye on the Grants.[54] A Manchester warehouseman once published a scurrilous pamphlet in which he ridiculed the elder brother William as "Billy Buttons." Later, when the man became a bankrupt, he had to apply to the same Grant to sign his certificate of bankruptcy in order that he might begin business again. Instead of throwing the document into the fire, William Grant signed it because of his libeler's honesty as a tradesman. Furthermore, upon discovering that the bankrupt had spent all of his money for the certificate of bankruptcy, William Grant gave him even more cause to repent having ridiculed him. Smiles records Grant's supposed reaction:

> "My good fellow, this will never do; your wife and family must not suffer in this way; be kind enough to take this ten-pound note to your wife from me; there, there, now—don't cry, it will also be well with you yet; keep up your spirit, set to work like a man, and you will raise your head amongst the best of us yet." The overpowered man endeavoured with choking utterance to express his gratitude, but in vain; and putting his hand to his face, he went out of the room sobbing like a child.[55]

In 1841 Lord John Manners and George Smythe visited the manufacturing districts in order to observe working conditions and to gauge the depth of Corn Law sentiment among the manufacturers. Stopping at Manchester, they met the Grants whom Manners described as "most exquisite old men," and calico printers who were proud of being able to print six colors at once.[56] That the Grants were sufficiently "Dickensian" in character is attested to by the observations of the Young Englander. Of all the manufacturers he saw, the Grants made the most lasting impression. In his journal he records that on the way to the Grant factory, children by the side of the road shouted "Hurrah for Grant." He also notes the affection of one brother for another expressed in taking leave of one another with a "Goodbye, love."[57] On the second day of his visit Manners saw an example of the Grant spirit when the brothers were discussing the matter of dispensing charity to some workingmen. The visitor records this scene: " 'I doubt, brother, whether you are, doing good by this.' 'Brother, brother,' answered William, ' the men can't starve you know; they would work if they could;' then turning to me [Manners] to explain, 'it's the mill up yonder, sir, has stopped; no, they mustn't starve, and if we, who can afford it, don't feed them they will get fed somehow else, and that perhaps wouldn't be so well. . . .' "[58]

Learning the history of the brothers, Manners relates that their father had attempted to apprentice the eldest son to Arkwright but he did not have the premium Arkwright wanted. Finding a less businesslike manufacturer to take him on as an apprentice, William worked early and late, saved his money, and took his brothers into partnership. From that time forward, William told his visitor, "we have had but one purse, one banking account, and what each wants, that he takes."[59] Manners then ends his journal entry with the following encomium: "this is the outline of this beautiful history . . . What a life has that man's been! From the boy wandering penniless by the banks of the uncontaminated Irwell—then without chimney in its valley—to the princely manufacturer-merchant, owning that very valley, and filling the remotest corners of the globe with the products of his industry and wealth, and still more wonderful, retaining all the guilelessness and simple-heartedness of childhood."[60]

IV

Hard Times

It was not until fifteen years after the writing of *Nicholas Nickleby* that Dickens fulfilled the vow he had made in his letter to Fitzgerald to strike a blow for the unfortunate victims of the factory system. By 1854 Dickens seems to have come to believe that his appeal to employers to follow the example of the Cheerybles had fallen on deaf ears. The forces of the new industrialism had negated the personal relationships that he sought to celebrate in his delineation of the Cheerybles, and it was apparent that the captain of industry preferred some form of the cash nexus relationship to that of paternalism. If, however, employers would not follow the pattern of the Cheeryble ideal, then they deserved to be represented in the light of their own ideal of laissez-faire individualism. *Hard Times* (1854) reflects Dickens's change of mood.[61]

The following analysis of the industrial magnate Josiah Bounderby will develop two points. First of all, in the caricature of Bounderby Dickens satirizes as "popular fictions" the simplistic, laissez-faire assumptions of captains of industry on the subject of factory legislation and employer-employee relations. Secondly, taking another "popular fiction," the myth of the self-made man, Dickens makes art out of the materials of polemic by permitting Bounderby to create a fictionalized version of himself as a self-made man. The Coketown industrialist's fantasy is a mixture of current notions of self-help (Smiles had begun in Leeds in 1845) and a romantic idealization of the self-made man of the early days of the Industrial Revolution. Thus, though an undisguised diatribe against the heartless employer, the characterization of Bounderby has an artistic quality that is generally absent from the industrial novel with a purpose.

Writing to Mrs. Gaskell in 1854, Dickens explained that in *Hard Times* he would be dealing in part with "The monstrous claims at domination made by a certain class of manufacturers, and the extent to which the way is made easy for working men to slide down into discontent under such hands. . . ."[62] Unlike Harriet Martineau's fictional employers, the Josiah Bounderbys of industrial England did not pretend to clothe class interests in the ideological garment provided for them by the rationalizations of political economy. If Harriet Martineau's industrialists do not feel, at least they think and are prepared to offer reasons in justification of their economic position. On the other hand, Josiah Bounderby neither thinks nor feels: he merely reacts with the stock responses of ignorant and unimaginative self-interest. This quality of mind is conspicuous in his dealings with employees, even when the issue at stake has little to do directly with the relations of capital and labor. When, for example, Bounderby's employee Stephen Blackpool approaches the magnate for advice in the matter of divorce, Bounderby, making it clear that he wants no complaints, reveals his lack of understanding by voicing an assumption about working class aspirations current among some employers:

> "Now, you know . . . we have never had any difficulty with you and you have never been one of the unreasonable ones. You don't expect to be set up in a coach and six, and to be fed on turtle soup and venison, with a gold spoon, as a good many of them do!" Mr. Bounderby always represented this to be the sole, immediate, and direct object of any Hand who was not entirely satisfied; "and therefore I know already that you have not come here to make a complaint. Now, you know, I am certain of that beforehand."[63]

But when Stephen calls a muddle the injustice of a law so structured that only the wealthy can afford to obtain a divorce on grounds of incompatibility, Bounderby is quick to "see traces of the turtle soup and venison, and gold spoon" in that (p. 68): "Pooh, pooh! Don't you talk nonsense . . . about things you don't understand; and don't you call the institutions of your country a muddle, or you'll get yourself into a real muddle one of these fine mornings. The institutions of your country are not your piece-work, and the only thing you have got to do is to mind your piece-work" (p. 67). As the novel progresses, Bounderby finds that he wants no part of a worker who, he believes, wants "to know how he could knock Religion over and floor the Established Church" (p. 165).

The factory workers of Coketown, who were "generically called 'the Hands,' a race who would have found more favour with some people, if Providence had seen fit to make them only hands" (p. 56), had no cause for complaint. Bounderby describes their work in the mills to James Harthouse, who was to have been future M. P. for Coketown: "Now, you have heard a lot of talk about the work in our mills, no doubt. . . . I'll state the fact of it to you. It's the pleasantest work there is, and it's the lightest work there is, and it's the best-paid work there is. More than that, we couldn't improve the mills themselves, unless we laid down Turkey carpets on the floors" (p. 113). As for the standard of living of the Coketown hands, Bounderby knew from personal experience "that they lived upon the best, and bought fresh butter; insisted on Mocha coffee, and rejected all but prime parts of meat . . ." (p. 21). Whenever trouble appears, it rises not out of the intolerable conditions of work, but is stirred up by "mischievous strangers who are always about—and who ought to be hanged wherever they are found" (p. 131). In contrast to the Hands who, in spite of the advantages Bounderby outlines, are perpetually dissatisfied, is the example of his employee Bitzer, the product of the Gradgrind school of political economy, and the logical consummation of the advice of that school to working men. Bitzer, coldly calculating his own interests, has none of the irrationalities of feeling and sentiment that prevent the ordinary working man from seeing the beauty of the science and subscribing to its principles. With these qualifications, we are told, Bitzer is admirably suited for the position of spy and general informer at Bounderby's bank. Following the advice of the economists who teach that every man can become a capitalist by saving, Bitzer does not understand why all working men cannot do the same: "This, again was one among the fictions of Coketown. Any capitalist there, who had made sixty thousand pounds out of sixpence, always professed to wonder why the sixty thousand nearest Hands didn't each make sixty thousand pounds out of sixpence, and more or less reproached them every one for not accomplishing the little feat. What I did you can do. Why don't you go and do it?" (p. 105).

With respect to factory legislation, the Bounderbys of Coketown were acutely hypersensitive. In the following passage, Dickens records the kind of response that, judging from Cobbett's list of millowners' objections to the Factory Act of 1833, was typical of the manufacturer's point of view before Parliamentary committees:

Surely there never was such fragile china-ware as that of which the millers of Coketown were made. Handle them never so lightly, and they fell to pieces with such ease that you might suspect them of having been flawed before. They were ruined, when they were required to send labouring children to school; they were ruined when inspectors were appointed to look into their works; they were ruined when such inspectors considered it doubtful whether they were quite justified in chopping people up with their machinery; they were utterly undone, when it was hinted that perhaps they need not always make quite so much smoke. Besides Mr. Bounderby's gold spoon which was generally received in Coketown, another prevalent fiction was very popular there. It took the form of a threat. Whenever a Coketowner felt he was ill-used—that is to say, whenever he was not left entirely alone, and it was proposed to hold him accountable for the consequences of any of his acts—he was sure to come out with the awful menace, that he would "sooner pitch his property into the Atlantic." This had terrified the Home Secretary within an inch of his life on several occasions. (pp. 98-99)[64]

It is Dickens's relentless interjection of the Coketown magnates' "popular fictions" that accounts in part for the harshness of *Hard Times*. But the element of comic irony in his dramatization of one popular fiction—the myth of the self-made man—relieves the sense of oppression generated by the bullying of Bounderby, the rationalism of Gradgrind, and the cynicism of the "fine gentleman" James Harthouse. Throughout the novel Bounderby's reiterations of his self-made manhood are the threads out of which the fabric of the myth is woven. The image of himself that he seeks to promote is that he, born in a ditch, was abandoned by his mother and left in the hands of a drunken grandmother who abused him and drove him away as a young child to a life of sleeping in pigsties and on paving stones. He pulled through, however, without anyone's aid and made his way to the top in the following succession: "Vagabond, errand-boy, labourer, porter, clerk, chief manager, small partner, Josiah Bounderby of Coketown. Those are the antecedents and the culmination" (p. 14). Never tired of boasting about his early poverty, his education in the school of hard blows, and his lack of refinement, he was "the Bully of humility" (p. 12). But when the mysterious old woman who is brought before him as a robbery suspect turns out to be his mother, who comes to town annually in order to catch a secret glimpse of him, all of Coketown learns that he is a "self-made Humbug" (p. 236). After Gradgrind accuses her of having left her son to be brought up in the gutter, Mrs. Pegler disposes of her son's "popular fiction." She describes what was more than likely the typical background of the self-made early Victorian businessman. Unaware of the falsehoods that her son published

about his start in life, the indignant Mrs. Pegler, a village shopkeeper, en-
lightens Gradgrind:

> Josiah in the gutter! . . . No such a thing, Sir. Never! For shame
> on you! My dear boy knows, and will give you to know, that though he
> come of humble parents, he comes of parents that loved him as dear as
> the best could, and never thought it hardship on themselves to pinch
> a bit that he might write and cipher beautiful and I've his books at
> home to show it! . . . And my dear boy knows, and will give you to
> know, Sir, that after his beloved father died, when he was eight years
> old, his mother, too, could pinch a bit, as it was her duty and her plea-
> sure and her pride to do it, to help him out in life, and put him 'pren-
> tice. And a steady lad he was, and a kind master he had to lend him a
> hand, and well he worked his own way forward to be rich and thriving.
> (p. 234)

After his humiliation Bounderby still remains unregenerate. Gradgrind
is spared because he meant to do right despite his wrong-headed cerebra-
tions. The mind that can reason, however mistakenly, is capable of acquir-
ing new wisdom, but the ego that has neither wisdom of head nor of heart
is bound to continue blustering until it collapses in a fit on a Coketown
street.

By exposing Bounderby as a humbug, Dickens undermined the notion
of rugged individualism in two ways. First of all, he hinted at the truth of
what R. H. Tawney has observed about self-made men and the social
order: "Few tricks of the unsophisticated intellect are more curious than
the naïve psychology of the business man, who ascribes his achievements
to his own unaided efforts, in bland unconsciousness of a social order
without whose continuous support he would be as a lamb bleating in the
desert."[65] Secondly, Dickens was obliquely commenting on the fact that
the self-made man has usually been the exception rather than the rule.
Despite the profession of Victorian employers that all could avail themselves of the opportunity of rising from the ranks, after 1825 the chances
of a working man's becoming the owner of a textile concern were few. A
family in the industrial North might attempt to rise on its own initiative
by opening a shop, but even so, a large proportion of those enterprises
failed.[66] Moreover, even during the entire period of the emergence of the
new class, it is erroneous to assume that industrialists were self-made men
in the sense that they arose, in Cobbett's words, "from the dunghill to
the chariot." A survey of 132 prominent manufacturers who operated between 1750 and 1850 reveals that one third came from working class or
farming families, while two-thirds came from an established business background.[67]

Dickens's treatment of Bounderby and his catalog of Bounderbyisms is another indication of the distortions to which the controversial figure of the industrialist was subjected. That the usefulness of *Hard Times* is lessened by Dickens's exaggerations is an objection that may be raised by fair-minded persons, just as the exaggerations of the Radical Snob Thackeray described raise a plea for fair play in the generous mind. Ruskin was of such a mind when he declared that Bounderby was a dramatic monster and not typical of the industrialist class. But Ruskin also insisted upon the truth behind the caricature, stating that Dickens was usually right: "[Readers] will find much that is partial and because partial, apparently unjust; but if they examine all the evidence on the other side, which Dickens seems to overlook, it will appear, after all their trouble, that his view was finally the right one, grossly and sharply told."[68]

v

William Langshawe, the Cotton Lord

In an attempt to balance the bad impressions of the manufacturing class that were fostered by visiting novelists who were friends of Shaftesbury, Elizabeth Stone, a native of Manchester, avoided partisanship and endeavored to make reason prevail in her work *William Langshawe, the Cotton Lord* (1842). Up to this point, the industrialist appears in a wholly good or in a totally bad light, according to his creator's attitude toward the factory system. Mrs. Stone, on the other hand, attempts to do the mill-owner simple justice by making a distinction between the worst, the best and the representative of the class:

> Light and darkness are scarcely more dissimilar than is the low-lived and ignorant, though shrewd, millowner of some out-lying district, from the cultivated denizen of the town; and the disgust with which the vulgar pleasures and brutal excesses of the former are regarded by the latter, are only equalled by the pitying contempt with which the magnate of the country looks upon the more refined gratifications of his compeer in the town. Between these two extremes there is a third class, a connecting medium, partaking in some degree both of the vices of one and the refinements of the other, formed as may be expected, from circumstances which draw it within the influences of both without entailing exclusive connection with either.[69]

The vulgar and tyrannical manufacturer and his sensual son appear in the characters of John Balshawe and his son John. Mrs. Stone, however, points out that they are the creatures of circumstances:

> those who, like Mr. Balshawe, had lived in secluded districts, had been the suns of a little sphere, the lords paramount among the

artizans whom their manufacture supported, and of the small shop-keepers around; and whose fiat could at once throng these shops with customers, or deprive them entirely of support . . . such men became demi-gods in their several districts. They had none to coerce, none to restrain them by precept or example where none other was on equal terms. They were frequently the only magistrates of their districts, and interpreted the law as it pleased them. Such plenitude of power did not soften an arbitrary disposition, nor render a hasty temper more gentle; and unless gifted with great natural goodness, these mushroom princes oftener enacted the tyrannical despot than the considerate master in their domain. (1:122-23)

The pleasures of a man like Balshawe consisted of a luxurious dinner followed by an all-night drinking bout (1:140-43). But Mrs. Stone was careful to point out that excessive drinking was characteristic only of the manufacturers of the outlying districts (1:142). As for John Balshawe Junior, "he was a low-lived libertine, carrying, in the indulgence of his brutal pleasures, shame and sorrow to the lowly hearths of those whom his father was bound by every tie of decency and morality to protect and cherish. Too often this is the case with the half-fledged sons of these secluded petty princes, who carry on a wasting warfare upon the morality and domestic comfort of their petty localities" (1:124-25).

In contrast to the Balshawes, Mr. Ainsley, angered as a youth at the ridicule cast upon cotton lords, became a self-made gentleman in his determination to prove that manufacturing was not inconsistent with refined manners:

> Now, the few real gentry who inhabit our environs, and the few aristocratic travellers who visit the town, are not victimized at my dinner-table, or wearied in my drawing room. But how little do any of them suppose that the man who can discourse of a Titian or Corregio, not indeed in the jargon of a connoisseur, but with taste and judgment—who can lead his own orchestra correctly in a concerted piece—or stand without wincing if a French satirist or an Italian poet be glanced at—how little do they think that the man who does this could not at twenty years old write an English sentence grammatically, and has acquired his hard-earned accomplishments entirely in the intervals of a laborious business! (1:67-68)

Between these two extremes is William Langshawe who is typical of the Manchester man. Langshawe's less agreeable traits are the ostentation and vulgarity that the refined Ainsley deplores. Langshawe's house is elaborately furnished, and at his sumptuous dinners which are devoured rather than elegantly trifled with, like Bounderby, he glories in his lack of refinement.[70] But these failings aside, Langshawe "was a man of kind

heart, and of rigid morality; a pattern of liberality and kindess and propriety in his domestic establishment, and of justice in his mercantile one. His
operatives respected him, his domestics loved him" (1:125). Langshawe,
then, falls somewhere between Balshawe and Ainsley: he possesses Balshawe's business acumen and lack of cultivation but shares the cultivated
Ainsley's refinement of morals.

Although Mrs. Stone's avowedly non-partisan readiness to distinguish
between good and bad manufacturers is commendable (especially since
she was a resident of Manchester), her justifications of the Manchester
manufacturer's attitudes would have lost her the sympathy of most novel
readers. It is doubtful whether the love of ostentation can be justified.
Nor is Langshawe's belief that a taste for literature is incompatible with
business likely to recommend him as a protagonist. As for the refined
Ainsley, his credibility is undermined elsewhere by Mrs. Stone's doubts
about the chance gentlemanly manners stand against the pushiness of
the Balshawes on the Cotton Exchange. As successful businessmen,
Langshawe and Balshawe are the heroes of this novel, and perhaps the
last word on them is best expressed by the book's lone reviewer: "There
may be Langshawes and Balshawes in Lancashire and elsewhere, who take
a pride in vulgarity, and who delight to proclaim that they are not gentlemen; but we have never met with any such, and common sense teaches
us that if such do exist, they must be regarded as 'Lusus Naturae'."[71]

In the face of an embarras de richesses of evidence from novelists, factory inspectors, Radical spokesmen, apologists for the factory system, and
reformers, it is difficult to ascertain the proportion of good and of bad
manufacturers in the 1830s and 1840s. Differences of opinion arise from
the use of different sources.[72] But a generalization can be made that might
suit all interested observers except perhaps Engels. The good manufacturer of these decades was likely to be the owner of a large concern with
reserves of capital for bad times. Such an establishment would efficiently
produce better goods, and its owner could afford to construct decent housing and offer other advantages which would help labor relations. On the
other hand, the bad manufacturer was often the small operator who was
short of capital and ability. He had to play fair with suppliers of raw
material and builders of machinery. In order to conserve resources the
only expedient left to such an employer was to turn to exploiting the
labor force made up largely of women and children.[73]

SIX

Plugson of St. Dolly Undershot

All work, even cotton-spinning, is noble.
Carlyle, Past and Present

In RETROSPECT, THE "GOOD" INDUSTRIALIST OF the political economist and the "bad" employer of the radical-humanitarian are representations which to a large degree do not rise above the topical polemic of the 1830s and 1840s. The task of treating but transcending the heated issues of the period by giving a visionary turn to the potential of the new class for good or evil is undertaken by Disraeli, whose projections of the industrialist suggest Carlyle's concept of a working aristocracy, and by Geraldine Jewsbury, who employed Carlyle's transcendentalism as an antidote to the materialism of the industrialist. Before considering the treatment of Carlylean ideas in fiction, it is necessary to outline Carlyle's assumptions about the place of his Plugson of Undershot in an industrial society.

Carlyle's prophetic utterances add a third dimension to the controversy over industrialism. He was in a sense both critic and apologist: he attacked the laissez-faire principle but without the kind of bias we have seen in the novelists of the last two chapters; he also envisioned the captain of industry, if shorn of his economic individualism, as a heroic figure who was the likely candidate for leadership in a country whose nominal aristocracy had relinquished this function through indifference and inactivity:

> Aristocracy has become Phantasm-Aristocracy, no longer able to do its work, not in the least conscious that it has any work longer to do. Unable, totally careless to do its work; careful only to clamour for the wages of doing its work,—nay for higher, and palpably undue wages, and Corn-Laws and increase of rents; the old rate of wages not being adequate now! In hydra-wrestle, giant "Millocracy" so-called, a real giant, though as yet a blind one and but half-awake, wrestles and wrings in choking

nightmare, "like to be strangled in the partridge-nets of Phantasm-Aris-
tocracy," as we said, which fancies itself still to be a giant. Wrestles, as
under nightmare, till it do awaken; and gasps and struggles thousand-
fold, we may say, in a truly painful manner, through all fibres of our
English Existence, in these hours and years!"[1]

But industrious millocracy does not deserve our unqualified sympathy
merely because it is the victim of the protectionism of a partridge-shooting
landed aristocracy, who seek to preserve unearned and artificial commercial privileges by supporting a Corn Law with arguments "such as might
make the angels and almost the very jackasses weep!"[2] Millocracy, too,
though it works for its privileges, is worthy of censure. Haunted by visions
of a private Hell—"The terror of 'Not succeeding' . . . chiefly of not
making money!"[3]—the disciples of the Gospel of Mammonism have overridden the considerations which distinguish a society of men from an
aggregate of atoms:

> True, it must be owned, we for the present have come to strange
> conclusions. We call it a Society; and go about professing openly the
> totalest separation, isolation. Our life is not a mutual helpfulness; but
> rather cloaked under due laws-of-war, named "fair competition" . . .
> it is a mutual hostility. We have forgotten everywhere that *Cash-pay-
> ment* is not the sole relation of human beings; we think, nothing doubt-
> ing, that *it* absolves and liquidates all engagements of man. "My starv-
> ing workers?" answers the rich mill-owner: "Did not I hire them fairly
> in the market? Did I not pay them, to the last sixpence, the sum cov-
> enanted for? What have I to do with them more?" Verily, Mammon-
> worship is a melancholy creed.[4]

Thus the world is divided between a working Mammonism which acknowledges no responsibilities and an idle landowning aristocracy which
refuses to do its work of governing. Of the two, however, Mammonism is
by far preferable: "Idleness is worst, Idleness alone is without hope:
work earnestly at anything, you will by degrees learn to work at almost all
things. There is endless hope in work, were it even to work at making
money."[5] Although there is no future for an idle aristocracy on this working planet, there is hope that the working aristocracy, not insensible to
trades unions and Chartist agitation, may reform.[6] Its first step is to
realize that the philosophy of profit and loss, and supply and demand can
never remain the basis for a permanent union between man and man.
The double entry of Plugson's ledgers must give way to the "quadruple
entry" of the Four Gospels of the New Testament: "For all human beings do require to have an Ideal in them; to have some Soul in them . . .
were it only to keep the body unputrified."[7] The "Brute-god Mammon"
must be dethroned and in his place a "Spirit-god" put. Up to now, un-

fortunately, the captain of industry has not been converted from his belief in the "Cash-Gospel":

> Hence these tears.—Plugson, who has indomitably spun Cotton merely to gain thousands of pounds, I have to call as yet a Bucanier and Chactaw; till there come something better, still indomitable from him. His hundred Thousand pound Notes, if there be nothing other, are to me but as the hundred Scalps in a Chactaw wigwam. The blind Plugson: he was a Captain of Industry, born member of the Ultimate genuine Aristocracy of this Universe, could he have known it! These thousand men that spun and toiled round him, they were a regiment whom he had enlisted, man by man; to make war on a very genuine enemy: Bareness of back, and disobedient Cotton-fibre, which will not, unless forced to it, consent to cover bare backs. Here is a most genuine enemy; over whom all creatures will wish him victory. He enlisted his thousand men: said to them, "Come, brothers, let us have a dash at Cotton!" They follow with cheerful shout; they gain such a victory over cotton as the Earth has to admire and clap hands at: but alas, it is yet only of the Bucanier or Chactaw sort,—as good as no victory! Foolish Plugson of St. Dolly Undershot. . . . Cotton is conquered; but the "bare backs"—are worse covered than ever![8]

In juxtaposition to the modern industrial captain, Carlyle puts William of Normandy who did not turn off his men after victory but told them instead: "Noble fighters, this is the land we have gained; be I Lord in it,— what we call *Law-ward*, maintainer and *keeper* of Heaven's *Laws* . . . and be ye Loyal Men around me in it; and we will stand by one another, as soldiers around a captain, for again we shall have need of one another."[9] William and his men were not united by a cash nexus but by a permanent contract, by laws of mutual obligation.

But the epic of the nineteenth century is no longer "Arms and the Man but Tools and the Man,"[10] and though the industrialist has up to this point lived under the "Laws of the Bucaniers,"[11] he is capable of nobler accomplishments. He is England's present hope, and therefore it is most essential that he be not hampered by the restrictive legislation of the owners of the soil. The Corn Laws should be repealed and this energetic but still barbarian Plugson must be civilized by factory legislation and the traditions of the old order:

> This is not a man I would kill and strangle by Corn-Laws, even if I could! No, I would fling my Corn-Laws and Shotbelts to the Devil; and try to help this man. I would teach him by noble precept and law precept, by noble example most of all, that Mammonism was not the essence of his or of my station in God's Universe. . . . By noble real legislation, by true *noble's*-work, by unwearied, valiant, and were it wage-

less effort, in my Parliament and in my Parish, I would aid, constrain, encourage him to effect more or less this blessed change."[12]

In order to reorganize a disordered industrial age, "an actual new Sovereignty, Industrial Aristocracy, real and not imaginary Aristocracy, is indispensable and undubitable. . . ."[13] Those who lead industry are, in sum, "Captains of the World," and if nobility does not exist in them, no aristocracy can ever again exist.[14] The world belongs not to the near-dead idle aristocracy but to the yet half-alive captain of industry. His hosts of industrial soldiers are in mutiny and must be put in order: "To order, to just subordination; noble loyalty in return for noble guidance. . . . Not as a bewildered, bewildering mob; but as a firm, regimented mass, with real captains over them will these men march anymore."[15] The contract between industrial captain and industrial soldier must be permanent, with a basis of mutual obligation and not the temporary contract that leaves the "free labourer" the liberty to starve when turned away.[16] In this manner, a "Chivalry of Labour" is created and though "despotism is essential in most enterprises," it can be reconciled with a manly freedom by being a just despotism.[17]

I

Coningsby, or the New Generation

Benjamin Disraeli, who according to J. A. Froude, studied and imitated Carlyle to such an extent that Carlyle considered him a "fantastic ape,"[18] set out to portray Plugson of Undershot along the noble lines that Carlyle had hoped the captain of industry would develop. In his first attempt at such a delineation, however, Disraeli proved to be more than a mere imitator. Together with Carlyle's concept of a working aristocracy, Disraeli also blended the myth of the Norman yoke and then as might be expected, translated these two concepts into terms of Whig and Tory politics. It is this imaginative handling of the industrialist as symbol and the assignation of plural meanings to that symbol that distinguishes the industrialist Millbank of Coningsby (1844) from the creations of novelists who, intent upon practical reforms, did not give a maximum of artistic realization to their characters.

In the course of his peregrinations, Harry Coningsby, the Young Englander who believes in a Tory party based upon principle and not expediency, visits Manchester. There he meets Millbank, a manufacturer and father of his Eton classmate, Oswald.[19] After dinner Coningsby is exposed to the manufacturer's political, social, and economic viewpoint, the essence of which is stated by Millbank as "all that we want in this

country is to be masters of our own industry; but Saxon industry and
Norman manners will never agree; and someday, Mr. Coningsby you will
find that out" (pp. 139-40). Puzzled by that enigmatic statement,
Coningsby asks the manufacturer whether he is then opposed to an aristocracy. Millbank answers that what he wants is a real and a natural
aristocracy:

> I do not understand how an aristocracy can exist, unless it be distin-
> guished by some quality which no other class of the community pos-
> sesses. Distinction is the basis of aristocracy. . . . That, however, is
> not the characteristic of the English peerage. I have yet to learn that
> they are richer than we are, better informed, wiser or more distin-
> guished for public or private virtue. Is it not monstrous that a small
> number of men, several of whom take the titles of duke or earl from
> towns which they never saw, which never heard of them, which they
> did not form, or build, or establish, I say is it not monstrous that in-
> dividuals so circumstanced should be invested with the highest of
> conceivable privileges—the privilege of making laws? (pp. 140-41)

The present peerage, continues Millbank, cannot trace its lineage back
to the Normans, yet it has adopted Norman manners as well as titles:
"They have neither the right of the Normans, nor do they fulfil the duty
of the Normans: they did not conquer the land, and they do not defend
it" (p. 142). But where is a natural aristocracy to be found? With an echo
of Carlyle's aristocracy of talent, or government by the wisest, who would
not, like the present aristocracy, take the wages of governing while they
misgovern, Millbank replies:[20]

> Among those men whom a nation recognizes as the most eminent
> for virtue, talents, and property, and if you please, birth and standing
> in the land. They guide opinion; and therefore they govern. I am no
> leveller; I look upon an artificial equality as equally pernicious with a
> factitious aristocracy; both depressing the energies, and checking the
> enterprise of a nation. I like man to be free; really free; free in his in-
> dustry as well as his body. (p. 142)

As the "Disciple of Progress," however, Millbank is essentially optimistic
about the possibility of a natural aristocracy, for the Reform Bill has
opened the way for remedying Norman political manners. Although such
evils as Corn Laws exist, they will in time disappear (p. 143). As a result
of the interview with the manufacturer, the Young Englander's views on
commercial policy are formed.

By a stretch of the historical imagination, Disraeli's association of the
new industry with Saxon England has overtones of the kind of assumption Paul Mantoux makes when he insists that if followed back far

enough, most manufacturing family trees would be found to have yeoman roots. But Disraeli did not attempt to trace the lineage of the industrial class. Instead, by equating industry with the Saxon and oppression with the usurping Norman, he was utilizing what Christopher Hill has called the theory of the Norman Yoke.[21] Involving a myth of a golden age of English equality, this popular theory looked backward to Anglo-Saxon times for lost rights and freedoms. According to the theory, before 1066 all Englishmen were free and equal citizens, and the people were represented in governing institutions. By bringing in the tyranny of a Norman king and alien landlords, however, the Norman Conquest changed all that. But Englishmen never forgot that they were once free-born Anglo-Saxons, and they struggled to recover their rights, which beginning with the Magna Carta, had to be extorted from their rulers.[22]

If, as Disraeli's Millbank avows, Saxon industry is enthralled by the Norman yoke, who are the Normans of the nineteenth century? For Disraeli, the political theorist, who because of his dissatisfaction with the state of contemporary parties, sought to found a new Tory party, the Normans are both the Tories who misgoverned England during the first three decades of the nineteenth century and their predecessors the Whigs, whose policy of commercial restriction they had followed.

Together with the other mediocrities in his Cabinet (1812-27), such men as Lord Castlereagh and Lord Sidmouth, Lord Liverpool had perverted Toryism. This faction, calling themselves Tories, had acted upon no principle, or upon principles that were contrary to those of the great Tory leaders. They had come to power during the latter years of the career of Pitt. This last of the great Tories had been forced to fall back on Whig measures during that time. The Liverpool Cabinet simply continued Pitt's errors: "Impudently usurping the name of that party of which nationality, and therefore universality is the essence, these pseudo-Tories made Exclusion the principle of their political constitution and Restriction the genius of their commercial code" (p. 56). Disraeli declares that these Whig principles,

> have really nothing in common with the ancient character of our political settlement, or the manners and customs of the English people. Confidence in the loyalty of the nation, testified by munificent grants of rights and franchises, and favour to an expansive system of traffic, were distinctive qualities of the English sovereignty, until the House of Commons usurped the better portion of its prerogatives [in 1688]. A widening of our electoral scheme, great facilities to commerce, and the rescue of our Roman Catholic fellow-subjects from the Puritanic yoke, from fetters which have been fastened on them by English parliaments in spite of the protests and exertions of English sovereigns;

these were the three great elements and fundamental truths of the
real Pitt system—a system founded on the traditions of our monarchy,
[whose Tory supporters] . . . had ever been anxious that the sovereign
of England should never be degraded into the position of a Venetian
doge. (pp. 61-62)

But Pitt had failed to make ancient English Tory principles flourish again
after the long domination of the Whigs in the eighteenth century. Since
the coming of the House of Hanover, the Whigs had governed England
by what Young England called a Venetian Constitution. Under the
Venetian Republic, an oligarchy composed of a number of noble families
ruled; the people were prevented by their constitution from having a
share in government; and the Sovereign was chosen and controlled by
the ruling families.

It is thus the spirit of Whiggism that Disraeli means by Norman manners. The Whigs have forced a foreign constitution upon the "ancient
English character of our political settlement." In a sweeping historical
summary, Disraeli dates the rise of Whiggism from the spoilation of the
Church and accounts for Millbank's plea for freedom for industry:

It is in the plunder of the church that we must seek for the primary
cause of our political exclusion, and our commercial restraint. That
unhallowed booty created a factitious aristocracy, ever fearful that they
might be called upon to re-gorge their sacriligeous spoil. To prevent
this they took to refuge in political religionism, and paltering with the
disturbed consciences or the pious fantasies of a portion of the people,
they organized them into religious sects. These became the unconscious Praetorians of their ill-gotten domains. At the head of these
religionists, they have ever since continued to govern, or powerfully
influence, this country. They have in that time pulled down thrones
and churches, changed dynasties, abrogated and remodelled parlia-
ments; they have disfranchised Scotland and confiscated Ireland. One
may admire the vigour and consistency of the Whig party, and recog-
nise in their career that unity of purpose that can only spring from a
great principle; but the Whigs introduced sectarian religion, sectarian
religion led to political exclusion, and political exclusion was soon accompanied by commercial restraint. (p. 62)

The Corn Laws, then, passed during the tenure of the pseudo-Tory Liverpool Cabinet, are inherently a Whig measure. A factitious aristocracy insisted that tribute be paid to it in the form of a bread tax; to both industrialist and workman such an act was worthy of a conqueror.

Millbank's dictum that Saxon industry must be free of Norman manners is perplexing on a first reading and is apt to be dismissed as a fantastic aping of *Ivanhoe*.[23] Yet in the light of popular theory and Young

England's political principles, the statement reveals itself to be pregnant with meaning. By endorsing the theory of the Norman Yoke, Disraeli reveals his sympathies with both the Chartists, one of whose leaders Feargus O'Connor had employed the "lost rights" argument in his demagoguery, and with the industrialists who pushed for Free Trade. Had Disraeli sought to be returned to Parliament from Manchester, it seems likely that he would have had a constituency.

In addition to Disraeli's imaginative treatment of Carlyle's concept of a working aristocracy, still another consideration related indirectly to Carlyle and important to the overall purpose of this study remains to be examined; namely, the social position of the industrialist in relation to the aristocrat. This aspect has not been treated by radical or humanitarian novelists in the preceding chapters dealing with controversy, largely because their immediate concerns were with the manufacturing class in relation to labor. In *Coningsby*, the presence of the son of an "infernal manufacturer," as one aristocratic classmate styles Oswald Millbank, at Eton would seem to prefigure the trend of the 1870s toward a gentleman's education, a factor which plays a major part in the aristocratization of the industrialist. But Oswald was not at that school for purposes of fraternization, but because of what seems to be sheer perversity of self-assertion on the part of his father:

> Millbank was the son of one of the wealthiest manufacturers of Lancashire. His father, whose opinions were of a very democratic bent, sent his son to Eton, though he disapproved of the system of education pursued there, to show that he had as much right to do so as any duke in the land. He had, however, brought up his only boy with a due prejudice against every sentiment or institution of an aristocratic character, and had especially impressed upon him in his school career to avoid the lightest semblance of courting the affections or society of the falsely held superior class.
>
> The character of the son, as much as the influence of the father, tended to the fulfilment of these injunctions. Oswald Millbank was of a proud and independent nature; reserved, a little stern. The early and constantly reiterated dogma of his father, that he belonged to a class debarred from its just position in the social system, had aggravated the grave and somewhat discontented humour of his blood. (p. 35)

His father's prejudices notwithstanding, Oswald Millbank secretly admires Coningsby for being the most accomplished boy in a school of aristocrats. The mystique of passionate schoolboy friendships is shown to overcome class prejudices. Upon his subsequent visit to the Millbanks, Coningsby becomes an admirer of not only the manufacturer who concerned himself with the moral and physical welfare of his workers, but also, Edith Millbank. The Young Englander, who represents a new generation of aristocracy which seeks to revive ancient allegiances between the owners of the soil and the people, marries a daughter of the working aristocracy untainted by the gospel of Mammon. Both Carlyle and Disraeli looked upon an aristocracy of the wisest as the natural leaders of the people, and in *Coningsby* the symbolic union of the landed aristocracy at its best with its equal among the manufacturing classes draws together the talents which promise that England's material prosperity will be accompanied by moral progress.

II

Sybil, or the Two Nations

In *Sybil* (1845) Disraeli resorts to Mrs. Trollope's and Charlotte Elizabeth's method of casting up examples of bad industrialists drawn from Parliamentary blue books; but his more imaginative portrayals reveal a Carlylean influence.[24] Once more Disraeli seems to be experimenting with Carlyle's concept of a working aristocracy. Having a twofold purpose, he exhibits this ideal in the person of Trafford and also demonstrates that by a working aristocracy is not meant an aristocracy of labor.

If Disraeli at times employed factual material similar to that of humanitarian novelists who purposed to expose the evil practices of certain manufacturers, he did not make the shrill arguments that are generally characteristic of those writers. Instead he sought to bring to light the abuse, rather than vilify the individual. We can predict, for example, what is to be expected of a firm named Shuffle and Screw, whose owners make no appearance and are known only by report. This pair of millowners are used to reveal the practice of paying wages equal to those of other manufacturers, but regularly deducting, through an intricate system of fines, enough money from the wages of labor to pay their overhead.[25] The same firm is used to expose the workings of another "Chactaw" maneuver —the cottage system, whereby workers were forced to rent their employers' cottages. Rent was automatically deducted from a worker's wages whether he lived in such a cottage or not (pp. 103-4). The notorious truck system of paying wages in exorbitantly priced goods receives attention in the Tommy shop scene (pp. 154-60). The Diggs are petty tyrants who run the shop with the approval of the colliery "mainmasters," who cannot stand the sight of a miner and therefore make themselves inaccessible to the pitmen (p. 145).[26] When dealing with such specific abuses, Disraeli seems to have added only a minimum of art to the material he had obtained from parliamentary reports. The economic historian C. R. Fay notes Disraeli's predilection for using the language of those who gave evidence to parliamentary committees. Fay writes that the Diggs' Tommy shop scene came out of the Midland Mining Commission Report of 1843, "now and then sentence for sentence, with Joseph Diggs in place of a certain coal proprietor in the Report named Banks. . . ."[27]

In the portrayal of Trafford, on the other hand, Disraeli developed in more detail the ideal of the working aristocracy that he had first sketched in the figure of Millbank in *Coningsby*. Admittedly, the conception of Trafford owes something to the tradition of the silver-fork novel, in which persons of consequence are of noble blood, as well as to Carlyle's notion. Unlike any other industrialist in the novels of this period, Trafford is a younger son of an aristocratic family. Such a qualification places him above the usual rivalry between industrialists and landed gentry.[28] As an idealization of the industrialist, then, Trafford, with the aid of literary convention, fulfills Carlyle's hopes:

> He was the younger son of a family that had for centuries been planted on the land, but who, not satisfied with the factitious consideration with which Society compensates the junior members of a territorial house for their entailed poverty, had availed himself of some opportunities that offered themselves, and had devoted his energies to those new sources of wealth that were unknown to his ancestors. His operations at first had been extremely limited, like his fortunes; but with a small capital, though his profits were not considerable, he at least gained experience. With gentle blood in his veins, and old English feelings, he imbibed, at an early period of his career, a correct conception of the relations which should subsist between the employer and the employed. He felt that between them there should be other ties than the payment and the receipt of wages. (p. 179)

As a model manufacturer Trafford first considered the physical advantages of his employees. His plant was constructed so as to eliminate the high temperature and close atmosphere that had been the major criticism voiced by Cobbett, Gaskell, and Engels, of the factory as a place of work. The problem of unwanted heat was solved by a single story construction with high ceilings. The difficulty of ventilation was surmounted by a process "not unlike that which is practiced in the House of Commons" (p. 179); that is, ventilation from below. As for the moral advantages of his system, Trafford appropriated a virtue of domestic industry, parental supervision, that P. Gaskell had complained was lost with the coming of the factories: "the child works under the eye of the parent, the parent under that of the superior workman; the inspector or employer at a glance can behold all" (p. 180).

Nor did Trafford's concern for the welfare of his workpeople stop at the gates of the factory. He also sought to revive in his factory village the spirit of the feudal manorial system and thus re-establish community over aggregation:[29]

> He knew well that the domestic virtues are dependent on the existence of a home, and one of his first efforts had been to build a village where every family might be well lodged. Though he was the principal proprietor, and proud of that character, he nevertheless encouraged his workmen to purchase the fee: there were some who had saved sufficient money to effect this; proud of their house and their little garden, and of the horticultural society, where its produce permitted them to be annual competitors. In every street there was a well: behind the factory were the public baths; the schools were under the direction of the perpetual curate of the church, which Mr. Trafford, though a Roman Catholic, had raised and endowed. In the midst of this village, surrounded by beautiful gardens which gave an impulse to the horticulture of the community was the house of Trafford himself, who comprehended his position too well to withdraw himself from vulgar exclusiveness from his real dependents, but recognized the baronial principle, reviving in a new form, and adapted to the softer manners and more ingenious circumstance of the times. (p. 180)

For Disraeli, then, the evils of an industrial society were to be eliminated by an introduction of the paternalistic values of a hierarchical, feudal society into the modern employer-employee relationship. The results would have been Utopian:

> The connection of a labourer with his place of work . . . is itself a great advantage. Proximity to the employer brings cleanliness and order, because it brings observation and encouragement. In the settlement of Trafford crime was positively unknown, and offences were very slight. There was not a single person in the village of a reprobate character. The men were well clad; the women had a blooming cheek; drunkenness was unknown; while the moral condition of the softer sex was appropriately elevated. (pp. 180-81)

Serving no other purpose in *Sybil* than that of a model employer, Trafford is known chiefly by his reputation. He speaks for himself, however, on the occasion of Lord de Mowbray's visit to his factory. When the nobleman compliments the millowner upon his uncommon establishment, adding that the outlay must have been great, Trafford reveals that he is in part a projection of Carlyle's Quaker captain of industry in *Past and Present*:

> "Why," said Mr. Trafford, "for my part I have always considered that there was nothing so expensive as a vicious population. I hope I had other objects in view in what I have done than a pecuniary compensation. They say we all have our hobbies; and it was ever mine to

improve the condition of my workpeople, to see what good tenements, and good schools, and just wages paid in a fair manner, and the encouragement of civilizing pursuits would do to elevate their character. I should find an ample reward in the moral tone and material happiness of this community; but really viewing it in a pecuniary point of view, the investment of capital has been one of the most profitable I have ever made; and I would not, I assure you, for double its amount, exchange my workpeople for the promiscuous assemblage engaged in other factories. (p. 184)[30]

Disraeli's account of Trafford's union of a modern technological mode of production with a social organization of the past and his aristocratic social background is a literal rendering of the idea of an "Industrial Aristocracy" that goes even beyond Carlyle's recommendation. Carlyle cared not for old blood; in the context of *Past and Present* it was synonymous with tired blood. Yet there remains another way of literally interpreting Carlyle's idea which would suit neither the celebrator of heroes nor the Young Englander. Might not a working aristocracy also signify an aristocracy of labor?

It goes without saying that by a working aristocracy Carlyle does not mean the rule of the working man. To him, "Democracy . . . means despair of finding any Heroes to govern you, and contented putting up with the want of them. . . ."[31] Moreover, democracy has taken the direction of a "chase of Liberty"[32] that at this point is concerned solely with freedom from oppression. But such a freedom is merely "one of the most insignificant fractional parts of Human Liberty,"[33] and purchased at the price of social isolation, it has turned out to be, for millions of working men, only the liberty to die of starvation.[34] In place of the guidance of "Real-Superiors," democracy offers only the false guidance of "Mock-Superiors."[35]

Nor did Disraeli believe that the people could wisely guide England. In *Sybil*, Egremont, the Young Englander, tells Sybil, who is confident that the Chartists will obtain their political demands, to dismiss that fancy: "The people are not strong; the people can never be strong" (p. 267). It is a new generation of aristocracy, Young England, who will vindicate their cause, for "They are the natural leaders of the people . . . the only ones" (p. 268). To Sybil's rejoinder that the people's leaders are their own representatives whom they trust, Egremont replies that the people may be betrayed by emancipators from their own class. Not all have the idealism and purity of heart and motive that Sybil's father, the Chartist leader Walter Gerard, possesses.

With these two negative attitudes toward democracy in mind, we can examine the puzzle of Disraeli's aristocracy of labor in the Wodgate of

Sybil. In this district governed by Bishop Hatton, an ironmaster, locks and files are manufactured. There are no large factories. Without the interference of capital, "Here Labour reigns supreme" (p. 162). The work of Wodgate is carried on by master workmen and their apprentices in their own houses: "These master workmen indeed form a powerful aristocracy, nor is it possible to conceive one apparently more oppressive. They are ruthless tyrants; they habitually inflict upon their subjects punishments more grievous than the slave population of our colonies were ever visited with . . ." (p. 162). But whether the apprentices are hardened to or unconscious of their degradation, or whether they are sustained by the thought of being oppressors in turn one day, they do not despise their masters, as the aristocracy is despised in many places. And why is this so? Ironically, Disraeli explains in Carlylean term: "In the first place, it is a real aristocracy; it is privileged, but it does something for its privileges. It is distinguished from the main body not merely by name. It is the most knowing class at Wodgate; it possesses indeed, in its way, complete knowledge; and it imparts in its own manner a certain quantity of it to those whom it guides. Thus it is an aristocracy that leads and therefore a fact" (pp. 162-63). Granted that here is a natural aristocracy in principle. But what kind of civilization can be expected from the supreme reign of labor? Only a state of society that would have an attraction for the anarchist: "Wodgate had advantages of its own, and of a kind which touch the fancy of the lawless. It was land without an owner; no one claimed any manorial right over it; they could build cottages without paying rent. It was a district recognized by no parish; so there were no tithes, and no meddlesome supervision" (p. 161). As a consequence Wodgate lacks a traditional structure of government or society:

> There are no land-lords, head-lessees, main masters, or butties in Wodgate. No church there has yet raised its spire; and, as if the jealous spirit of Woden still haunted his ancient temple, even the conventicle scarcely dares show its humble front in some obscure corner. There is no municipality, no magistrate; there are no local acts, no vestries, no schools of any kind. The streets are never cleaned; every man lights his own house; nor does anyone know anything except his business. (p. 162)

And when not attending to their business, which consists of long hours of hard work for four days a week, all of the inhabitants of Wodgate are drunk, their only restraint being involuntary exhaustion. Without any higher authority to preach to them or control them, the people are amoral brutes:

> It is not that the people are immoral, for immorality implies some

forethought; or ignorant, for ignorance is relative; but they are animals; unconscious; their minds a blank; and their worst actions only the impulse of a gross or savage instinct. There are many in this town who are ignorant of their very names; very few who can spell. It is rare that you meet with a young person who knows his own age; rarer to find the boy who has seen a book, or the girl who has seen a flower. Ask them the name of their sovereign, and they will give you an unmeaning stare; ask them the name of their religion, and they will laugh; who rules them on earth, or who can save them in heaven, are alike mysteries to them. (p. 163)

Stephen Morley, the Chartist, in search of Bishop Hatton meets a young couple who, because there is no church in Wodgate, have been married by Hatton, the "governor." The ceremony consisted of a sprinkling of salt over a gridiron and a reading of the "Our Father" backwards. Unlike her husband Tummas, Suky is proud of being Wodgate's sole "Christian" and of teaching her husband to believe in "our Lord Saviour Pontius Pilate, who was crucified to save our sins; and in Moses, Goliath, and the rest of the Apostles" (p. 166).

Unlike the set piece characterization of Trafford, Bishop Hatton has a plot function. When the Chartists resolve to stop work in all of England, one of their emissaries ingratiates himself with Hatton and convinces him that he is the man who can gain the Five Points of the Charter for the working men of England. Having nothing to do but make a superfluous lock and only vaguely understanding the meaning of the Charter, Hatton undertakes the role of "Liberator" and with his Hell-Cats sets out on a path of destruction. After being turned away from Trafford's mill by Walter Gerard, Hatton fulfills his function by storming Mowbray's castle and being instrumental in obtaining from its muniment room the documents which prove that Sybil and her father are the rightful owners of the Mowbray estate. The conventions of the silver-fork school demand that aristocrat marry aristocrat, and thus Hatton provides Sybil with the requisite pedigree to marry Charles Egremont. As Raymond Williams observed about this union, "the marriage bells ring out not over the achievement of One Nation but over the uniting of the properties of Marney and Mowbray."[36]

At this point we may wonder what the Wodgate setting and Hatton's role as the "Liberator" contribute to the total meaning of a novel treating the concept of "Two Nations." It has been shown that the account of living conditions at Wodgate was, with a degree of latitude, drawn from the evidence of Parliamentary blue books describing the squalor of the district of Willenhall.[37] Thus Disraeli may have intended that the English public should see the nadir of human degradation produced by a certain kind of industrialism. Hatton, as we have seen, was useful to the working out of plot. That both the squatters' district and its "governor" are grotesques is evident. But the two could be excused as serving their respective purposes if Disraeli had not added his statement that the master workmen of Wodgate formed a real, a working aristocracy. Disraeli had too much respect for the idea of aristocracy, not to mention Carlyle, to reduce Carlyle's concept to an absurdity by playing with a literal interpretation of it. No aristocracy, idle or working, could conceivably break the heads of its dependents with hammers, locks, and files, or allow them to remain without the civilizing traditions of government, religion, or education. What then does Disraeli's aristocracy of labor signify? I should like to suggest that the rule of the master workmen of Wodgate is an imaginative, serio-comic recreation of vague fears of what was to be called by Marx later in the decade, the dictatorship of the proletariat.[38]

Since the 1830s, the discontent of the working classes on the Continent was viewed with the possibility that the proletariat might overturn the existing order. In 1831 the silk workers of Lyon arose in desperation and had to be put down by force. A French critic compared the uprising to the "barbarian invasions" that had destroyed Rome. The expression took hold and was repeated in France and Germany throughout the next two decades.[39] After 1840, communist and socialist Utopian thought, which was characterized by a belief in peaceful change through an appeal to all classes, had declined in reputation. In its place a new strategy of mass uprisings and revolution by force took the place of Utopian belief in reasonableness and the susceptibility of men to persuasion. Reason was feckless; reform was to be instituted by seized power.[40] Along with this change of outlook arose a fear of communism, however the term may be defined, on the part of those who abhorred sudden and violent change.[41] Just what this communist or anarchist sentiment was is not easy to define. (In Germany anarchism and communism were not precisely distinguishable.)[42] Unlike the Utopian socialists whose faith in human reason led them to propose schemes that were, if not practical, at least tangible, the communists tended not to draw blueprints of their society, but to thrive on a mystic belief in the triumph of the proletariat.[43] After 1840 in any case, communism was accepted by revolutionary thinkers as the final stage of human society, and when Marx summoned in 1848 a "spectre of communism" to haunt Europe, he was affirming a fact which, though exaggerated as a threat to the existing order, held true for France and Germany. Exaggeration notwithstanding, the fear of communism was even greater in the years before 1848.[44]

Despite the fact that these attitudes toward communism reflected European rather than English experience, it is safe to say that fear is a

readily importable commodity. Assuredly, Englishmen who were aware
of developments on the Continent must have watched the course of
European unrest in the same way that, in his *Review*, Defoe was accustomed to tracing the progress of the plague from one European capital
to another and attempting to foretell when it would arrive in London.
We have seen how Charlotte Elizabeth held the "Beast of Socialism"
more in abomination than the factory system responsible for its manifes-
tation. In spite of her tendency toward hysteria in art as well as politics,
that novelist is, in the opinion of G. M. Young, representative of a body
of educated English opinion.[45] Moreover, noting that assassination was
not typical of the English even in the "hungry forties," Raymond Williams calls the murder of Harry Carson "a dramatization of the fear of
violence."[46]

One would be hard put to find a novelist more likely to be acquainted
with the trend of European political thought than Disraeli. That he was
aware of avant-garde thinking is evidenced by some of the principles of
society announced in *Sybil* by the Chartist intellectual Stephen Morley,
whose ideas have a vaguely socialistic or communistic tinge. Morley denounces Trafford's attempts at instilling a feeling for a patriarchal society
by providing his working men with homes in order to stem the tide of
vanishing domestic feelings. The Chartist explains his position to Egremont.

> You lament the expiring idea of Home. It would not be expiring, if
> it were worth retaining. The domestic principle has fulfilled its pur-
> pose. The irresistible law of progress demands that another should be
> developed. It will come; you may advance or retard, but you cannot
> prevent it. It will work out like the development of organic nature. In
> the present state of civilization, and with the scientific means of hap-
> piness at our command, the notion of home should be obsolete. Home
> is a barbarous idea; the method of a rude age; home is isolation; there-
> fore anti-social. What we want is Community. (p. 190)

Disraeli, however, did not sympathize with such inexorable laws of
progress. His voice is heard through the Chartist Walter Gerard, who
answers with, "It's all very fine . . . and I dare say you are right, Stephen;
but I like stretching my feet on my own hearth" (p. 190). And in another instance Gerard, speaking not just for himself but for all Englishmen, informs his daughter Sybil of the real reason for his objection to his
friend Morley's ideas of society:

> Stephen is prejudiced. . . . He is a visionary, indulging in impos-
> sible dreams, and if possible, little desirable. He knows nothing of the
> country or the character of his countrymen. Englishmen want none of

his joint-stock felicity; they want their rights—rights consistent with the rights of other classes, but without which the rights of other classes cannot and ought not be secure. (pp. 286-87)

Because he believed that Englishmen wanted only their lost rights, Disraeli, who for the writing of *Sybil* had access to the correspondence of Feargus O'Connor, the most vociferous of the Chartists demanding a reinstatement of lost rights, did not seriously feel the fear of communism that disturbed Europeans who believed in the inevitability of a new social order. As a consequence, the implication of a barbarian dictatorship of the proletariat in the rule of the "Liberator" of Wodgate, where "Labour reigns supreme," is treated comically. Hatton is more a poltergeist than a "spectre of communism." As long as there are such manufacturers as Trafford who, in addition to establishing old English feudal values, gives a "fair day's wages for a fair day's work" and who does not operate by the "laws of the Bucanier" nor count scalps like a "Chactaw," there will be honest workmen who will barricade his factory gates and play the water hoses upon Hatton's Hell-Cats, who would destroy the old English social system and values that their employer worked so diligently to recreate and to instill in them.

III

The Half Sisters

Writing in 1887 about his connection with the Carlyles, J. A. Froude summarizes the relationship between Geraldine Jewsbury and the Carlyles:

> "Geraldine Jewsbury was Mrs. Carlyle's most intimate and most confidential friend. Their correspondence, a large part of which is now in my possession, proves sufficiently how close the confidence was. Geraldine herself was a gifted woman. She had been attracted by Carlyle's writings, had introduced herself to him as one of his most ardent worshippers, which to the end of her own life she continued to be in spite of all which she saw and knew. She was about Mrs. Carlyle's own age. She was admitted to Cheyne Rowe on the closest terms. Mrs. Carlyle in her own troubles, spoke and wrote of Geraldine Jewsbury as her Consuelo.[47]

In *The Half-Sisters* (1848), Geraldine Jewsbury reveals the extent of her discipleship to the author of *Sartor Resartus* by taking as her themes, work versus idleness and the relation of both to the reality of the spirit.[48] These themes are developed through the characters of William Bryant, an ironmaster, his wife Alice, and her half-sister Bianca.

The late Phillip Helmsby, father of Alice and Bianca, was an iron-master from Newcastle who, having been sent on business to Genoa, fell in love with an Italian woman. They took matters into their own hands and Bianca was born illegitimate. Upon his father's death, Helmsby came home to take over the ironworks; and the affairs of business left no room for thoughts of love which "can thrive only in idleness."[49] Blotting out his Italian dream, he married his partner's daughter, a sensible if prosaic woman. Shortly after Alice was born, he died; and the iron works were sold. To her eventual regret, Alice did not lose touch with the world of business. She and her mother continued to move in the circle of her late father's business acquaintances. But Alice, who seemed to have inherited the nature that her father exhibited at Genoa before he entered the real world of work, was unhappy with her existence. One of the reasons for this was that the men of her acquaintance, occupied with business, had no interest in the graces and refinements of feminine society:

> Society in a prosperous commercial town is a raw material not worked up into any social or conventional elegances. . . . Labour has never yet been made to look lovely, and those engaged in labour have nothing picturesque or engaging in their manners. . . . The men engaged all day in business operations on a large scale, frequently with several hundred workpeople to manage, were not likely to feel any interest in small refinements and elegances for which there was no tangible use. Consequently, female society went for very little. To manage the house well, and to see that dinner was punctual and well appointed; to be very quiet and not talk nonsense, or rather to talk very little of anything; were the principal qualities desired in wives and daughters. . . . [The men] were tired and harassed when they came home from business, and were in no mood for anything more exalted than to make themselves comfortable; their energies were all engrossed in one direction, namely, towards their business, which was the object "first, last, midst, and without end" of their life; and they were not up to taking any trouble for the sake of society. (p. 31)

Alice, on the point of suffocation from boredom and given to reverie, is captivated by William Bryant, an ironmaster many years her senior. As Othello did to Desdemona, he tells her of his business travels on the Continent and of the strange races of people he had encountered, with the result that, "William Bryant became the hero of her desert" (p. 39). Bryant thought Alice "charmingly romantic" but, believing that she would outgrow it and become the sensible woman her mother was, he married her.

Nevertheless, Alice's new station did not alter her existence. She was depressed by the idleness expected of her as the wife of a prosperous man, and Bryant did not perceive her state of mind.

> He was essentially a practical matter-of-fact man, and had no conception of the morbid sinking of heart and deadly sadness which so easily beset imaginative temperaments, whose owners are not subject to the stern tonic of the *necessity* to work. Alice sank under the weight of a golden leisure, which she had not the energy adequately to employ. Worldly prosperity is a much greater drain upon our energies than the most severe adversity; there is no spring, no elasticity; it is like walking through life upon a Turkey carpet. Large and noble faculties are required to make a wise use of worldly prosperity; there is little stimulus in, and no excitement beyond, what the individual can furnish for himself; his days are rounded with security, and softly cushioned against all the harsh realities of life. (p. 81)

Engrossed in business activities which required all his energy, Bryant, a kind and affectionate man, loved Alice, but had no leisure to provide companionship or occupation for her. She wished to please him in some way and he desired only that she amuse herself: "Constantly occupied himself with affairs of deep importance, he had no idea of the weight of *ennui* which was eating the life out of Alice. He was not in the least insensible to Alice's demonstrations of affection, although it was not in his nature to be demonstrative himself; and he sometimes wished his wife to be a little less sensitive and romantic" (p. 141). Unaware that idleness can take a mischievous turn, Bryant invites a young gentleman without occupation, Conrad Percy, to spend a few days at his home. On one occasion when they are alone, Alice, offering a glimpse into the despondency of soul in a woman without a regular occupation or duties, discusses with Conrad the employment of her time.[50] When Conrad asks her what she does all day, Alice replies that she does nothing, that every day, like an unstrung bead, has no connection with the one before or after, that each does not transcend the Actual by being a part of a larger goal or Ideal:

> I hardly know . . . I have nothing to do that seems worth doing. I am depressed under a constant sense of waste, a vague consciousness that I am always doing wrong, and yet I can find out nothing that I ought to do. . . . I used to think that I should be so happy, if I might have all my time to improve myself, and spend as I like; but now that I have it, I do not know what to do with it. My whole life is one cloud, and I have a sense of responsibility which I can neither adequately discharge nor deliver myself from. I have nothing to look forward to. When I get up in the morning, I know all that is likely to happen before night; one day is like another, and the weight of life that lies upon me is intolerable. (p. 204)

Bryant's unceasing proccupation with business, which makes him blind to Alice's soul's need, leads to her taking the fatal step of running away with Conrad, who has insinuated himself into the family by becoming an investor in Bryant's concern. The climactic moment arrives when Bryant must leave home to look into the failure of one of his correspondents. He is silent and abstracted by business anxieties. Alice, not trusting herself with Conrad, appeals to her husband to take her with him. The harassed Bryant tells her not to be childish, to be reasonable, and to stop making such scenes: " 'I should be in the way,' sobbed she, as soon as she was alone, 'he is quite tired of these scenes—business, business, always business—I am nothing, or at best of secondary importance. Well, be it so, be it so; I need feel no more remorse; he has lost me by his own fault' " (p. 217). Overcome by guilt, however, Alice collapses in the midst of the preparations for her departure and dies of a seizure shortly afterwards.

Because of her lack of spiritual resources, Alice had been unable to transcend the world of the Actual in which she was trapped by the inertia of idleness. She had never attained the state of mind with which she could respond to Carlyle's dictum that, "Doubt of any sort cannot be removed except by Action."[51] or to his other precept, " 'Do the Duty which lies nearest thee,' which thus knowest to be a Duty! Thy second Duty will already have become clearer."[52] Though not concerned with states of unbelief, Geraldine Jewsbury seems to have applied to Alice's predicament Carlyle's notion that the Ideal, a contemplation of which brings spiritual peace, exists only in the Actual. The following passage from Sartor seems to suggest what Alice was unable to perceive. Writing about the moment of "Spiritual Enfranchisement," Carlyle explains: "The Situation that has not its Duty, its Ideal, was never yet occupied by man. Yes here, in this poor, miserable, hampered, despicable Actual, wherein thou even now standest, here or nowhere is thy Ideal: work it out therefrom; and working, believe, live, be free. Fool! The Ideal is in thyself, the impediment too is in thyself: thy Condition is but the stuff thou art to shape that same Ideal out of. . . ."[53] Carlyle then exhorts the "tempest-tost Soul" who is imprisoned in the chaos of the Actual to create a world out of chaos by following his well-known advice, "Whatsoever thy hand findeth to do, do it with thy whole might."[54]

Alice's husband, Bryant, though having found something to do and having done it with all his might, has not performed his whole duty. Working with Mammon as his god, he too has, like Alice, been living a day-to-day existence confined to the Actual, for him the practical world of business. The death of Alice is a profound experience that liberates him from a totally material existence. His new found belief in the Ideal is expressed in a fusion of the Christian concept of a life after death with Carlylean transcendentalism:

> Men must lose some dear object by death before they can realise the invisible world: we must have a stake in it before we can believe it.
>
> Sitting there, beside his dead wife, Bryant was admitted to the threshold of the unseen state. What now to him was the dream of life, with all its highly-coloured appearances? Hope and fear were alike dead: he sat in the presence of the Invisible and calmness came gradually to his soul.
>
> Alice's weakness—Conrad's treachery—his own wounded pride—all seemed now hushed to insignificance in the presence of the great mysterious fact of Death; even his grief seemed small and idle. What was he that he should complain? The tumult and glare which had surrounded all things subsided before the cold, colourless light of death.
>
> He left that chamber in the early dawn of the next morning with some portion of the eternal calmness on his soul. (p. 227)

The spiritual experience of a glimpse into the invisible world transforms Bryant into Carlyle's noble captain of industry who renounces a Mammonish for a God-like spirit.[55] He reveals his future plans to a Lord Melton:

> As long as I live, I must be doing something. I do not care for making money now; it is the work I care for. I shall live in the mountains among the miners. Since I have been in sorrow, I have thought of many things that never struck me before, especially since I have been lying here. We have many hundred workmen in our employ—we paid them their wages—they did our work—the rest was their concern. I think we should have considered something more than making money out of them. They are a sad wild set. I have not much faith in benevolent schemes, but I shall see what can be done about them. (pp. 286-87)

Bryant continues his work with the sole object of ameliorating the condition of his working men.

In contrast to Alice's complete failure to perceive the Ideal and Bryant's realization that came too late, Bianca is successful from the start. Arriving penniless in England, she meets with a company of actors. Faced with the necessity of working, she struggles to make good as an actress. Far from considering her profession solely as a livelihood, Bianca, inspired by an old actor who loves his work, aspires to an ideal of her art:

> I care for perfecting myself in my art more than for any praise or credit. Oh! to be able to realize the idea of which you gave me a glimpse when I beheld you acting for the first time! To enter into that world, which, as it were, lies unseen around us, and bring out thence

the thoughts and conceptions that are hidden there, and force them into a visible shape, a bodily expression, I would consent to dwell in darkness my whole life." (p. 123)

She is also encouraged by Lord Melton's advice on the insufficiency of happiness as a life's goal (p. 171).[56] Thus having found her work, Bianca achieves a transcendent spiritual peace.

In all, *The Half-Sisters* is a curious novel even for its time. Though it is permeated by the spirit of the Everlasting Yea, it successfully embodies philosophical states of mind into characters without making those characters into abstractions. Alice, Bryant, and Bianca work out their separate destinies with a minimum of intrusion of philosophic ideas. Carlyles' notions aside, the novel might be called an anatomy of boredom, a subject that has not been searchingly treated by other novelists of the time. Even Charlotte Brontë who published *Shirley* in 1849 does not so much examine the agony of female ennui as describe female annoyance at having no serious work to do in a man's world. We may remember in that novel Caroline Helstone's aunt, who passes much of her time straightening the contents of her bureau. The world of *The Half-Sisters*, with its busy ironmasters living in an atmosphere where workmen must be managed and schedules and bills of exchange must be met, does not permit women fulfilment through any avenue other than the kitchen or dining room. Nor does it allow them a share in the feeling of engrossment in work that pervades such an atmosphere. Next to the highborn ladies of the fashionable novel who spend their time reciprocating morning calls, Alice Bryant stands uneasily. We have entered the modern world in which idleness for the wealthy woman of sensibility is no longer a badge of class status but a curse.

SEVEN

Social Peace

My principles of Political Economy . . . were all
summed in a single sentence in the last volume of
Modern Painters—"Government and cooperation
are in all things the Laws of Life; Anarchy and
competition the Laws of Death."

Ruskin, *Unto This Last*

WITH THE EXCEPTION OF DICKENS'S BELATED
attack in *Hard Times*, the figure of the industrialist in the novels after
1850 is no longer the subject of controversy. After the dwindling of
propagandistic portrayals, the millowner is depicted with a degree of
sympathetic realism not possible during the heat of polemic conspicuous
in many of the novels preoccupied with the Condition of England question. The advent of an era of social peace in the early 1850s would seem
unnaturally abrupt, however, if there were not good reasons for the rela-
tively sudden change. Before proceeding with a discussion of the fiction
of social peace, we might trace the outcome of the controversy and also
consider other developments responsible for the change of mood.

The passage of long-awaited legislation is assuredly one of the most
important factors which contributed to the easing of tensions between
landlord, industrialist, and working man. The Repeal of the Corn Laws,
which in 1846 dealt a signal, though not final, blow to aristocratic privilege, silenced that powerful agency of the manufacturing interests, the
Anti-Corn Law League. Both the free-trading industrialist and the workman benefited by cheap bread. The employer might feel a slackening in
trade union demands for cost of living wage raises, and the employee had
more money to spend on other necessities. Contrary to what landowners
expected, agriculture was not depressed. Opponents of Free Trade had
predicted that the home market would be deluged by foreign foodstuffs
after the Repeal, but British farmers met the challenge with new techniques of production. The result was a prosperous agriculture which

contributed to commercial expansion, and the early 1850s became in the words of Lord Ernle, "the Golden Age of English agriculture."[1]

If the industrialist secretly rejoiced at the check given to landed privilege, his sense of satisfaction was short-lived, for the limit of his power was also circumscribed by legislation. In 1847, the Ten-Hours Bill was passed, giving women and children the benefit of a shorter working day and putting an end to fifteen years of Lord Shaftesbury's agitation. The shortening of the working day was followed by an increase of employer interest in the moral and physical welfare of employees. Efforts to better the working conditions were made not only in the textile mills but also in all classes of manufacturing.[2] In a glance at his birthplace, W. H. Ainsworth, fondly noting the ugliness as well as the prosperity of Manchester, describes the change: "And it is only right to add that, of late years, considerable ameliorations have been made by the millowners, and the hours of labour limited, from which causes the health, condition, and morals of the persons employed, especially the girls and children, have been materially improved."[3]

In addition to the tangible effects of legislation, more impersonal factors were conducive to tranquillity. The year 1848 saw the collapse of Chartism. Divided leadership, diversity of interests and aims, and to some extent the opposition of Wesleyans to subversion, all played a part in the eventual disintegration of this movement.[4] On account of the expansion of trade which began in the late 1840s, steady work reduced strikes to a few. The Preston strike notwithstanding, trade union aggressiveness gave way to harmony between labor and capital in the years 1850-57.[5] Malthusians were comforted by the high rate of emigration at mid-century. During the period 1835-69, the greatest wave of emigration occurred between 1850-54, when 1,600,000 people left for Canada, America, New Zealand, and Australia.[6] The discovery of gold in America (1849) and in Australia (1850) helped ease social and economic pressures by furthering the expansion of trade as well as encouraging emigration.[7] Less easy to gauge as a factor tending to lessen social tensions was the cumulative effect of the educational provisions of the Factory Act of 1833. Government inspectors seemed to believe that the two hours of daily schooling had made an improvement by the 1850s.[8] The rise in literacy was accompanied by the growth of the popular press. Perhaps, as Altick observes, the working man was more amused than made wiser by the increasing supply of reading matter; but, Altick concludes, the unequalled spread of the reading habit among the mass reading public between the years of the Reform Bill of 1832 and the Great Exhibition of 1851 contributed in some part to the relative stability of mid-Victorian society.[9] Finally, the

Exposition of 1851 symbolized not only England's prosperity in manufacturing but also "the realization of the unity of mankind" and the passing of "a great crisis in the world foreshadowing universal peace."[10]

I

Jane Rutherford; or the Miners' Strike

In the first of the novels of social peace *Jane Rutherford; or the Miners' Strike* (1853), Fanny Mayne reflects the mood of reconciliation that is characteristic of mid-century.[11] By asserting that progress has taken place in the mining districts since the time of *Sybil*, she seeks to convince the reading public of the purified periodical press that the spirit of class antagonism has been supplanted by that class association:

> "One half of the world knows not how the other half lives," was the talismanic key that opened at once the brotherhood of humanity, and "what can I do for my neighbour?" is now the cry of the neighbourly in all classes; the young and the old, the pious and the philanthropic, the lord and the squire, the merchant and the lawyer, the physician and the scribe, all will meet together now on the common ground of working for their neighbour's weal. Therefore, "one half of the world knows not how the other half lives," is no longer true, although it is still reechoed by the maudlin sentimentalist, and the radical socialist, to uphold the theories of the latter or make a happy turn to the rhapsodies of the former. (July 14, p. 867)[12]

In *Jane Rutherford* the unapproachable and the absentee mineowners of *Sybil* have been replaced by the responsible resident; and the iniquitous truck system, which Disraeli had exposed in the Diggs' Tommy Shop episode, has given way to wages paid in cash (June 9, p. 786). Moreover, Miss Mayne's mineowners are aware of the injustice of the tied cottages system of Disraeli's Shuffle and Screw, and instead furnish cottages without automatically deducting rent from a worker's wages (Sept. 22, p. 111).

Desiring above all to avoid setting class against class, Fanny Mayne refuses to stereotype masters and men along class lines. In her attempt to draw realistic rather than propagandistic portraits, she seeks to prove that it is not class interest that motivates employer and employed; but rather, in this novel, the human failings of vanity in a workman, and the naivete of an absentee mineowner's good faith in his agents.

Jonathan Rutherford, the leader of the strike, is a somewhat more complex figure than the usual stereotype of the agitator as incompetent workman. On the contrary, Rutherford was the best workman at his job. His besetting sin, however, was vanity. Having read radical newspapers and having been entranced by the rhetoric of their sweeping attacks upon employers, Rutherford daydreamed about being the leader of a strike.[13] His ambitions were not at all satisfied when the colliery owner, Lord Westerland, willingly agreed to the trade union's demands (June 23, pp. 818-19). Impelled thus by motives of personal aggrandizement and not by a true desire to vindicate the rights of labor, Rutherford continued to make unreasonable demands. Having made a general nuisance of himself, he was disliked by masters and men alike. Finally, he revenged himself on both by rattening a mineshaft and escaped to America.

Lord Westerland does not remain for long the sort of absentee mine-owner depicted in *Sybil*. Ignorant of what his agents had done after he had agreed to raise wages, he was surprised when a strike was called. Upon investigating he discovered that the middlemen, or butties, who managed his collieries, had granted the raise in pay but had also demanded that the colliers dig more coal during their working shift (July 14, p. 866). At a meeting with the miners, Lord Westerland promises to redress the wrong that has been committed without his sanction. Moreover, assuming a further interest in his men, he takes up residence in the mining districts and resolves to visit other proprietors in order to get them to raise their wages (July 14, pp. 867-68). He insists that it is a mistake to think of class interest as separate, and seeks to encourage class association with a view of giving a check to the "socialistic" tendency toward class conflict, reflected in Rutherford's labelling the masters tyrants and the workers, slaves (July 21, p. 882). Together with Stephenson, a self-made millowner and colliery proprietor who "fulfills the *New Zealander's definition of a gentleman:* . . . "One who speaks kind words and does kind actions'" (Aug. 25, p. 47), Lord Westerland gives a new meaning to the political economist's abstraction regarding an identity of interests. The two employers make available for purchase small parcels of land as freeholds, "rightly judging that the man who has strength of mind, forethought, and self-denial sufficient to enable him to lay out of his weekly wages enough to make himself a proprietor of a freehold and the power of voting in parliamentary elections consequent upon it, will be the last, even though he should continue a labourer at weekly wages, to try to overthrow the true rights of property" (Sept. 22, p. 111). Thus the interests of capital and labor can be considered identical only when labor too, in the words of the economist, obtains fixed capital through ownership of property.

In the mineowners' plan lies the key to Fanny Mayne's attitude toward industrial society. Opposed to the omnipotence of either masters or trade unions, the self-styled "Friend of the People" sought to inculcate in the working man the idea of self-help. As part of her strategy, she edited *The True Briton* for two years (1853-54), filling her editorials with exhortations to the working classes to attain economic independence through thrift and self-denial.[14] But though her parlance was the same as that of the political economist, her purpose differed (no doubt because of the prosperity of the times). For instead of encouraging workmen to save their money solely as a provision for subsistence during bad times, she desired that they invest it in property.

The rationale behind Fanny Mayne's attempts to portray her masters and men realistically was noble. But by striving scrupulously to avoid the exaggeration and sensationalism which she believed set one class against another, her editorship was short-lived. As Dalziel has concluded, *The True Briton* failed because it pleased no one. It offended the ultra evangelicals because it was not dogmatic enough. And the seekers after tales of adventure and romance would have found her periodical lacking in these qualities. Such a heroine as Jane Rutherford, who "was no maudlin sentimentalist, no pining, dreamy heroine of a fanciful romance" (June 16, p. 810), had little appeal for such readers. And finally, "those who wanted outspoken and uncritical support of the working classes against the rich would not be satisfied by it either."[15]

II

Lights and Shadows of English Life

Also seeking to convey an impression of class harmony is the anonymous author of *Lights and Shadows of English Life* (1855), who is zealously bent upon fostering goodwill, not only between employer and employed, but also between manufacturer and landed gentleman. This novelist's stated purpose is to discredit what he considers misrepresentations of the manufacturing class in fiction. He may have in mind *Hard Times* which appeared the year before when he writes:

> I, here, would pause one moment in my tale to express my wish, that a more experienced pen than mine, were employed to illustrate this truth, and happy, shall I deem myself, if the picture I endeavour to draw of factory-life, and the mutual good feeling existing between the server and the served, may tend to eradicate some of those prejudices against the master-manufacturers which have been fostered, by unjust, I might almost use the stronger term of untrue statements which, though under the garb of fiction, assume to be those of reality and nature.
>
> This tale shews the opposite side of the picture and the true one, in the opinion of those who live in the immediate neighbourhood of those great factories, and whose influential names, if I thought right to give them, would at once stamp my statements with authenticity.[16]

In keeping with the writer's aim, the relation of the millowner, Mr. Leslie, to his employees approaches a state of perfection. First observed in the "baronial principle" of Disraeli's Trafford, an intimation of the aristocratization of the industrialist is seen in the character of Leslie, who "takes the same interest, and watches over the welfare of each individual as earnestly as the landed proprietors among our aristocracy do, or ought to do, of their tenantry" (1:29). In spite of the temptations which accompany untold wealth, Leslie's chief occupation is the good of his workmen (1:38). Actuated by a spirit of benevolence, he persists in superintending his factory, even though he might just as easily resign his business to an agent (1:57-59). In times when work is slack, he keeps his men at full employment and full pay (1:199). His factory is well ventilated; the grounds boast a sculptured fountain, flower beds, and cottages with flower and kitchen gardens which even Prince Albert might have used as patterns for his model cottages. Adjacent to the factory is a playing field where the maypole is raised every spring. In addition, Leslie has spared no expense in building a factory church in an elaborate style of architecture (1:206-9). So that the seating arrangement in the church would be democratic, he insisted that no "squire's seat" be built for himself. Revered by his employees as a "beloved sovereign" and not a tyrant, Leslie respected them in return, and as a consequence has never met with any insubordination from them nor found them with Chartist sympathies (1:238). Showing no inclination to strike, his workers are possessed of a "real, genuine John Bull good feeling" (3:42). With such men as himself setting an example for other manufacturers to follow, even if on a smaller scale, it is not surprising that Leslie can say to Colonel Dudley, a leader of militia:

> The whole tone of the factory-system is very generally improved of late years, and much less of bad feeling exists between the employer and the employed than formerly. A good master is sure to have good men, and, when their separate interests are once felt to be bound into one, then the dangers of disunion and distrust are over. These north-country people are very warm-hearted, and very obstinate in either good or bad, and thus once convince them that the master of their works means well and honestly by them, that he seeks their prosperity as well as his own, and a tie exists between them which cannot be broken. No fear of a strike on their side, or a sordid grinding-down of their wages on his. (3:41)

To which Colonel Dudley adds that there is no longer a need for the militia (ever present in Harriet Martineau's fiction) to keep the peace between master and man (3:42).

While Mr. Leslie promotes kindly feeling among his workmen, Mrs.

Leslie strives to improve the relations between manufacturers and the old
aristocratic county families. Because she is the daughter of a clergyman
of old family, she is acceptable in the role of mediator. On one occasion,
she conciliates Lady Lansmere, who has a "horror of parvenuism" by
reassuring the patrician that all she needs to do is "try the agreeability"
of the class she seems to despise (1:271). To effect this, Mrs. Leslie
urges Lady Lansmere, at one of the Leslies' mixed social gatherings, to
seek out Mrs. Monroe, the wife of a manufacturer. It might be added
that to these social functions, Mr. Leslie invites different grades of society,
from shopkeepers to aristocrats, in hopes that class relationships will improve upon acquaintance. Agreeable to her hostess's advice, Lady Lansmere approaches the manufacturer's wife:

> Mrs. Leslie could scarcely repress a smile, when she saw the haughty
> peeress advance to Mrs. Monroe, and with an attempt at cordiality,
> place her hand within her arm, as she conducted her out of the room
> to her own apartment, an approach to friendliness never before granted.
> After a rather prolonged absence, Mrs. Leslie again smiled, as she saw
> the two return, with a very different expression of countenance to
> that with which they left the room. The cold, distant frigidity had
> passed from Mrs. Monroe's, and the assumption of civility from that
> of her hostess. (2:139)

Upon discovering that Mrs. Monroe sketches, plays the piano, and loves
children, Lady Lansmere is grateful to Mrs. Leslie for opening her eyes
to the virtues of such a talented neighbor (2:139-41). Agnes, Mrs. Leslie's
sister, later comments upon her sister's ability to promote a better relationship between the middle and the higher classes: "it is curious to see
how well Geraldine has succeeded in bringing [Mrs. Monroe] out and
making her appreciated by those in this aristocratic neighbourhood, who
before the genial thaw of the [Leslie] influence encased themselves in
worse than a panoply of steel, and thought no one whose riches did not
consist in land, could be fit to associate in any way with those native lords
of the soil" (3:286). To which Mr. Leslie replies that it is to his wife's
aristocratic lineage that improved relations are due:

> Yes, it is curious to see what a little good example, judiciously ad-
> ministered, can effect . . . but I believe Geraldine owes something to
> her own aristocratic blood in being able to effect the improvement
> which she has certainly brought about. If even Mrs. Leslie of Scansdale
> Manor had been a manufacturer's daughter, it is a chance if she had
> been received on the terms of equality with which she has been by the
> "county families," as they call themselves par excellence, in the neigh-
> bourhood, and on no other terms, certainly, would I have allowed my
> wife to have been visited. (3:286-87)

Perhaps the harshest comment in this novel is Mr. Leslie's last sentence quoted above. *Light and Shadows of English Life* presents an idealized picture of class relations, improved on all levels; and, though the novel reveals a trace of what was later to be called Victorian smugness and its self-proclaimed realism strains the probable, it is significant as one expression of the mood of social peace that prevailed in the 1850s. The fiction of the previous two decades had in many instances attempted to suggest the evil of which the industrialist was capable. With the cessation of hostilities, his potential for good was given full treatment and, with it, the promise that he was as capable of behaving like "a fine old English gentleman, all of the olden time" (1:217) as any owner of ancestral acres.

III

North and South

When Mrs. Gaskell's second novel dealing with industrialism was published in *Household Words* (1854-55), it is said that the sales of that weekly dropped. Dickens would not have been surprised at the truth of this, for he himself found the novel "wearisome to the last degree."[17] But we must remember Dickens was judging it in comparison with the kind of novel that would lend itself to being presented in weekly installments. *North and South*, however, was almost wholly unsuited for serialization chiefly because it is concerned with the slow process by which John Thornton, a millowner of the North, gains an education in sensibility through his association with Margaret Hale, a representative of the cultural and moral values of the agricultural South. With the possible exception of the unfeeling Carson's rather sudden conversion through suffering, the good and bad manufacturers that we have seen thus far have been static characters who do not change in the course of the narrative. Indeed, the extreme of this type, the millowner known only by report, might be said to resemble the seventeenth century Overburian character. On the other hand, John Thornton is a dynamic character who first appears as the champion of the principles of laissez faire; but in the course of the narrative, he gradually sheds his ideas of economic individualism for a sense of social responsibility. Beginning with a strong belief in a cash-nexus relationship between master and man, he ends attempting to conduct experiments in industrial relations which will bring all concerned into personal contact with each other.

Although Thornton is not portrayed in an attractive light throughout much of *North and South*, Mrs. Gaskell's sympathy for the manufacturer is assured. Unlike the Bounderbys of industry, Thornton is more hard headed than hard hearted; and at the outset of the novel the possibility of his regeneration is hinted at when, dissatisfied with being a successful manufacturer only, he engages Margaret Hale's father as his tutor in the classics. He is thereby also exposed to Margaret Hale and a way of life wholly unknown to him.

Having thrown up his Church of England living in the South because of religious doubts, Mr. Hale moved to Milton Northern (Manchester), where he was to support his family by tutoring. Upon her father's disclosure of his plan, his daughter, who prefers people whose occupations have to do with land, exclaims, "What in the world do manufacturers want with the classics, or literature or the accomplishments of a gentleman?"[18] To which her father replies, "some of them really seem to be fine fellows, conscious of their own deficiencies, which is more than many a man at Oxford is. Some resolutely want to learn, though they have come to man's estate. Some want their children to be better instructed than they themselves have been" (p. 34). Knowing little about the North, Margaret falls into the genteel error of confusing manufacturers with tradesmen. She objects to "all who have something tangible to sell" (p. 59) as governed by the principle of *caveat emptor* and by the erroneous assumption that credit is real wealth (p. 292). Mr. Hale, however, mildly reproves her for her confusion of economic groups: "Don't call the Milton manufacturers tradesmen, Margaret. . . . They are very different" (p. 59).

In the course of her frequent contacts with Thornton at Milton Northern, Margaret learns a good deal about manufacturers. At the same time, Thornton's economic views are exposed to the criticism of the refined tutor's daughter from the South. Echoes of Bounderby are heard in Thornton's emphasis on the need to undersell, in his belief of leaving the country if a fair profit is not to be had, and in his dislike for factory legislation (pp. 77, 138-39). With respect to the chances for self-made success, however, Thornton is aware that the heroic age of entrepreneurship is over. But if every man can no longer become a master, he can at least become what is known in the parlance of the modern American trade union as a company man: "every one who rules himself to decency and sobriety of conduct and attention to his duties, comes over to our ranks; it may not be always as a master, but as an overlooker, a cashier, a book-keeper, a clerk, one on the side of authority and order" (p. 78). Success is the reward of prudence and good conduct; and failure, of improvidence and ignorance. Luck, merit, or talent are not essential to success; what is necessary is the regular habit of self-denial. To be poor is to lack character. The suffering of the poor, argues Thornton, "is but the natural punishment of dishonestly-enjoyed pleasure, at some former period of their lives. I do not look upon self-indulgent, sensual people as worthy of my hatred; I simply look upon them with contempt for their poorness of character" (p. 79).

After a period of exposure to social values so different from her own, Margaret begins to take issue with Thornton's assumptions. For one, she resents his despising people for wasteful improvidence without exhibiting, on his part, a sense of responsibility for teaching them the frugal habits that made him a success: "And the poor men around him—they were poor because they were vicious—out of the pale of his sympathies because they had not his iron nature, and the capabilities that it gives him for being rich" (p. 82). The arrogant pride that disinclines masters from giving to their men reasons for their actions also comes under attack. When Margaret asks Thornton why workers cannot be told of his expectation of a slump in trade as a reason for denying them a raise in wages, the millowner replies, "Do you give your servants reasons for your expenditure, or your economy in the use of your own money? We, the owners of capital, have a right to choose what we do with it" (p. 112). Margaret counters with a notion characteristic of Mrs. Gaskell, the idea of the rich man as the steward of wealth: "there is no human law to prevent employers from utterly wasting or throwing away all their money if they choose but there are passages in the Bible which would rather imply . . . that they neglected their duty as stewards if they did so" (p. 112). The exaggerated respect for independence which serves as the rationale for Thornton's anti-paternalism is also subject to Margaret's critical scrutiny. Thornton, expecting his workmen to be as obedient as children during working hours, would grant them the independence of adults only on their own time:

> Now certainly, the time is not come for the hands to have any independent action during business hours. . . . And I say, that the masters would be trenching on the independence of their hands, in a way that I, for one, should not feel justified in doing if we interfered too much with the life they lead out of the mills. Because they labour ten hours a day for us, I do not see that we have any right to impose leading-strings upon them for the rest of their time. I value my own independence so highly that I can fancy no degradation greater than that of having another man perpetually directing and advising and lecturing me, even planning too closely in any way about my actions. He might be the wisest of men or the most powerful—I should equally rebel and resent his interference. I imagine this is a stronger feeling in the North of England than in the South. (pp. 115-16)

But Margaret refuses to accept Thornton's notions of independence. The South stands for friendship and mutual dependence: it is un-Christian to think of masters and men as isolated individuals: "God made us so

that we must be mutually dependent. We may ignore our own dependence, or refuse to acknowledge that others depend upon us in more
respects than the payment of weekly wages. . . . The most proudly independent man depends on those around him for their insensible influence on his character—his life. And the most isolated of your Dark-
shire Egos has dependents clinging to him on all sides. . . ." (pp. 116-17)

In the course of these colloquies the millowner gives no evidence of
responding to Margaret's arguments. The outcome of a near riot at his
mill, however, reveals that he is more vulnerable than he appears. Having
sent for soldiers, Thornton is content to barricade himself in his home
and wait for the military to deal with the mob. Thinking this measure
unmanly, Margaret exhorts him to go out to talk to the workers. Stung
by her accusation of cowardice, Thornton faces his dissatisfied workers
like a statue. But when she sees some boys picking up missiles, Margaret,
ashamed of having goaded him, shields him and is struck with a stone
(pp. 170-74). After the dispersal of the workers, Thornton makes a
declaration of love to her; but Margaret, lest others should think she was
throwing herself in his way, rejects him, saying that she would have done
the same for any man threatened by a crowd (pp. 187-88). Moreover,
though attracted to the kind of energy and purpose that animates the millowner, Margaret is not in love with this man whose lack of sympathy for
his fellow men fits badly with her concept of the whole duty of man.
During the second half of *North and South*, Thornton silently and gradually makes himself over according to Margaret's views. Shortly after his
rebuff, a change is perceptible. Though looked upon by his workmen "as
what the Bible calls a 'hard man'—not so much unjust as unfeeling; clear
in judgment, standing upon his 'rights' as no human being ought to
stand. . . ." (p. 160), the millowner does not want to press charges
against the rioters. Unlike Harriet Martineau, whose rioters must be
legally punished as well as proscribed by employers, Thornton thinks
legal revenge unnecessary. The strike leader Higgins reports to the Hales,
Thornton's statement in court: "[The rioters] are well known; they will
find the natural punishment of their conduct in the difficulty they will
meet wi' getting employment. That will be severe enough" (pp. 222-23).

It is through the black-listed Higgins that Margaret bridges the gulf
between master and man. She sends Higgins, who has taken on the
responsibility of raising the family of the suicide rioter Boucher, to ask
Thornton for work. The millowner declines at first but relents upon
learning that Higgins waited half of a day to see him. After making inquiries into Higgins's character and the account of his duty toward the
Bouchers, Thornton hires him (pp. 314-15). From this outspoken and

independent Lancashire working man, Thornton comes to understand the viewpoint of the labor force, and both master and man learn that "we have all of us one human heart" (p. 408). Margaret Hale's belief in mutual dependence becomes the cornerstone of Thornton's thinking with respect to his men. The millowner decides to explore the possibilities of a new relationship with his employees: "My only wish is to have the opportunity of cultivating some intercourse with the hands beyond the mere 'cash nexus'. . . . I have arrived at the conviction that no mere institutions, however wise, and however much thought may be required to organize them and arrange them, can attach class to class as they should be attached, unless the working out of such institutions bring the individuals of the different classes into actual personal contact. Such intercourse is the very breath of life" (pp. 419-20). Although he is not optimistic about class association as a preventative of future strikes, at least such a relation ". . . may render strikes not the bitter, venomous sources of hatred they have hitherto been" (p. 420).

As Thornton lays aside his economic individualism, he does not, as might be assumed, become the kind of benevolent employer who we find is the "good" manufacturer in fiction. Mindful of the pitfalls of paternalism outlined by Sir Arthur Helps and W. R. Greg, Thornton adds a new dimension to the character of the good employer. His former attitude of respect for the independence of his employees, divested of its laissez-faire implications, leads him to shun acts of paternalistic philanthropy. After building a dining room for his men, Thornton buys provisions wholesale, as Robert Owen had done before him.[19] But unlike the benevolent autocrat Owen, who did not perceive that the working masses needed to create their own environment and not merely respond gratefully to plans laid above,[20] Thornton does not want to force any scheme, however benevolent, upon his employees, since such a move would interfere with their freedom of choice. Nor does the working man want that kind of philanthropic interference. When Thornton, for example, proposes to Higgins a plan for a dining room, the workman finds fault with the entire scheme. Thornton then lays it aside with the following consequences as related to Mr. Bell:

> suddenly this Higgins came to me and graciously signified his approval of a scheme so nearly the same as mine that I might fairly have claimed it. . . . I was a little "riled," I confess, by his manner, and thought of throwing the whole thing overboard to sink or swim. But it seemed childish to relinquish a plan which I had once thought wise and well laid, just because I myself did not receive all the honour and consequence due to the originator. So I cooly took the part assigned to me,

which is something like that of steward to a club. I buy in provisions
wholesale and provide a fitting matron as cook. (p. 351)

The men in turn pay rent for the equipment and the dining room. By
espousing such a course of action, Thornton reveals a new concept of employer-employee relations, in detail unlike that of any other "good" employer in the novels of this study. It is a combination of the best of the
two opposing attitudes of cash-nexus and paternalism: he has tempered
the isolated economic independence of the cash payment relationship
with the concern for the welfare of employees inherent in benevolent
paternalism, by discarding the selfishness of the former and eschewing
the tendency toward patronization of the latter.

The change in Thornton's outlook is welcome to Margaret. As the
heir to Mr. Bell's property, she becomes the landlord of Thornton, whose
mill was built on Bell land. The subsequent marriage of Thornton and
Margaret unites the driving force of the Industrial Revolution in the
North with the cultural and moral tradition of the South. The novel ends
on the note of social harmony with which the era of the 1830s and 1840s
ends: class antagonism is replaced by class association, and foreshadowing an era that goes beyond the confines of this study, master and man
meet as equals.

EIGHT

The Two Aristocracies

> The revolution in society has reached this class.
> The great powers of industrial art have no exclu-
> sion of name or blood. The tools of our time;
> namely, steam, ships, printing, money, and popu-
> lar education, belong to those who can handle
> them: and their effect has been, that advantages
> once confined to men of family, are now open to
> the whole middle class. The road that grandeur
> levels for his coach, toil can travel in his cart.
>
> Emerson, *English Traits* (1856)

IN THE PRECEDING CHAPTER WE HAVE OBSERVED
that the relationship between employer and employee presents a picture
of reconciliation. The harmony that exists between the two classes is
largely the result of the masters' acceptance of a new sense of social responsibility and their realization that power ought not be exercised for un-
worthy aims. The novels of the 1850s which focus upon the relationship
between the industrialist and the aristocrat also reflect a mood of class
harmony which is the consequence of a balance of power. Such a state of
affairs justifies in part W. L. Burn's calling the mid-Victorian era "the
age of equipoise."[1] Along with twenty years of post-Reform Bill political
changes and the general acceptance of the belief, reflected in the Exhibition of 1851, that England's future power and wealth lay in maintaining its position as the "workshop of the world," the captain of industry
had become the virtual peer of the landed aristocracy, where money power
was concerned. Since public opinion (outside genteel circles) tended, in
the presence of immense riches, to make few distinctions regarding ancestry, it was not surprising that affluent industrialists came to be styled,
quite seriously, as an aristocracy of wealth.

I

The Two Aristocracies

In the realm of fiction Catherine Gore, a popular writer of silver-fork novels, who might be expected to be the last to admit an intruder into the circle of her society fiction, gave currency to the notion of a legitimate aristocracy of industrial wealth. In her novel *The Two Aristocracies* (1857), Mrs. Gore presents the history of the relationship between the industrial aristocracy and the aristocracy of birth over three generations of the nineteenth century. If her superficial use of the convention of marriage is taken as a standard of measurement, she seems to suggest that at mid-century the two classes were on a par. In the second generation a marriage takes place between the two but results in estrangement because of inequalities of fortune in the one, and of rank in the other. It is only in the third generation that a marriage of social equals can take place.

The novel begins at the close of the Napoleonic wars. Matthew Lambert, the owner of an ironworks in Birmingham and a Dissenter of serious and rigid demeanor, legally adopts a bright young clerk into his family at the dying wish of his son Zack, who is mortally wounded in a brawl at Le Havre, where he was sent to deliver machinery to a French sugar refinery. The clerk, Mark Barneson, gives evidence of one of the qualities needed for success: he is not an inventor but has a facility for putting other peoples' inventions to work. True to their Nonconformist background, the elder Lamberts, considering public entertainments sinful, confine their activities to business and to the conventicle. When old Lambert dies, Mark Barneson and the two Misses Lambert, Rhoda and Lettice are made joint owners of the ironworks. In his will Lambert stipulated both that no capital was to be withdrawn from the firm within the lifetime of the girls, and that one of the girls should marry Mark Barneson as an example to the other that she should not marry out of her station.

Under Mark's direction the prosperity of the firm enables the Lamberts to settle in a country retreat near Arden Hall, home of Sir Arscott Littlecote who exemplifies the attitude of aristocratic prejudice toward the manufacturing capitals in the unliberalized England of the post-Napoleonic but pre-Reform Bill era:

> The business of Birmingham was to make nails, tea-boards, and door-handles,—arms, when war was brisk,—steam-engines, when it could find a purchaser:—but to hold its tongue.—Manchester was bound to supply us with servants' sheeting and fast-coloured calicoes. . . . Out of business hours, we were not on bowing terms with the Great Unwashed. Once a year, the political lion of the day went down and roared them a speech. . . . But for the ensuing eleven months and

twenty-nine days, the manufacturing or commercial city became only a word on a map; a name in the Gazetteer, or the city article. Its millions might find their way into the public coffers: its hundred of thousands of living souls were, like Viola's history—'a blank, my lord!'[2]

Sir Arscott forbids any intercourse between his family and the Lamberts, but that interdict does not hinder his son Rupert from paying court to Rhoda Lambert, who has acquired all the scorn of a Sir Arscott for her manufacturing background. Longing to ornament the world of fashion, Rhoda marries Rupert. At the outset of their marriage, however, they are immediately estranged. Rhoda discovers that Rupert married her only after being satisfied with the surreptitious inquiries he had made regarding her fortune as one-third owner of the Bracknell Ironworks. Pressed for debt because of spendthrift living, Rupert seeks to gain power of attorney over her income. All of Rupert's earlier claims to be a member of a new race of liberal aristocrats were those of a fortune-hunting opportunist. After Rhoda's refusal to sign documents giving him control over her fortune, Rupert too is convinced his marriage was a mistake: "Never again was she to hear from his lips the endearing name of 'Rhoda.' His Rhoda had ceased to exist. He no longer loved her as a wife. An insurmountable barrier, a hateful thought was perpetually interposed between them.—'You married me for money,' was written on the face of Rhoda. 'You married me for rank,' replied the scarcely repressed sneer of her husband" (1:244).

Since the second generation did not succeed in overcoming the disparity between the two classes, the task remains for the third. Lettice Lambert, true to old Lambert's wish, married Mark Barneson and a daughter Barbara was born. After the Reform Bill Barneson rose in the political world, having become popular in a former rotten borough and in his native seat of Birmingham as well. As the third generation grows to maturity, the aristocracy, bowing to the inevitable, affects a spirit of liberalism. Thus when the prosperous engine-builder buys a country estate adjacent to Lord Ullesmere, that nobleman, though "he accepted what he called the 'fusion of classes,' as a victim suffering from the toothache shakes hands with the inevitable dentist" (2:68), is delighted to be able to show his superiority to the prejudices of his order. Mrs. Gore delivers his public sentiments on the subject in the rhetoric of the political time-server. The Marquis desires his colleagues in the Cabinet to know that,

it was his "dooty" to notice the nailer [Barneson];—"a man to whom the commerce of the country was so largely indebted; a man whose industry and intellect were the means of pouring thousands,—millions—

into the Exchequer;—a man whose establishment, (he was informed—
he had never visited Birmingham) afforded model "institootions" of
enlightened benevolence;—a man whose engines were steaming across
the Atlantic, and his locomotives across the wilds of—of—India,—that
is—Hindostan—". . . "Mr. Barneson might be regarded as one of the
ablest appropriators of Steam Power;—the creation, if he might be so
permitted to speak, that followed nearest in importance to mankind
after that recorded in Genesis." (2:70)

The Marquis' neighborliness, however, yields results that he did not expect. His son Bernard falls in love with Barneson's daughter. But a marriage is "utterly and totally out of the question;" that is, until Barneson
offers a handsome settlement, together with his country estate, as a dowry.
As objections are removed by gold, the Marquis makes one of his semi-
public pronouncements which is understood to be further proof of his
advanced views: " 'In these times,' he said, 'it was the dooty of very
man whose position in life rendered him an example, to promote to the
utmost the fusion of classes;'—and he was overjoyed to be able to welcome
into his family the daughter of a most excellent and enlightened man"
(2:135). And he adds later, "the union of the 'two aristocracies'—that is,
the marriage of a Marquis's son with the daughter of a man holding
marquessatorial [sic] rank in the world of trade was a victory for liberalism" (2:166). A generation earlier such a match, as we have seen, would
not have come off so well. Bob Gresham, who had been Rupert's creditor
and who had engineered the match between Rupert and Rhoda, comments upon the marriage of Barbara Barneson and Lord Bernard: "By
Jove, the counter is beginning to bowl over the board of green-cloth.—
Twenty years ago, when I made the match between [Rupert] and her
aunt, the world turned up its nose, or rather held its nose,—at the mere
notion of the connection" (2:136).

Marriage as an expression of equality of social station is frequently
employed by Mrs. Gore. Like the novel under present discussion, her
Peers and Parvenus (1846) and her *Cromer Hall: or Old Families and
New* (1846) each contain a final paragraph which is a set piece celebrating
a wedding. We can only conclude that marriage in Mrs. Gore's works
seems to be a convention of fiction which provides a tidy end to a novel
and is somewhat suspect as a symbolic gesture expressing union, as in
the case of *North and South*. If her inveterate matchmaking offers little
symbolic value as a reflection of the spirit of the age, the tone she takes
toward the landed aristocracy in this novel is indicative of a change of
taste in fiction. And Mrs. Gore, best known as a prolific chronicler of
the sayings and doings of high life, is in a sense as much a time-server as
her Lord Ullesmere.[3] In *The Two Aristocracies* the selfish motives that

she ascribes to the old order, as opposed to the uprightness of the iron-master, are a remove from the silver-fork tradition with which she is associated. It may be that she is following in the wake of *North and South*, which appeared two years earlier, but the resemblance between the two novels noted by Matthew Rosa[4] is extremely vague. In any event, it seems that the use of an industrialist as protagonist, by a novelist whose concerns were normally with high society and who was not a polemicist, is another indication of the fact that, after 1850, the industrialist had entered the society of fiction as the representative of a class which was fast becoming a respectable addition to English society and which was no longer the whipping boy of social problem novelists.

II

Bleak House

In an attempt to describe the prevailing spirit of the 1850s and 1860s, a noted British historian makes the following generalization: "The word 'balance' was one of the key words of the period both in relation to politics and to society."[5] With respect to the relative positions of the landed and the manufacturing classes, Dickens seems to have locked the scales at precisely that point at which the two power groups were in a state of equilibrium. This is evident in the brief confrontation between Rouncewell, the ironmaster, and Sir Leicester Dedlock in *Bleak House* (1853).

Rouncewell, the son of Sir Leicester's housekeeper, seeks an interview with Sir Leicester and Lady Dedlock respecting the matrimonial interest of his son in Rosa, Lady Dedlock's protege. Ushered into their presence Rouncewell is unruffled, though he regrets having to be brief because business calls him to superintend workmen in several places. He explains to his aristocratic hosts that his son has fallen in love with Rosa, but that marriage is presently out of the question. The ironmaster will consent to their marriage only upon condition that Rosa leave Chesney Wold. If, however, her departure would inconvenience Lady Dedlock, the iron-master would gladly drop the whole subject. Sir Leicester is taken aback at this seemingly odd request. Like Bounderby, the aristocrat is given to stock responses: "Not remain at Chesney Wold! Make it a condition! All Sir Leicester's old misgivings relative to Wat Tyler, and the people of the iron districts who do nothing but turn out by torchlight, come in a shower upon his head: the fine grey hair of which, as well as his whiskers, actually stirs with indignation."[6] But controlling his initial urge, he asks the ironmaster whether Rosa is likely to injure her prospects by remaining with Lady Dedlock. Rouncewell then explains his plans for Rosa. He begins by informing Sir Leicester that he has educated his son and daughters so that they are worthy of any station. Rosa is not their equal in this respect. But, he continues, unequal marriages are quite frequent among his class. Often the son of an employer falls in love with a factory girl. If the girl has a good character, she is commonly sent for two years to a school of the kind that the employer's children have attended. If at the end of that time the girl profits from the experience and is on terms of equality with her intended husband in the matter of education, the father of the boy will give his consent. Knowing several cases like this, Rouncewell has resolved to do the same for Rosa and his son. Calm in his indignation, Sir Leicester cannot believe anyone would draw a parallel between Chesney Wold and a "factory." But it is Sir Leicester who makes the comparison, and when Rouncewell, who has avoided discussing the matter in comparative terms, is put to it, he is forced into shocking the aristocrat by his dismissal of Dedlock patronage. The following quotation illustrates this, along with the implications Rouncewell's attitude has for the world of the Dedlocks:

> "Are you aware, Sir, that this young woman whom my Lady—my Lady—has placed near her person, was brought up at the village school outside the gates?"
> "Sir Leicester, I am quite aware of it. A very good school it is and handsomely supported by this family."
> "Then, Mr. Rouncewell," returns Sir Leicester, "the application of what you have said is, to me, incomprehensible."
> "Will it be more comprehensible, Sir Leicester, if I say," the ironmaster is reddening a little, "that I do not regard the village school as teaching everything desirable to be known by my son's wife?"
> From the village school of Chesney Wold, intact as it is this minute, to the whole framework of society: from the whole framework of society, to the aforesaid framework receiving tremendous cracks in consequence of people (ironmasters, leadmistresses, and what not) not minding their catechism, and getting out of the station unto which they are called, necessarily and for ever, according to Sir Leicester's rapid logic, the first station in which they happen to find themselves; and from that, to their educating other people out of *their* stations, and so obliterating the landmarks, and opening the floodgates, and all the rest of it; this is the swift progress of the Dedlock mind. (p. 365)

Seeing their views on duty, station, and education completely opposed, Sir Leicester requests that the subject be dismissed. Rouncewell courteously replies that he will urge his son to forget Rosa and, declining an offer of overnight hospitality because of pressing business in another part of England, rushes off on an all night journey (p. 366).

Sometime later, the "iron gentleman" is summoned by Lady Dedlock, who sensing that her exposure lies at hand, does not want Rosa in the way when her world crumbles. The ironmaster is told by Lady Dedlock that Rosa is still in love and is insensible to the advantages of her connection with Chesney Wold. Upon hearing this, Sir Leicester, who had at first objected to Rosa's leaving because she should not be deprived of the good fortune to be under the patronage of the Dedlocks, concurs. With a straightforward manner and good humored politeness that amply cloaks his irony, Rouncewell is apologetic about troubling the Dedlocks with so "unimportant" a matter as the happiness of his son. With this last ironic expression of an exaggerated respect for their privacy, he leaves with the future wife of his son, to whom as a playful little joke upon Sir Leicester's misgivings about a change in the social order, Dickens has given the name Wat:

> Sir Leicester and Lady Dedlock . . . I beg to take my leave, with an apology for having again troubled you, though not of my own act, on this tiresome subject. I can very well understand, I assure you, how tiresome so small a matter must have become to Lady Dedlock. If I am doubtful of my dealing with it, it is only because I did not at first quietly exert my influence to take my young friend here away, without troubling you at all. But it appeared to me—I dare say, magnifying the importance of the thing—that it was respectful to explain to you how the matter stood, and candid to consult your wishes and convenience. I hope you will excuse my acquaintance with the polite world. (pp. 603-4)

In their dealings, the aristocrat and the ironmaster exhibit a mutual aversion that is thinly covered by a veil of civility on both sides. Sir Leicester's feelings are evident in Dickens' transcription of his thoughts, and Rouncewell's, through his polite irony. But a mutual respect is also indicated by the restraint which distinguishes their brief relationship.

In contrast to our knowledge of Sir Leicester, our acquaintance with Rouncewell is limited; but despite the small part assigned to him by Dickens, it is possible to make some generalizations about this industrialist, who is neither a Cheeryble nor a Bounderby. Rouncewell thinks highly of himself and his accomplishments. He is not ashamed of his mother's long and devoted service as housekeeper to the Dedlocks, "because such an instance bespeaks high worth on two sides; on the great side assuredly; on the small one, no less assuredly" (p. 363). By praising his mother he is also aknowledging his own merit. In another era he might have worn Sir Leicester's livery, but the Industrial Revolution changed all that. Although his mother will not leave the abode which

she has called home for half a century, Rouncewell is independent of
Dedlock patronage and desires to make certain that the younger generation of his family shall not be dependent upon the favor of a moribund
aristocracy. Still, he can afford to be charitable in his attitude toward Sir
Leicester, for time is on the side of the "iron gentleman." Although we
know little about Rouncewell, R. J. Cruikshank, in the manner of Dickens's foretelling the future of his characters in an epilogue, confirms this
writer's suspicions when he predicts the outcome of the Dedlock-Rounce-
well relationship:

> In the end, the heirs of Mr. Rouncewell almost certainly inherited
> Sir Leicester Dedlock's place in Lincolnshire, and one feels confident
> that the third generation was magnificently represented by a Sir
> Leicester Rouncewell, M. P. for the county, a great gentleman of the
> old school who was adored by his tenantry, and whose speeches deplor-
> ing the revolutionary sentiments of Mr. Gladstone delivered in the
> unstrung voice of the true aristocrat, recalled to elderly members the
> primeval Conservatism of Colonel Sibthorpe of Lincoln.[7]

III

Hugh Vernon, the Weaver's Son

A reviewer of Mrs. Gore's *The Two Aristocracies* had this to say about
her descriptive technique: "Mrs. Gore cannot draw manufacturers and
their establishments like one who is to the manner born, but she does it
well enough for the purposes of a novel."[8] Unfortunately, Mrs. Gore's
limitation in the matter of drawing industrialist's "establishments" is also
that of the majority of novelists treated in this study. Yet again, as the
review adds, the novel does not demand a faithful record of a certain kind
of inanimate particular. On this last point, it may be further argued that
detailed descriptions of the interiors of homes tend to impede the flow
of narrative. But as Mark Twain has shown in his chapter "The House
Beautiful" in *Life on the Mississippi*, the furnishings of a home are an
index to the minds of its occupants. And where a writer has taken pains
to make such a description contribute to our knowledge of his characters,
his effort has not been merely a gratuitous accumulation of detail.

This last is the case with the anonymous author of *Hugh Vernon, the
Weaver's Son* (1853).[9] Not only does this writer present a meaningful
description of the interior of a manufacturer's home, but he also compares his taste in furnishings to that of an aristocrat, thus providing us
with an insight into the differing temperaments of the two aristocracies.

The primary concern of the author of *Hugh Vernon* is to demonstrate

that to a working man without education or the refinement of generations
the unearned acquisition of wealth through, in this case, a legacy, represents "simply an increase in sensual pleasures" (Nov. 10, p. 222). Set
against the clutter of uneconomical and badly chosen purchases found in
the home of the working man John Vernon, recent heir to a cousin's estate, are the furnishings of Mr. Chester, a gentlemanly silk manufacturer
and those of the aristocratic Lacys. The following description of what is
not in the drawing room of the manufacturer gives some indication of
what Mr. Chester considers in bad taste:

> There was no false art in this room of Mr. Chester's; no sprawling
> nymphs, or Titans caricatured out of all likeness with muscular hu-
> manity. There was no glaring taste of scarlet, and gold, and purple, and
> green, and orange, all on the same piece, such as people call "warm"
> and "rich;" no voluptuous trickeries of heavy draperies, softening the
> day into a mysterious twilight, over Ledas and Danaes, and Venuses, in-
> nocent of millinery and contemptuous of appearances; no coarse mix-
> tures of velvet and worsted, and linen and gold, to give a more dashing
> effect than the value of the stuff warranted; no costly china placed side
> by side with mock Dresden; no ormolu on stands of ragged cotton-vel-
> vet; no papier mache, next to imitated Japanese work; no Indian curi-
> osities, manufactured in Thames-street. (Nov. 10, p. 222)

Mrs. Chester, we are told, was in her tastes a true artist, "an artist of the
simple Greek school,—one who preferred the pure Ionic pillar to the
richness of the Corinthian capital . . ." (Nov. 10, p. 222), and her drawing room was furnished accordingly:

> All was simple and elegant, perfect in its kind, and chaste in its spirit;
> the colours—pale green and gold—pure and fresh, and the ornaments
> artistic, and each complete in itself. Not a tint was too harsh or too in-
> sipid, not a piece too surcharged or too poor. . . . Everything was
> tranquil, everything was pure; the spirit of beauty and of love—the
> spirit of peace and of knowledge, breathed out from all around; as the
> spirit of disorder and license is felt in the households of the careless and
> the vicious. . . ." (Nov. 10, p. 222)

Hugh Vernon had visited the Chester home when his father had been
employed at Chester's silk mill. After John Vernon had received his inheritance, Hugh was sent away to school and there became acquainted
with Herbert Lacy, an aristocrat. Invited to the Lacys' home during a
school holiday, Hugh had an opportunity to see the difference between his two "grand houses:"

The house was beautifully furnished but in quite a different manner to Mr. Chester's, which, as the only well-kept house that Hugh knew of, was naturally his measure of comparison. The Chesters had various objects of art, all perfect, but almost all modern—the Lacys disdained modern art; the Chesters had filled their rooms with English manufactures—the Lacys theirs with foreign. Vases from Wedgwood, tables from Jeunesse and Bettridge, porcelain from Minthorn, and all other things from the best home manufacturers, were in the Chester's inventory;—Florentine marbles, Sevres china and Dresden marqueterie, of the real Louis Quinze time, carved oak, black and old, French tablecloths, and French chairs, all that was foreign and historic was in the Lacys'. (Nov. 24, p. 254)

At bottom both classes are represented as having refined taste, the difference being that among furnishings of equal aesthetic worth, the one (without being a Podsnap, but perhaps out of an economic class bias) buys English, while the other prefers the Continental products long associated with an aristocratic sensibility. Despite the difference, both have more in common with each other than the manufacturer of the 1850s has with the early industrialist. To see how far the manufacturer was removed from his counterpart of two generations earlier, it is only necessary to look at a description of the "House Beautiful" of the self-made man of the early nineteenth century. Mr. Wilcox in *Marian Withers* was one of the old race of spinners who had risen from the ranks. Though he owned two mills, he continued to live in the simple and frugal style that had been his wont twenty years before:

> The house, a substantial stone-building, adjoined the mill. The front-door opened into a passage, covered with a strip of oil cloth, from which all trace of pattern had long since been trodden away. On one side of this passage was a large kitchen, which in its furniture was partly a sitting-room; a sofa, covered with print, and stuffed with feathers, stood beneath the wide low window, which was neither sash nor casement; two large, three-cornered armchairs, with semicircular backs stood opposite to each other in the chimney corner. The ceiling was covered with a frame, upon which a good store of oatcakes were drying; a few wooden book-shelves were put up in one corner, and round the walls hung coloured prints representing the execution of some of the mutineers at the Nore, the death of Nelson, and the funeral of Princess Charlotte, the likenesses of sundry Methodist ministers, and an almanack in a black frame; some wooden chairs, a settle, and a carved oak chest, which held the family linen, and a large old-fashioned dining-table, completed the furniture. The only attempt at luxury was a cushion placed in the broad window sill, and a piece of carpet in the centre of the white stoned floor. Over the chimney-piece there was a bright array of shining tin and copper kettles. (*Marian Withers*, 2:7-8)

As we have endeavored to demonstrate, some of the novelists of the 1850s viewed the industrialists and the aristocrats as power groups having reached a state of equilibrium. The increasing political influence of a Mark Barneson, the economic emancipation of Rouncewell from, to use Cazamian's phrase, "le Toryisme stupide"[10] through Free Trade, and the aesthetic sensibility of Chester, all suggest that the captains of industry had become a social force which might be considered, in many quarters, a second aristocracy.

NINE

The Idea
of a Gentleman

It is as a manufacturer and to mark the interest
which the Queen takes in the manufacturing pursuits of the country, that Mr. Strutt is metamor-
phosed into Baron Belper. . . . It shows a wise
appreciation of the signs of the times. It is something for those who claim to be regarded as the
descendants of the mailed barons of England to
admit into their order a man who not only has
made but is making his fortune by spindles and
looms. . . . Lord Belper is the first "millowner"
who has been elevated to the peerage. . . .
London Times, Aug. 2, 1856[1]

W. L. BURN HAS CONJECTURED THAT THE
popularity, in the earlier nineteenth century, of the genealogist Burke
was the natural reaction of landed families to the presence of the new
industrialists; that is, it was an expression of a desire to keep the concept
of gentility distinct from that of affluence. An individual possessing the
distinction of birth was thereby assured of a social position unaffected by
economic status or, for the most part, personal conduct.[2] Interest in
pedigree as a standard of judgment continued, for in 1847 Burke began
publishing an annual supplement.[3] But while established families sought
to preserve the time-honored notion of an aristocracy of titled and untitled gentry connected with land, the word "aristocracy" had accumulated associations of meaning that had little to do with lineage. In *Past
and Present*, for example, Carlyle was not thinking along class lines when
he called for an aristocracy of talent, the rule of the wisest and the best.
A quotation from the *Times* is a further instance of an extension of the
traditional category of meaning. The *Times* affirms that the strength and

dignity of a country depends on the quality of its best, but "this aristocracy is not an aristocracy of blood, not an aristocracy of fashion, not an aristocracy of talent only; it is an aristocracy of Character. That is the true heraldry of man."[4] The tendency to regard the concept of an aristocracy in terms other than those of acres and blood bespoke the need of a broader basis for judging who were England's best.

In connection with this concern for defining an aristocracy, there is ample evidence that the concept of the gentleman had assumed a paramount importance, especially to the mid-Victorians. Wingfield-Stratford goes so far as to state that during the decades 1830-70, "the dominant feature of the Victorian Age . . . is that the English mind has become gentleman conscious in a way that it has never been before."[5] In a chapter devoted to the "balance of interests" of mid-Victorian society, another modern historian writes that, "the idea of the 'gentleman' is the necessary link in any analysis of mid-Victorian ways of thinking and behaving . . ."[6] The gentlemanly ideal, continues this historian, founded on a belief in a moral code and drawn according to what should be rather than what was, "helped make the Victorian social balance what it was, something quite different from the social balance of any other country in any other period of prolonged prosperity."[7] And Ruskin, marking somewhat peevishly the increase of individual social mobility, wrote that the aspiration to gentility had become a compulsion for Victorians:

> The very removal of the massy bars which once separated one class of society from another, has rendered it tenfold more shameful in foolish people's, *i.e.*, in most people's eyes, to remain in the lower grades of it, than ever it was before. . . . Now that man may make money, and rise in the world, and associate himself, unreproached, with people once far above him . . . it becomes a veritable shame to him to remain in the state he was born in, and everybody thinks it is his duty to try to be a "gentleman."[8]

Among "everybody" was the industrialist. Having gained an equality of status based upon both an increase of political power and the accumulation of wealth, the captains of industry eventually aspired to be worthy of the best tradition of the old order—the idea of a gentleman. In addition to its usual application to birth, the word "aristocracy," as we have seen, was employed in connection with talent and character. Using the concept of meritocracy as a justification for rank, the wealthy industrialists in time assimilated with the traditional rulers of the land to form what was needful to a society that had outgrown the uncomplicated concept of the Three Estates; namely, a new gentry.

A selection of novels of the 1850s and 1860s suggests a logical process through which the idea of a gentleman was broadened and a new gentry formed. This line of reasoning may be briefly summarized thus: Anthony Trollope treats the complexity of the problem by acknowledging that talent is meritorious, but emphasizing the difficulty of assessing it as a measure of gentility; Dinah Mulock simplistically asserts that character is the measure of a gentleman; and Mrs. Henry Wood establishes a modus vivendi by making a public school education the test of a gentleman.

I

Dr. Thorne

Noting the continuing importance of deference even to a highly mobile industrial society, Asa Briggs declares that the idea of a gentleman was "extremely complicated both to define and to disentangle."[9] Reflecting this complexity, Trollope expresses both the necessity of restricting the application of the term and the hazards involved in using it.

> There are places in life which can hardly be well filled except by "Gentlemen." The word is one the use of which almost subjects one to ignominy. If I say that a judge should be a gentleman, or a bishop, I am met with scornful allusion to "Nature's Gentlemen." Were I to make such an assertion with reference to the House of Commons, nothing that I ever said again would receive the slightest attention. A man in public life could not do himself a greater injury than by saying in public that commissions in the army and navy, or berths in the Civil Service, should be given exclusively to gentlemen. He would be defied to define the term,—and would fail should he attempt to do so. But he would know what he meant, and so very probably would they who defied him."[10]

Certain positions, then, were the prerogative of gentlemen, but this did not mean that only certain individuals might be gentlemen. On the contrary, any man might become one if he chose, but some had a better chance than others:

> It may be that the son of a butcher in the village shall become as well fitted for employments requiring gentle culture as the son of a parson. Such is often the case. When such is the case, no one has been more prone to give the butcher's son all the welcome he has merited than I myself; but the chances are greatly in favor of the parson's son. The gates of the one class should be open to the other; but neither to one class or the other can good be done by declaring that there are no gates, no barrier, no difference.[11]

Owing in large part to his "advanced conservative Liberal views,[12]

Trollope was hard put to define the gentleman, once he ventured beyond the traditional category of birth. This difficulty is reflected in *Dr. Thorne* (1858) where he makes such an attempt. Though Mary Thorne's mixed notions are the outcome of her position as an illegitimate child, and subject to the demands of story, nevertheless, the conflict in her mind reflects the complexity of Trollope's own attitude toward the meaning of "gentleman." Mary, raised by Dr. Thorne, whose gentlemanly status was secure, believes (as her guardian would approve) that no one by virtue of his material advantages is her superior. But her attitude toward gentility alternates between democratic and aristocratic feelings:

> If she were born a gentlewoman! And then came to her mind those curious questions: what makes a gentleman? what makes a gentlewoman? What is the inner reality, the spiritualized, quintessence of that privilege in the world which men call rank, which forces the thousands and hundreds of thousands to bow down before the few elect? What gives, or what can give it, or should give it?
> And she answered the question. Absolute, intrinsic acknowledged, individual merit must give it to its possessor, let him be whom, and what and whence he might. So far the spirit of democracy was strong within her. Beyond this it could be had but by inheritance, received as it were secondhand, or twenty second-hand. And so far the spirit of aristocracy was strong within her. All this she had, as may be imagined, learnt in early years from her uncle. . . .[13]

Considering Frank Gresham's profession of love a young man's folly, yet regretting that her nameless status should impede her matrimonial prospects with an aristocrat, Mary reveals her aristocratic bias more clearly as she muses over Frank's offer:

> She said to herself, proudly, that God's handiwork was the inner man, the inner woman, the naked creature animated by a living soul; that all other adjuncts were but man's clothing for the creature; all others, whether stitched by tailors or contrived by kings. Was it not within her capacity to do as nobly, to love as truly, to worship her God in heaven with as perfect a faith, and her god on earth with as leal a truth, as though blood had descended to her purely through scores of purely-born progenitors? So to herself she spoke; and yet, as she said it she knew that were she a man, such a man as the heir of Greshamsbury should be, nothing should tempt her to sully her children's blood by mating herself with any one that was baseborn. She felt that were she an Augusta Gresham, no Mr. Moffatt [heir to a tradesman's fortune], let his wealth be what it might, should win her hand unless he too could tell of family honours and a line of ancestors.
> And so, with a mind at war with itself, she came forth armed to do

battle against the world's prejudices, those prejudices she herself still loved so well. (pp. 87-88)

The complexity of Mary's attitude toward the requisites of gentility is also evident in Trollope's treatment of Roger Scatcherd, Mary's maternal uncle, unknown as such to her. In the character of Scatcherd, the railway contractor, individual merit appears as the talent necessary to undertake and successfully perform tasks that are indispensable to a society becoming increasingly complex. Trollope clearly admires Scatcherd's capacity for getting work done, but at the same time he shows some of his limitations:

> Roger Scatcherd had . . . a reputation, but not for beauty or propriety of conduct. He was known for the best stonemason in the four counties, and as the man who could, on occasions, drink the most alcohol in a given time in the same localities. As a workman, indeed, he had a higher repute even than this: he was not only a good and very quick stonemason, but he had also a capacity of turning other men into good stonemasons: he had a gift of knowing what a man could and should do; and, by degrees, he taught himself what five, and ten, and twenty-latterly, what a thousand and two thousand men might accomplish among them: this, also, he did with very little aid from pen and paper, with which he was not and never became, very conversant. (p. 21)

Scatcherd, who earlier in his life had killed in a drunken rage Dr. Thorne's brother Henry, the seducer of his sister, Mary Scatcherd, had, by virtue of his executive ability, subsequently become an important and wealthy man:

> He had become a contractor, first for little things, such as half a mile or so of railway embankment, or three or four canal bridges, locks, docks, and quays, and had latterly had his hands in the making of whole lines of railway. . . .
> And he acquired more than wealth. There had been a time when the government wanted the immediate performance of some extraordinary piece of work, and Roger Scatcherd had been the man to do it. There had been some extremely necessary bit of a railway to be made in half the time that such work would properly demand, some speculation to be incurred requiring great means and courage as well, and Roger Scatcherd had been found to be the man for the time. He was then elevated for the moment to the dizzy pinnacle of a newspaper hero and became one of those "whom the king delighteth to honour." He went up one day to court to kiss Her Majesty's hand, and came down to his new grand house at Boxall Hill, Sir Roger Scatcherd, Bart. (p. 101)

But as Trollope reveals elsewhere, talent alone, however remarkable and needful to an industrial society, though it earns its possessor a baronetcy, is not enough to make a man a gentleman. Instead, talent tends to isolate him; and isolation carries with it a destructive element. The habit of drink, which was once the solace of the hard working stonemason, becomes indispensable to the contractor living under the pressure of maintaining a reputation for speed and efficiency twice that of his competitors. Thus during the entire week preceding bidding on a construction project, the crucial time of calculating his costs and profit with an eye to underbidding others without sacrificing the quality of his work, Scatcherd goes on a solitary drinking spree (p. 101). Another factor contributing to his isolation is Scatcherd's political bias, his democrat's antagonism toward the aristocracy. The Radical opinions that he held as a workman he retained as a master, so that he had friends neither among the Whigs, whom he "hated as knaves" nor the Conservatives who "should be laughed at as fools" (p. 73). His only friend in the world is the man who treats him after his prolonged bouts with alcohol; namely, Dr. Thorne. After one of these periods, Scatcherd sends for Thorne, and in the ensuing scene, Trollope drops the tone of irony with which he had earlier treated the contractor's alcoholism.[14] Here he reveals in a sympathetic straightforward manner the abysmal isolation of a man who has raised himself to an eminence by talent alone:

"Why do you take it then? Why do you do it? . . . Oh, Scatcherd! Scatcherd!" and the doctor prepared to pour out the flood of his eloquence in beseeching this singular man to abstain from his well-known poison.

"Is that all you know of human nature, doctor? Abstain. Can you abstain from breathing, and live like a fish does under water?"

"But Nature has not ordered you to drink, Scatcherd."

"Habit is second nature, man; and a stronger nature than the first. And why should I not drink? What else has the world given me for all that I have done for it? What other resource have I? What other gratification?"

"Oh, my god! Have you not unbounded wealth? Can you not do anything you wish? be anything you choose?"

"No," and the sick man shrieked with an energy that made him audible all through the house. "I can do nothing that I would choose to do; be nothing that I would wish to be! What can I do? What can I be? What gratification can I have except the brandy bottle? If I go among gentlemen, can I talk to them? If they have anything to say about a railway, they will ask me a question: if they speak to me beyond that I must be dumb.[15] If I go among my workmen, can they talk to

me? No; I am their master, and a stern master. They bob their heads
and shake in their shoes when they see me. Where are my friends?
Here!" said he, and he dragged a bottle from under his very pillow.
"Where are my amusements? Here!" and he brandished the bottle
almost in the doctor's face. "Where is my one resource, my one gratification, my only comfort after all my toils? Here, doctor; here, here,
here!" and, so saying, he replaced his treasure beneath his pillow.
(p. 112-13)

Thorne believes that Scatcherd is either foolish or mad for being indifferent to the inevitably fatal consequences of alcohol. In reply, Scatcherd
reveals a sentiment that has been expressed audibly by no other captain
of industry in this study: a desire to abdicate the position of power which
he has struggled to attain:

> Folly enough, perhaps, and madness enough, also. Such a life as
> mine makes a man a fool, and makes him mad, too. What have I about
> me that I should be afraid to die? I'm worth three hundred thousand
> pounds; and I'd give it all to be able to go to work tomorrow with a
> hod and mortar, and have a fellow clap his hand upon my shoulder,
> and say: "Well, Roger, shall us have that 'ere other half-pint this
> morning?" I'll tell you what, Thorne, when a man has made three
> hundred thousand pounds, there's nothing left for him to do but to
> die. It's all he's good for then. When money's been made, the next
> thing is to spend it. Now the man who makes it has not the heart to do
> that. (p. 113)

Ultimately, the circumstances of Scatcherd's isolation cost him his life.

The objection that the railway contractor is not a representative Trol-
lopian character can be made, and therefore his usefulness as an expression of his creator's attitude toward gentility is limited. Bradford Booth
has written that the Scatcherd story is out of place in Barset and that it
is an element of Victorian sensationalism more in keeping with the melodrama of popular Victorian novelists.[16] After examining Trollope's other
works for similar characters, Michael Sadleir's findings tend to substanti-
ate the opinion that the figure of Scatcherd stands alone. Financial ad-
venturers, money magnates, and inheritors of tradesmen's fortunes appear
in Trollope's novels; but despite the dramatic effectiveness of Scatcherd
and Trollope's awareness of the frequency with which such men appeared
on the changing social scene, the railway contractor is Trollope's only
portrait of the self-made man. Sadleir explains this by pointing out that
the plot of *Dr. Thorne* was Tom Trollope's idea.[17]

Despite Scatcherd's anomalous position among Trollope's predominantly aristocratic characters, the contractor is more than merely a foreign

element borrowed from another tradition: Anthony Trollope, successful at two careers, is in part Roger Scatcherd. As the progress of English civilization demanded men to build better transportation facilities, so it also needed those who would improve its communications system. Trollope was proud of his achievement in this latter capacity. When he retired from the Post Office, he revealed how intimately concerned he had been about ensuring good postal service:

> That the public in little villages should be enabled to buy postage stamps; that they should have their letters delivered free and at an early hour; that pillar letter-boxes should be put up for them (of which accommodation in the streets and ways of England I was the originator, having, however, got authority for the erection of the first at St. Heliers in Jersey); that the letter-carriers and sorters should not be overworked; that they should be adequately paid, and have some hours to themselves especially on Sundays; above all, that they should be made to earn their wages . . . these were the matters by which I was stirred to what the Secretary was pleased to call energetic performance of my duties.[18]

The age demanded, then, men who had the talent for devising "pillar letter-boxes" as well as those who, like Scatcherd, could construct "a harbour to hold all the commerce of Lancashire" (Dr. Thorne, p. 101). But here the resemblance between Trollope and Scatcherd ends, for the contractor did not have his creator's resources. It was Trollope's second career which enabled him to be one of "Nature's gentlemen." He tells us that he was motivated to write novels because the greatest reward of the literary man was the opportunity to move among distinguished people. Not only was the writer free from the fixed hours of other professions, but also gentlemen afforded him the respect of an equal: "But it is in the consideration which he enjoys that the successful author finds his richest reward. He is, if not of equal rank yet of equal standing with the highest; and if he be open to the amenities of society, he may choose his own circles. He without money can enter doors which are closed against almost all but him and the wealthy."[19]

We have seen that the idea of a gentleman was for Trollope neither easy to define nor apply. Although he possessed aristocratic sympathies, he acknowledged that a specialized talent was socially valuable to a society that required complicated and difficult tasks to be done.[20] As such, the talented merited distinction. Trollope trusted to his literary career for "equal standing with the highest," but in the case of Scatcherd, expertise in transportation services, without culture or education, did not, nor could it, make the gentleman.

II

John Halifax, Gentleman

In a chapter of *Self-Help* (1859) entitled "Character—The True Gentleman," Samuel Smiles voices his belief that the only true aristocracy is one of character. For him, the test of a "true gentleman" was his moral superiority: "His qualities depend not upon fashion or manners, but upon moral worth—not upon personal possessions, but upon personal qualities. The Psalmist briefly describes him as one 'that walketh uprightly, and worketh righteousness and speaketh the truth in his heart.' "[21] The gentleman's sense of honor teaches him to avoid mean actions: "His law is rectitude, action in right lines."[22] And because "humanity is sacred in his eyes," he is kind, charitable, and forbearing.[23] Nor is there any necessary correspondence between wealth and rank and gentlemanly qualities: "The poor man may be a true gentleman,—in spirit and in daily life. He may be honest, truthful, upright, polite, temperate, courageous, self-respecting and self-helping,—that is, be a true gentleman."[24] Most important of all for Smiles, the writer of industrial biographies, is a notion that is one of the keystones of this study of the aristocratization of the industrialist; namely, that the true gentleman is known by the way in which he treats his dependents:

> There are many tests by which a gentleman may be known; but there is one that never fails—How does he *exercise power* over those subordinate to him? . . . How does the officer treat his men, the employer his servants, the master his pupils, and man in every station those who are weaker than himself? The discretion, forbearance, and kindliness, with which power in such cases is used, may indeed be regarded as the crucial test of gentlemanly character.[25]

Smiles' equation of *aristos* with character had been dramatized three years earlier by Dinah Maria Mulock (Mrs. Craik) in her novel, *John Halifax Gentleman* (1856), a Victorian best-seller that by 1897 was reported to have reached a sale of 250,000 copies.[26] Moreover, not unlike *Self-Help*, Dinah Mulock's work became "to many a draughtsman, tradesman, and hard-handed toiler, on both sides of the Atlantic, a dear companion and a household name."[27] Lacking the kind of worldly experience that had complicated Trollope's view, Dinah Mulock, like Smiles, simply asserts the centuries-old argument that moral attributes make the gentleman. For her, a gentleman may be recognized not by the accidents of fortune but by absolutes; namely, the virtues enumerated by Smiles and seconded by English evangelical Christianity. If in Trollope's Scatcherd merit appears as talent unsupported by moral sentiment, the merit of John Halifax is the moral worth of the Christian gentleman.

At the opening of her novel the antecedents of Dinah Mulock's self-made gentleman are hastily passed over. Young John Halifax's sole heritage is a Greek Testament that belonged to his father, who died in John's infancy. On the flyleaf are recorded the dates of his parents' marriage and their deaths. With respect to John's ancestry, the narrator of the novel Phineas Fletcher, John's life-long friend, writes: "This was all I ever heard of the boy's parentage: nor do I believe he knew more himself. He was indebted to no forefathers for a family history: the chronicle commenced with himself and was altogether his own making. No romantic antecedents ever turned up: his lineage remained uninvestigated and his pedigree began and ended with his own honest name."[28] John, a fourteen year old illiterate when he meets Phineas, has for the past three years following his mother's death managed to survive as an underemployed farm hand. He has based his own ideal of character on the scant fact that his father had written the word "gentleman" after his name in John's Bible. With this ideal as John's polestar, Dinah Mulock illustrates how a half-starved, homeless orphan becomes a prosperous millowner, possessing always—in poverty, in riches, and in the struggle between—the integrity and loftiness of purpose which mark him as one of Nature's true gentlemen.

In the course of their initial meeting, the demeanor of John Halifax discloses to Phineas that the ragged boy is no mere vagabond. Unemployed for the present, John earns a groat by assisting the invalid Phineas home from his father's tan-yard. Impressed by the gentleness in strength of the orphan, Phineas' father, Abel Fletcher, offers John, in addition to the groat he has earned, a shilling for his kindness. The nearly starving boy keeps the agreed-upon groat but returns the shilling declaring that he does not expect payment for kindness (p. 8). At the request of his son, Abel Fletcher offers John, who has no trade, a job in the tan-yard. Because it constitutes honest employment, the orphan, proudly self-dependent and unwilling to beg, gladly accepts the meanest work in the tan-yard—that of collecting the malodorous skins from neighboring farmers. Although it is a disagreeable task, John philosophizes, "I would like to be anything that was honest and honourable. It's a notion of mine, that whatever a man may be, his trade does not make him—he makes his trade" (p. 31).

Sensitive to the objections of his housekeeper to making his father's cart boy a companion, the lonely Phineas does not for a time see as much of John as he would like. On such occasions when he does, Phineas, reflecting the feminine sensibility of his creator, records the gentlemanly qualities which endear him to John. At one point it is John's tenderness: "a quality different from kindliness, affectionateness, or benevolence; a quality which can exist only in strong, deep, and undemonstrative natures, and therefore in its perfection oftenest found in men. John Halifax had it more than any one, woman or man, that I ever knew" (pp. 23-24). At another time Phineas calls attention to John's "natural deference," not the homage paid by the employee to the master's son, but the respect offered by the younger to the elder and by the strong to the weak (p. 28). On still another occasion Phineas notes that John possessed "a character the keystone of which was that whereon is built all liking and all love— *dependableness*. He was one whom you may be long in knowing, but whom the more you know the more you trust; and once trusting you trust forever" (pp. 29-30).

Along with the personal qualities which Phineas enumerates, John possesses the determination and perseverance which will enable him to carry out the boyish boast: "If I get one foot on the ladder, perhaps I may climb" (p. 30). While driving his cart along country roads, John teaches himself to add and to read. Phineas sends him appropriate reading matter: the primer of the economic man, *Robinson Crusoe*, together with *Pilgrim's Progress* and the Bible (pp. 38-39). When his employer learns how profitably he has spent his leisure time, John is promoted to collecting money instead of skins. During a flood John demonstrates that he has his employer's interests at heart, by alarming Abel Fletcher to the danger. The outcome of this episode is his master's realization that John is virtually indispensable to the tanning concern. John is placed on a more equal footing with his employer when Fletcher decides to take him on as an apprentice, with the view that he might someday manage the tan-yard for the invalid Phineas. This arrangement is quite satisfactory to the young man, who nevertheless has other dreams of his own. Among the books in his room is the model of a loom (pp. 80-81).

After several years of work in the tannery, John earns a month in the country with Phineas. While there, two significant events transpire: John meets his future wife, Ursula, and he has an opportunity to visit the cloth mill at Enderley, of which in time he will be the master. Ursula March, the daughter of a former governor of the West Indies, is taken with the gentlemanly courtesy of Halifax, who performs the office of a friend while her father is dying. Upon his death, Ursula, alone in the world, takes up residence with her aristocratic relatives in Norton Bury, where Fletcher's tan-yard is located. An elderly couple who know of John's kindness to Ursula invite him to a social gathering. There he encounters Squire Brithwood, Ursula's cousin, who regards anyone connected with trade as an inferior, and he objects to the presence of his cousin's benefactor. Resenting the "tanner-lad's" refusal to acknowledge the superiority of his rank, the Squire strikes Halifax, an insult, we are told, that the code of the aristocrat considered a matter of honor. The middle class Evangelical author points up the falsity of this code by showing that the Christian gentleman will not return blow for blow. Proudly and calmly John extricates himself without loss of dignity. His action earns him the favor of Ursula who later remarks, "You have but shown me what I shall remember all my life—that a Christian can only be a gentleman" (p. 181). After a love sickness equal to that of Troilus, John recovers quickly when, at the instigation of Phineas, Ursula visits him and declares her love (pp. 195-96). When Squire Brithwood hears of their marriage plans, he vows that, as trustee for her father's estate, he will not allow Ursula one penny of her fortune, and John is too proud to exercise his legal right lest he be deemed a fortune hunter. Moreover, it is unchristian to fight even a legal battle.

For a dozen years the couple live modestly on John's income from his partnership in the tan-yard. John continues tinkering with his models and dreams about the possibility of applying steam power to a cloth mill (p. 213). One day he is approached by Lord Luxmore who owns the land on which the Enderley mill is built. Knowing of John's ambition to lease it and also of his lack of capital, Lord Luxmore influences Squire Brithwood to release Ursula's fortune. The earl counts upon John's popularity as a peacemaker among the people of Norton Bury to help him send his henchman to Parliament. A boarder in the Halifax home after his father's death, Phineas Fletcher is overjoyed at the prospect of John as a mill-owner. He sees a Christian God's hand in this: "That one bad man, for his own purposes, should influence another bad man to an act of justice—and that this double evil should be made to work out our good! Also that this should come just in our time of need—when John's strength seemed ready to fail" (p. 242). After taking out a lease on the mill, however, John Halifax foils Lord Luxmore by exposing his man as unqualified for Parliament. The aristocrat has a temporary revenge by diverting the stream that turns the water wheel of the Enderley mill. But once more good comes out of evil when John counters by making his dream of a steam driven mill a reality. That stroke symbolizes his final independence of the aristocracy. Now he can devote himself to a career of usefulness to his mill hands:

> At last, his long life of duty was merging into the life he loved. He looked as proud and as pleased as a boy, in talking of the new inventions he meant to apply in cloth-weaving; and how he and his wife had agreed together to live for some years to come at little Longfield, strictly

within their settled income, that all the remainder of his capital might
go to the improvement of Enderley Mills and mill-people.

"I shall be master of nearly a hundred—men and women. Think
what good we may do! She has half-a-dozen plans on foot already—
bless her dear heart!" (p. 259)

With respect to his work people, the new millowner acts the friend as
well as master. He gives consideration to all they say and remembers
each by name. To his children, he explains the reason for the consequent
contentment of his employees:

> "Our people will work the better, because they will work from love.
> Not merely doing their duty and obeying their master in a blind way,
> but feeling an interest in him and all that belongs to him; knowing
> that he feels the same in them. Knowing, too, that although, being
> their superior in many things, he is their master and they his servants,
> he never forgets that saying, which I read out of the Bible, children, this
> morning: 'One is your master—even Christ, and all ye are brethren.'"
> (p. 277)

As John Halifax's fortunes grow, he desires to extend his sphere of usefulness by moving from the confines of Longfield to the "great house" at
Beechwood Hall, in the village where his factory is located. His son Guy is
delighted with the prospect of aristocratic pastimes and his daughter
Maud, with visions of numerous visiting carriages. Their father, however,
does not have those objects in mind. During the conversation in which
he explains his reasons for moving to an aristocratic mansion comes the
thematic climax of Dinah Mulock's story of a man who has never de-
valued the moral worth of the virtuous Christian and who at the same
time has successfully met the popular standard of a gentleman:

> "When I was a young man, before your mother and I were married,
> indeed before I had ever seen her, I had strongly impressed on my mind
> the wish to gain influence in the world—riches if I could—but at all
> events, influence. I thought I could use it well, better than most men;
> those can best help the poor who understand the poor. And I can; since,
> you know, when your Uncle Phineas found me, I was—"
> "Father," said Guy, flushing scarlet, "we may as well pass over
> that fact. We are gentlefolks now."
> "We always were, my son." (p. 333)

By making gentility synonymous with respectability, Dinah Mulock
pays tribute to the noblest ideal of that element of the English middle
classes which was nurtured by the Evangelical revival. If, however, we

recognize that the author's social and religious attitudes are rooted in this background, we might further detect a form of snobbery at work in the novel. John Halifax is desirous of being on an equal footing with the old county families, but he wants them to conform to his view of morality. He accepts their virtue, which in his eyes is their being in a position of power to do good; but at the same time he scorns their frailties. Thus, he takes great pains to discourage Ursula's occasional aristocratic visitor, the clever and accomplished but adulterous Lady Caroline, daughter of Lord Luxmore. At one time he tactfully, but somewhat ungallantly, denies her entrance into his home (pp. 214-16). And at another, he sternly upbraids her for planning to run away with a lover from her drunken and impossible husband, Squire Brithwood (pp. 252-53). And when her brother William, the future Earl or Luxmore, reveals an interest in John's daughter, he is denied her hand. John points to their disparity in rank, but the implication is that the nobleman, despite his innocuousness, is faulted for his aristocratic birth.

To appreciate fully the virtues of the middle station in life toward which he is looking, the aristocrat must undergo John's experience of life in reverse. Becoming the new Earl of Luxmore upon his father's death, the peer makes himself penniless when he espouses a middle class view of honor—he sells his estate to pay off the former earl's creditors. After a two years penance in America as plain William Ravenel, hard working but unsuccessful, the humbled nobleman returns to England. He is regarded as a wiser and better man for the experience and is now an acceptable husband for Maud Halifax (p. 426, 451-54).

As viewed in this episode, Dinah Mulock's opinion of the nobility reveals an affinity with that of the religious revivalist Hannah More, who best summarizes this prevalent middle class attitude. In her *Thoughts Concerning the Manners of the Great* (1809), Hannah More insisted that the higher orders of society were in need of moral fibre, as well as social graces and accomplishments: "Mere decorum of manners . . . without a strict attention to religious principle is a constant source of danger to the rich and the great." It was a mistake to consider respectable those who observed only the outward forms of religion.[29] Accordingly, Dinah Mulock's true gentleman was distinct from the ordinary nobleman. Making his pattern of behavior the living embodiment of the chapters of the New Testament, the Christian gentleman protected the weak, the defenseless, and the dependent. In addition to the public virtue of power responsibly exercised, he also had a private virtue which Dinah Mulock equally extolls: a devout commitment to "home-love, married love, love among children and at the fireside" (p. 251).

III

Mrs. Halliburton's Troubles

The idyllic picture of moral worth as the qualification not only for true gentility, but also the factor that, with the aid of Providence, leads to worldly success is not without its charm and no doubt accounts for the popularity of such a work as *John Halifax*. But beyond the world of the Evangelical and the gospel of Smiles, moral excellence as a measure of the gentleman was much too difficult to evaluate:

> There existed generally a vague idea that the conception of a gentleman ought to include moral attributes; it was indeed an idea which hovered through much nineteenth century thought and was not without its influence on social values, but as a conception, it was unlikely to be precise enough or powerful enough to be the ruling principle in determining social position. People were not going to test a man's gentility solely by the touchstone of his morals or his behaviour; the results of an attempt to do this would be too revolutionary and inconvenient. . . .[30]

Still, the spirit of self-help that Smiles represented had linked moral attributes with the success of industrialists, engineers, and inventors. To a civilization that was becoming increasingly complex, the men who built its railways, constructed machinery for its factories, and clothed its population performed complicated services that warranted social recognition. But how was it to be granted? That such men as these, along with the commercial classes in general, were numerous enough to have changed in the 1860s the character of the Lower House was a reality noted by Walter Bagehot in 1872:

> The Reform Act of 1867 has, I think, unmistakeably completed the effect which the Act of 1832 began, but left unfinished. The middle class element has gained greatly by the second change, and the aristocratic element has lost greatly. . . . The Spirit of our present House of Commons is plutocratic, not aristocratic; its most prominent statesmen are not men of ancient or of great hereditary estate; they are men mostly of substantial means, but they are mostly, too, connected more or less closely to the new trading class wealth.[31]

Political reforms only emphasized the multiplication of these individuals. As the members of this category took their places in Parliament, a new ruling caste which included the professional classes and the leaders of commerce and industry, as well as the old landed gentry, came into being. With the formation of a new gentry, "some tests were needed which would extend the number of new gentlemen, and which would rationalize and moralize the conception of a gentleman to a generation for whom the old naïve touchstones of blood, or heraldry, or landownership would by no means suffice."[32]

A test which would provide a suitably objective standard of judgment was that of a liberal education in the public schools and the Universities of Oxford and Cambridge.[33] Bagehot had held that the sons of the middle classes could be made into gentlemen if sent to the right school. In this connection, Harold Nicolson explains, "The public school was regarded as a melting pot in which the rich industrials could be fused with the old aristocracy by somewhat drastic means. Bagehot entitled the method 'removable inequality.'"[34] And in contrast to the professional education found in German and Scottish universities, Oxford and Cambridge provided a liberal education and thus served as a bulwark against materialism and professionalism. The graduates of English institutions acquired a uniformity of culture and manners, and as G. M. Young summarizes, "the Universities broke the fall of the aristocracy by civilizing the plutocracy."[35] By 1875, and most likely even earlier, the wealthy inhabitants of the industrial districts appear to have had their sons educated in the public schools. In his account of the formation of a new gentry, Kitson Clark sees the assimilation of the industrials as the last stage of the consolidation of the new gentry:

> First there had been the broadening of the conception of a gentleman by the emphasis on the test of the education of a gentleman, a broadening of which the professional classes had made use. Then there had been the development and multiplication of the institutions which could give that education, and now the sons of the leaders of industry were drawn in also. They were very often drawn to places of education remote from the places where their parents had made or were making their money; they mixed with the sons of men of different traditions; they learnt a new way of talking and of thinking; they were trained in disciplines which often had no relation to the scientific side of their work; they were drawn away from the men who must continue to be the rank and file and non-commissioned officers of industry, and they became acclimatized to a life which very often drew them out of industry altogether.[36]

The fact that industrialists were the last to be assimilated into the new gentry lends credence to what might seem an all too simple generalization on the part of Kitson Clark. In order to validate that historian's conclusion, we might examine the objections and obstacles which account in part for the lag.

First of all, throughout a good part of the nineteenth century there had existed the belief that a public school or university education was unsuitable for the sons of millowners. In *North and South* (1856), Mrs. Gaskell suggests as much when she makes Mr. Hale's position as tutor dependent upon this prejudice. Describing some of his pupils, Mrs. Gaskell observes:

> They were mostly of the age when many boys would be still at school, but, according to the prevalent and apparently well-founded notions of [Manchester], to make a lad into a good tradesman, he must be caught young, and acclimatized to the life of the mill, or office, or warehouse. If he were sent even to the Scotch Universities, he came back unsettled for commercial pursuits: how much more so if he went to Oxford or Cambridge where he could not enter till he was eighteen? So most of the manufacturers placed their sons in sucking situations at fourteen or fifteen years of age, unsparingly cutting away all off-shoots in the direction of literature or high mental cultivation, in hopes of throwing the whole strength and vigour of the plant into commerce. (p. 63)[37]

The manufacturer's objection to literature and culture was a decided rejection of the classical curriculum which formed the backbone of liberal education.[38] The Spartan mother of John Thornton in *North and South*, for example, did not approve of the revival of interest in Greek displayed by her son, even after he had become a successful manufacturer. She told his tutor, Mr. Hale: "I have no doubt that classics are very desirable for people who have leisure. But I confess, it was against my judgment that my son renewed his study of them. The time and place in which he lives, seems to me to require all his energy and attention. Classics may do very well for men who loiter away their lives in the country or in colleges; but [Manchester] men ought to have their thoughts and powers absorbed in the work of today" (p. 107). In spite of the fact that he is currently studying Greek, John Thornton agrees with the substance of his mother's argument. Character, especially the traits of self-denial and perseverance, not a classical education are the essentials for the man struggling to succeed. His tutor Mr. Hale, however, somewhat naïvely insists upon attributing Thornton's success in some degree to his earlier exposure to a classical education; but Thornton remains unconvinced:

> "But you had had the rudiments of a good education," remarked Mr. Hale. "The quick zest with which you are now reading Homer shows me that you do not come to it as an unknown book: you have read it before and are only recalling your old knowledge."
> "That is true—I had blundered along it at school; I dare say I was even considered a pretty fair classic in those days, though my Latin and Greek have slipped away from me since. But I ask you what preparation they were for such a life as I had to lead? None at all. Utterly

none at all. On the point of education, any man who can read and write starts fair with me in the amount of really useful knowledge that I had at that time."

"Well, I don't agree with you. But there I am perhaps somewhat of a pedant. Did not the recollection of the heroic simplicity of the Homeric life nerve you up?"

"Not a bit!" exclaimed Mr. Thornton, laughing. "I was too busy to think about any dead people with the living pressing alongside of me, neck to neck in the struggle for bread." (pp. 79-80)

But lest Thornton appear the Philistine, Mrs. Gaskell, later in the novel, allows the manufacturer an intellectual justification for his attitude toward the classics. He tells Mr. Bell, a tutor at Oxford:

If we do not reverence the past as you do in Oxford, it is because we want something which can apply to the present more directly. It is fine when the study of the past leads to a prophecy of the future. But to men groping in new circumstances, it would be finer if the words of experience could direct us how to act in what concerns us most intimately and immediately; which is full of difficulties that must be encountered; and upon the mode in which they are met and conquered— not merely pushed aside for the time—depends our future. Out of the wisdom of the past, help us over the present. But no! People can speak of Utopia much more easily than of the next day's duty; and yet when that duty is all done by others, who [is] so ready to cry, "Fie, for shame!" (pp. 324-25)

Still another factor which tended to discourage a university education for the sons of the "rich industrials" was the obstacle of religion. Throughout the nineteenth century, Nonconformity was strong in the industrial North. Although some of the second generation of industrialists joined the Church of England (as is the case with the son of a dissenting cotton manufacturer in Kingsley's *Yeast*), the Oxford Movement had the effect of confirming Nonconformists in their dissent.[39] It was not until the Acts of 1854 and 1856 that Dissenters were permitted to matriculate without signing the Thirty-Nine Articles. Still, fellowships and colleges or university offices were denied to them. (The senior wranglers at Cambridge were barred from fellowships in 1860 and 1861 because of religious tests.) From 1863 onward, annual bills were introduced to repeal the remaining tests and by 1871, writes E. L. Woodward, "the citadel was taken."[40]

Through her portrait of the gentleman manufacturer Mrs. Henry Wood reflects the historical trend toward assimilation discussed above. In *Mrs. Halliburton's Troubles* (1862), Thomas Ashley, a second generation glove manufacturer, possesses wealth, moral worth and, above all, a liberal education. As such he is for Mrs. Wood the complete English gentleman. Early in the novel a Quakeress describes Ashley's affluence and moral stature to his new tenant Mrs. Halliburton:

> Thomas Ashley is one of the first manufacturers in the city, as his father was before him. When thee shall know the place and the people better, thee will find that there is not a name more respected throughout Helstonleigh than that of Thomas Ashley. . . . His household is an expensive one, and he keeps his open and his close carriage. . . . It is not for his riches that Thomas Ashley is respected, but for his high character. There is not a juster man living than Thomas Ashley; there is not a manufacturer in the town who is so considerate and so kind to his workmen. His rate of wages is on the highest scale, and he is incapable of oppression.[41]

But Mrs. Halliburton has cause to doubt the character of Ashley when his lawyer, Anthony Dare, pretending to act on Ashley's orders, threatens to evict the widow from her rented cottage for reasons of his own. When she describes her plight to the Quakeress, Patience is nonplussed and offers an example of Ashley's demonstrated charitableness:

> It is not like Thomas Ashley. I will give thee an instance of his disposition and general character. There was a baker rented under him. . . . The baker got behind with his rent; other bakers were more favoured than he; but he kept on at his trade, hoping times would mend. Year by year he failed in his rent—Thomas Ashley, mark thee, still paying him regularly for the bread supplied to his family. "Why do you not stop his bread-money?" asked one, who knew of this, of Thomas Ashley. "Because he is poor, and he looks to my weekly money, with that of others, to buy his flour," was Thomas Ashley's answer. Well, when he owed several years' rent, the baker died, and the widow was going to move. Anthony Dare hastened to Thomas Ashley. "Which day shall I levy a distress upon the goods?" asked he. "Not at all," replied Thomas Ashley. And he went to the widow, and told her the rent was forgiven, and the goods were her own, to take with her when she left. That is Thomas Ashley. (p. 93)

Patience advises Mrs. Halliburton to apply directly to Ashley: "Thee art his tenant. As to hearing thee, that he certainly would. Thomas Ashley is of a courteous nature. The poorest workman in our manufactory, going to the master with a grievance, is sure of a patient hearing" (p. 94). The widow takes her friend's advice and her first glimpse of Ashley convinces her that he is a "thorough gentleman" (p. 95). When she beseeches him not to oppress her for failing to pay her rent, Ashley quietly replies, "I have never oppressed any one in my life" (p. 96). And we can guess that when Ashley discovers his lawyer's high-handed treatment of the widow, he reproves him and offers her a rental on generous terms.

Thus far there is little difference between this employer and the stereotype of the ideal employer that Disraeli delineates in Trafford, who resembles the paternalistic, feudal landlord. Yet what differentiates the figure of Thomas Ashley from most of the other industrialists in this study is the attention his creator devotes to his education. Mrs. Halliburton discovers that Ashley was trained as a classical scholar at the college school attached to the town cathedral. His father desired him to enter a profession, rather than the business of manufacturing gloves, but Ashley insisted upon succeeding his father (p. 135). Intending to provide the same kind of education for her sons, the widow inquires about the cathedral school that Ashley attended. She learns that the school is no longer highly thought of, since its curriculum consists of the study of Latin and Greek exclusively. With wise forethought Ashley's father made up for this deficiency by providing his son with tutors for the subjects not taught at the college school, and for sundry undefined "accomplishments." Ashley's factory manager describes his employer as "one of the most accomplished men of the day," adding that, "few are so thoroughly and comprehensively educated as is Thomas Ashley" (p. 136). Although Mrs. Wood does not designate what subjects Ashley studied in addition to the classics, we can judge the nature of his comprehensive education by what Jane Halliburton notes is slighted by the classical curriculum.

> But though the classics are essential parts of a liberal education, they do not comprise all its requisites. And nothing else was taught at the college school. There certainly was a writing-master, and something like an initiation into the first rules of arithmetic was attempted; but not a boy in the charity school, hard by, but could have shamed the college boys in adding up a column of figures or writing a page. As to their English—. You should have seen them attempt to write a letter. In short, the college school ignored everything except Latin and Greek. (p. 207)

Greatly concerned by this state of affairs, Mrs. Halliburton resolves to tutor her sons in history, geography, astronomy, and particularly English composition.

Despite the inadequacy of the exclusively classical education for the man of business, the study of Latin is omnipresent in this novel as the hallmark of the gentleman. The language, the knowledge of which saved Ben Jonson from punishment for manslaughter, still has a talismanic power through which the eldest Halliburton boy William gains the respect of Thomas Ashley, who is, according to his son Henry, "one of the best classical scholars of the day—although he is a manufacturer" (p. 150). William, who works in Ashley's glove factory in order to support his widowed mother and his brothers, had learned Latin from his father. On one occasion he is sent by the factory manager on an errand to the Ashley home. While waiting to deliver his message, William instructs his employer's son Henry in the cases of Latin nouns. After William departs, Henry declares to his father that it is a pity that a boy that knows Latin so well should work in a factory. Ashley reminds his son that the education of a gentleman is not inconsistent with factory work:

> "The only 'pity' is that he is in it too early," was the response of Mr. Ashley. "His Latin would not be any detriment to his being in a manufactory or the manufactory to his Latin. I am a manufacturer myself, Henry. You appear to ignore that sometimes."
> "The Dares go on so. They din it in my ears that a manufacturer cannot be a gentleman."
> "I shall cause you to drop the acquaintance of the Dares if you allow yourself to listen to all the false and foolish notions they may give utterance to. Cyril Dare will probably go into a manufactory himself." (p. 151)

After his employer discovers William's interest in Latin, the young man is given his evenings free to pursue his studies. The remainder of the novel treats, on the one hand, the grooming of young Halliburton as Ashley's successor and, on the other, the degeneration of Lawyer Dare's family, with their false notions of gentility. Halliburton's upright conduct and his learning eventually earn him a partnership along with the envy of the Dares, who had expected their scapegrace son Cyril to have filled that place. Ashley informs Lawyer Dare of his son's idleness and deceitfulness, and in the matter of a successor, the manufacturer continues, " 'Whoever I take must be a man of probity and honour: and a gentleman,' he added with a stress upon the word. 'William Halliburton is all that' " (p. 421). By striving to equal Ashley in character and the estimation of his fellow citizens, William earns both the position of manager of the glove manufactory and the hand of his employer's daughter. Upon his retirement from the firm, Ashley is appointed high sheriff of the county. In the pageantry of the high sheriff's procession at the assizes, Mrs. Wood displays the reverence of the town of Helstonleigh for their gentleman-manufacturer. In a rare narrative paragraph she fuses the estimation in which Ashley is held with the physical fact of the approaching procession:

> A blast, shrill and loud, from the advancing heralds, was borne on the air of the bright March afternoon, as the cavalcade advanced up

East Street. The javelin-men rode next, two abreast, in the plain dark Ashley livery, the points of their javelins glittering in the sunshine hardly able to advance for the crowd. A feverish crowd. Little cared they to-day for the proud trumpets, for the javelin bearers, for the various attractions that made their delight on other of these days; they cared but for that stately equipage in the rear. Not for its four prancing horses, for its shining silver ornaments, for its portly coachman on the hammer-cloth, not even for the very judges themselves; but for the master of that carriage, the high sheriff, Thomas Ashley. (p. 464)[42]

IV

Marquis and Merchant

A more superficial sign of assimilation was the purchase of country estates by industrialists.[43] Indeed, much to the chagrin of the landed gentry, such acquisitions are commonplace in the novels we have considered. For example, the elder Millbank succeeded in his deliberate attempt to vex Coningsby's grandfather Lord Monmouth by purchasing an adjoining estate. In The Two Aristocracies, Mark Barneson unwittingly produces the same effect upon Sir Arscott Littlecote. And the presence of a manufacturer in another of Mrs. Gore's novel Cromer Hall (1846) so discomfits the resident Squire that he sells his ancestral lands and moves to Bath. Nor were the Greshams pleased at having Roger Scatcherd buy neighboring Boxhall.

Mortimer Collins's Marquis and Merchant (1871) also reveals that sort of land hunger, but its greater significance and appropriateness as the work which brings this study to a close lies in its expression of a changing aristocratic attitude toward the genteel aspirations of the captain of industry during the period of the formation of a new gentry.

Collins was not without aristocratic prejudices, but these were tempered with a general respect for trade. A self-styled bohemian, Collins considered himself a poet and a novelist but he earned his living chiefly as a journalist. Of his political interests his wife writes: "He was an able political writer, and wrote so many political squibs, that he was once shown a small room, almost entirely papered with them. He was always a Tory, and boasted that while yet a school-boy, he managed to change the politics of a provincial paper from Liberal to Conservative."[44] In a letter written to a friend in 1875, Collins records that he did not begin writing fiction "till after a long pull at journalism," and exults in his fights with publishers and the abuse heaped upon him by Radical critics because of his having been a "Tory editor" all his life.[45] During the last ten years of his life he was a Conservative journalist for the Globe and a weekly contributor to the St.

James Chronicle. His liberal attitude toward London commerce is revealed in an article entitled "Trade Union, True and False (1874)." In it he proposed that the twelve City Companies of London create a "Civic University" and by granting degrees ennoble trade. He continues: "Trade is an honourable vocation. It is the occupation of many gentlemen of the highest character and standing. If this were more completely and generally recognized it would be a great benefit."[46]

In *Marquis and Merchant* Collins offers two uncomplicated reasons for a Manchester millionaire's purchase of a country estate. For one, he desired to glorify himself in the eyes of his associates in the "City of Cotton" by playing the country gentleman. For another, he intended to thwart a marquis who had planned to buy the same estate.[47] Mowbray, the millionaire, "courteous and genial with his equals, and very generous to his inferiors . . . acknowledged no superior" (1:97). Harboring a dislike for the peerage, he "wanted to be a thorn in aristocratic flesh" (1:115). His first meeting with his aristocratic neighbor, however, leaves him temporarily puzzled. Adrian, son of Lord Waynflete welcomes him: "My father wanted to buy the property . . . but he will soon get over his disappointment. You are going to build; you will set the people's blood circulating; you will do good among them, and stimulate others to do good" (1:69). Such liberal views coming from a member of a family he considers staunchly Tory surprise Mowbray. Believing that a sinister, ulterior motive lies behind Adrian's gracious welcome, the Manchester millionaire chooses to be churlish rather than civil in his dealings. He prohibits turf cutting on his estate and will not permit gypsies to camp there annually. As a final gesture, he encloses Ashridge Common with an iron fence. Resentful of his infringement upon their time honored privilege, the gypsies kidnap his daughter. When Adrian recovers her, the millionaire buries his contempt for the House of Lords, and thus trade and rank are reconciled.

If we regard Collins, the Tory editor, as representative of a body of Conservative opinion, his novel suggests that the principle of aristocratic exclusiveness has changed since the time when the writer of Arkwright's obituary (1791) complimented that pioneer industrialist solely for his utility. "A Tory," states Collins's marquis to the Manchester millionaire, "is a man who believes England should be governed by gentlemen. A Liberal is a man who believes any Englishman may become a gentleman if he likes. I am both" (1:171). This echo of the idea of advanced Conservative Liberalism, which for Trollope signified a tendency toward the equalization of social conditions as civilization progressed, has another, less lofty meaning for Collins and for many of his countrymen. With the consolidation of land, commerce, and industry into a new gentry, a new ruling caste, England—strengthened by the union of formerly antagonistic economic groups—shall become the aristocracy of nations, "a sacred island . . . the cradle of the world-governing race" (3:233). The march of civilization shall see "the triumph of the highest race. . . . the development of the English race everywhere" (3:232). On the other end of the world's social hierarchy will be Chinese, who will henceforth be its day laborers (3:232). Frances Collins once praised her husband's novels for their original ideas. Although some of them appear far-fetched in print, Collins is the herald of a new era—the age of imperialism.

Notes

INTRODUCTION

1. (London, 1963), p. 704. Matthew Boulton to James Boswell on the latter's visit in 1776 to the Soho Iron Works where Boulton and James Watt manufactured steam engines.

2. Henry Adams, *The Education of Henry Adams* (New York, 1964), 2:297.

3. *The Making of Victorian England* (Cambridge, Mass., 1962), p. 273.

4. In John Galt's *Annals of the Parish* (1821), the factory workers who came to the new cotton mill at Cayenneville in 1788 brought a new spirit to the Reverend Micah Balwhidder's parish. They subscribed to a London newspaper, which presumably was congenial to their democratic ideas, and questioned orthodox beliefs about government and religion. *The Works of John Galt*, ed. D. S. Meldrum and W. Roughead, 1 (Edinburgh, 1936): 183-84. By 1802 Galt's chronicler notes that in addition to the London daily newspaper subscription, Cayenneville now had a bookseller's shop, magazines, reviews and other new writings. Balwhidder observes that "mankind read more, and the spirit of reflection and reasoning was more awake than at any time within my remembrance." Galt, *Works*, 2:30. The extraordinary popularity of Paine's *Rights of Man* at the turn of the century gives some indication of the kind of reading matter that interested Galt's democratic weavers. "No single piece of nonce literature," writes Richard Altick, "so far as the few available records indicate, had ever approached such a circulation." *The English Common Reader* (Chicago, 1963), pp. 70-71. Tom Paine along with Hannah More "had opened the book to the common English reader." Altick, p. 77. The northern factory worker's contempt for the aristocrat's dependent, the agricultural laborer of the South, is expressed in his Lancashire dialect by Mrs. Gaskell's strike leader, Nicholas Higgins (to Margaret Hale): "I know naught of your ways down South. I have heerd they're a pack of spiritless, down-trodden men; welly clemmed [starved] to death; too much dazed wi' clemming to know when they're put upon. Now, it's not so here. We know when we're put upon; and we'en too much blood in us to stand it. We just take our hands fro' our looms, and say, 'Yo may clem us, but yo'll not put upon us, my masters!' " *North and South* (London, 1961), p. 127.

5. See Emerson on "Aristocracy" in his *English Traits* (1856), *English Traits, Representative Men, and Other Essays* (London, 1919), pp. 98-99. (Emerson viewed the middle classes an an "untitled nobility [who] possess all the power without the in-

conveniences that belong to rank."); and "Manifesto of the Communist Party (1848),"
in *Basic Writings on Politics and Philosophy. Marx, Karl, and Friedrick Engels,* ed.
Lewis S. Feuer (New York, 1959), pp. 9-10.

6. G. von Schulze-Gaevernitz, *Social Peace,* trans. C. M. Wicksteed (London,
1893), pp. 18-19.

7. "The England of Marx and Mill as Reflected in Fiction," *Journal of Economic
History,* Supplement 8 (1948), 43. For a similar warning against the uncritical use
of social novels as sources of economic and social history, see W. H. Chaloner, "Mrs.
Trollope and the Early Factory System," *VS,* 4 (1960), 166.

8. "Social Background and Social Thought," in *The Reinterpretation of Victorian
Literature,* ed. Joseph E. Baker (Princeton, 1950), p. 9. Neff also notes the need to
explore Victorian fiction "for evidence of the increasing fluidity of classes . . . of the
relative social standing of the professions, of trade, finance, and manufacture." Ibid,
p. 16.

9. The relative scarcity of novels dealing with industrialists written during the
period 1760-1830 is perhaps explained as a lag. Norbert Gossman has examined part
of the period in his study, "Political and Social Themes in the English Popular Novel,
1815-1832," *Public Opinion Quarterly,* 20 (1956): 531-41. Gossman has found that
the Industrial Revolution was rarely mentioned in fiction, that the old agrarian life was
preferred because of a desire for the stability of the past, and that social problems were
those of the old order; for example, absentee landlordism. He concludes that popular
opinion continued to reflect a respect for the aristocracy because of its important social
role in society. Judging from Gossman's results, it would appear that Jane Austen was
not alone among novelists in her indifference to the social problems and political questions of the Napoleonic era and its aftermath.

10. Peter Gaskell, *The Manufacturing Population of England* (London, 1833),
pp. 40-42. Paul Mantoux, *The Industrial Revolution in the Eighteenth* Century (New
York and Evanston, 1962), p. 370.

11. *The Age of Improvement, 1783-1867* (New York, 1964), p. 411.

CHAPTER ONE

1. Friedrich Engels, *The Condition of the Working Class in England* (1845),
trans. and ed. W. O. Henderson and W. H. Chaloner (Oxford, 1958), p. 9.

2. Quoted in A. L. Morton, *The Life and Ideas of Robert Owen* (New York,
1963), p. 16.

3. The phrase is Henry Nash Smith's. See his *Virgin Land* (New York, 1957), p.
154. Chapter 12 of that work treats the idea of the yeoman in America.

4. Paul Mantoux, *The Industrial Revolution in the Eighteenth Century* (New
York and Evanston, 1962), pp. 369-73.

5. In the course of explaining the Englishman's land hunger, Disraeli provides a
useful breakdown of the successive waves of new wealth in England over the centuries:

In a commercial country like England, every half century develops some new and
vast source of public wealth, which brings into national notice a new and powerful
class. A couple of centuries ago, a Turkey Merchant was the great creator of wealth;
the West India Planter followed him. In the middle of the last century appeared the

Nabob. These characters in their zenith in turn merged in the land, and became English aristocrats; while, the Levant decaying, the West Indies exhausted, and Hindostan plundered, the breeds died away, and now exist only in our English comedies, from Wycherly and Congreve to Cumberland and Morton. The expenditure of the revolutionary war produced the Loanmonger, who succeeded the Nabob; and the application of science to industry developed the Manufacturer, who in turn aspires to be "large-acred" and always will, as long as we have a territorial constitution; a better security for the preponderance of the landed interest than any corn-law, fixed or fluctuating. *Sybil* [1845] (Harmondsworth, 1954), pp. 81-82.

6. Arnold Toynbee, *The Industrial Revolution* (Boston, 1960), pp. 30-39. This work was originally published in 1884. For a brief account of the gradual extinction of the yeoman class in Yorkshire, see Mrs. Elizabeth Gaskell's *The Life of Charlotte Brontë* (London, 1960), pp. 12-13. The desirability of land ownership as a basis of power is evident in the virtually omnipotent position of the eighteenth-century country squire, whose functions extended to most aspects of country life. In addition to serving as justices of the peace at Quarter or Petty Sessions, they licensed public houses, levied county rates, administered the Poor Law, and were responsible for the maintenance of bridges and prisons. From the Glorious Revolution to the Reform Bill, the squirearchy "were the real rulers of England." Kenneth C. Slagle, *The English Country Squire as Depicted in English Prose Fiction from 1740-1800* (Philadelphia, 1938), p. 7.

7. Mantoux, pp. 370-71.

8. Ibid., p. 370. Ironmasters seem to have come from small workshops, but even so, Mantoux maintains, "a further inquiry into the origins of their families would more than once bring us back to the country and the peasant class." Ibid., p. 372.

9. Peter Gaskell, *The Manufacturing Population of England* (London, 1833), p. 41. Gaskell (d.1841) was a surgeon who practised near the cotton district of Lancashire.

10. Another historian of industrial society holds that the origins of the manufacturing class tend to be obscured "by the flow of capital from one economic field to another; by the rapid economic change; and by the interlocking and overlapping connections of the new manufacturers with merchants, landlords, and farmers, artizans, and the old petty manufacturers." Witt Bowden, *Industrial Society in England Towards the End of the Eighteenth Century* (New York, 1925), pp. 138-39.

11. T. S. Ashton, *The Industrial Revolution: 1760-1830* (London, 1962), pp. 16-17. For the various sources of industrial capital, see pp. 94-95 of Ashton's study.

12. *Memoir of Edmund Cartwright* (1825), quoted in Bowden, p. 155.

13. Ashton, p. 17.

14. Bowden, pp. 136, 146, 142-44. The industrialist's economic rise, moreover, was made possible not by monopoly but by the enormous productivity of the new machinery. Evidence of the rapid accumulation of capital both by the small owner of machinery and the large-scale manufacturer is found in Robert Owen's account of his career during the 1790s, first as the possessor of only three cotton spinning mules and then as the manager of Drinkwater's mill. *The Life of Robert Owen by Himself* (New York, 1920), pp. 32-36, 48. This work was originally published in 1857.

15. Mantoux, p. 367.

16. Cited by L. G. Johnson in his book, *The Social Evolution of Industrial Britain: A Study in the Growth of Our Industrial Society* (Liverpool, 1959), p. 1.

17. *Manifesto of the Communist Party* (1848) in *Basic Writings on Politics and*

Philosophy: Marx, Karl, and Friedrich Engels, ed. Lewis S. Feuer (New York, 1959), p. 14.

18. Bowden, p. 159. William Cobbett later caustically expatiates upon the barrier between classes imposed by employers who had risen from the "dunghill to the chariot." *The Opinions of William Cobbett*, ed. G. D. H. Cole and Margaret Cole (London, 1944), pp. 86-87.

19. Peter Gaskell, pp. 20-21.

20. Ibid. Gaskell also notes in the same passage that, along with the squirearchy and part of the same social system, "the Yeomanry of England, the small farmers, have fallen victims to the breaking up of a condition of society, and a state of property, which secured a flourishing rural population."

21. Esmé Wingfield-Stratford, *The Squire and His Relations* (London, 1956), p. 239.

22. *Communist Manifesto*, pp. 9-10. In spite of the Carlylean echoes in the passage, Carlyle was critical of both the aristocracy, who put game laws and Corn Laws ahead of their social obligations and the captains of industry, who were of the "Bucanier or Chactaw sort." *Past and Present* (New York, 1918), p. 223.

23. Mantoux, pp. 373-74. Contrary to what one might expect, the great manufacturers were not the great inventors. Hargreaves, Crompton, and Cartwright did not succeed in establishing themselves as industrialists. The only example of the inventor-manufacturer in this period is the dynasty of ironmasters, the Darbys. James Watt was an inventive genius and a manufacturer, but his success as the latter was due to his partnership with Matthew Boulton. It was, then, the manufacturer as entrepreneur who profited from improvements in the techniques of production. Ibid., p. 368.

24. Beginning humbly necessitated personal involvement in one's work and proved an advantage over accumulated capital: "There is a singularity attending the rise of some of these individuals [early cotton manufacturers], showing very strongly how infinitely superior is personal endeavour to accumulated wealth. *Few of the men who entered the trade rich were successful. They trusted too much to others—too little to themselves* [italics mine]; whilst, on the contrary, the men who did establish themselves were raised by their own efforts—commencing in a very humble way, and pushing their advance by a series of unceasing exertions, having a very limited capital to begin with, or even none at all save that of their own labour." Peter Gaskell, p. 45.

25. *The Philosophy of Manufactures*, quoted in Reinhard Bendix, *Work and Authority in Industry: Ideologies of Management in the Course of Industrialization* (New York and Evanston, 1963), p. 59. Continuing his panegyric on Arkwright, Ure makes a comparison which Emerson was to elaborate upon subsequently: "It required, in fact, a man of a Napoleon nerve and ambition to subdue the refractory tempers of work-people accustomed to irregular paroxysms of diligence, and to urge on his multifarious and intricate constructions in the face of prejudice, passion, and envy." Ibid. A decade later, Emerson in *Representative Men* (1844) characterized Napoleon as the prophet of the spirit of commerce, money, and material power, of "the class of business in America, in England, in France . . . the class of industry and skill." *English Traits, Representative Men, and Other Essays* (London, 1919), pp. 260-71. Napoleon's virtues of punctuality, personal attention, courage, and thoroughness (p. 272) are also those generally ascribed to the successful self-made industrialist.

26. Mantoux, p. 377.

27. *Life of Robert Owen*, pp. 39-40. This was not the first time Robert Owen was utterly at a loss as to how to proceed but still able to function successfully. The year

before he became Drinkwater's manager, Owen had left his clerkship and with a borrowed £ 100 ventured into the business of making cotton spinning machinery with a partner, Jones, who professed to be an engineer:

> I soon found however that Jones was a mere working mechanic, without any idea how to manage workmen, or how to conduct business on the scale on which he had commenced.

> I had not the slightest knowledge of this new machinery—had never seen it at work. I was totally ignorant of what was required; but as there were so many men engaged to work for us, I knew that their wages must be paid, and that if they were not well looked after, our business must soon cease and end in our ruin. Jones knew little about book keeping, finance matters, or the superintendence of men. I therefore undertook to keep the accounts—pay and receive all; and I was the first and last in the manufactory. I looked very wise at the men in their different departments, although I really knew nothing. But by intensely observing everything, I maintained order and regularity throughout the establishment. pp. 32-33.

28. Bowden, pp. 160-61.

29. *Thomas Carlyle's Collected Works*, 10 (London, 1869): 398-99. Nor did Carlyle season his admiration for the man who revolutionized cotton spinning with his water frame, for in 1843, he wrote another panegyric, juxtaposing past and present: "Certain times do crystallize themselves in a magnificent manner; and others, perhaps, are like to do it in rather a shabby one!—But Richard Arkwright too will have his Monument, a thousand years hence: all Lancashire and Yorkshire, and how many other shires and countries with their machines and industries, for his monument! A true pyramid or 'flame-mountain,' flaming with steam fires and useful labour over wide continents, usefully towards the Stars, to a certain height;—how much grander than your foolish Cheops Pyramids or Sakhara [sic] clay ones!" *Past and Present* (New York, 1918), p. 69.

30. Bowden, p. 155.   31. Ibid.

32. *Chartism, Works*, 10:398.

33. Bowden, p. 155. By 1787, however, Watt was anything but a mere mechanic, for the Soho firm of Boulton and Watt (visited by Boswell in 1776), was supplying steam engines and machinery to the British Isles and the Continent. Watt's tone of self-deprecation is characteristic of his tendency toward diffidence and despondency and probable proof that without the confident Boulton as a partner, Watt might have remained only a "poor mechanic."

34. Ibid.   35. Ibid.

36. Bowden, pp. 156-57.   37. Emerson, p. 274.

38. Ashton, p. 132. Such anti-labor legislation as the Combination Acts of 1799, which called conspiracy any attempt on the part of workmen to form societies and clubs in order to bargain for improved working conditions from a position of strength, was more a political reaction to the fear of Jacobin revolutionary fervor than collusion on the part of government and manufacturing interests to suppress labor. J. H. Plumb, *England in the Eighteenth Century: 1714-1815* (Harmondsworth, 1959), p. 158.

39. *Lord Beaconsfield* (London and New York, 1914), p. 91. This work was originally published in 1890.

40. *The Opinion of William Cobbett*, pp. 171, 174. Cobbett plays upon the term "cotton lords" in a mock address to "My LORDS SEIGNEURS of the Twist, sovereigns of the Spinning-Jenny." p. 171. From the point of the propertyless working man, who made no distinction between sources of wealth and who thought of all rich

men as gentlemen, "The Three Estates of the Realm were now Crown, Landlord, and Industrial Employers." J. L. Hammond and Barbara Hammond, *The Town Labourer: 1760-1832* (London, 1918), p. 209.

CHAPTER TWO

1. *The Industrial Revolution: 1760-1830* (London, 1962), pp. 16-17.

2. Because full-length portraits of the industrialist in novels written during the period of initial emergence (1760-1832) are rare, it has been necessary to use historical novels written by Victorians between 1836 and 1874. Note 9 of the Introduction accounts in part for writers' lack of interest in industrial matters in the early nineteenth century.

3. Irvin G. Wyllie uses the phrase to describe the American far-right who opposed the idea of self-help on the grounds that it was radical and subversive. See Wyllie's *The Self-Made Man in America* (New Brunswick, 1954), p. 133.

4. John Galt, *The Literary Life, and Miscellanies of John Galt* (Edinburgh, 1834), 1:155-56.

5. *The Autobiography of John Galt* (London, 1833), 2:219.

6. J. G. Lockhart, *Memoirs of the Life of Sir Walter Scott, Bart.* (Edinburgh, 1837), 5:82.

7. *The English Novel: A Panorama* (Boston, 1960), p. 217.

8. *Literary Life*, 1:152.

9. "Annals of the Parish" *Quarterly Review* 25 (April 1821): 147-48.

10. "Secondary Scottish Novels," *Edinburgh Review*, 39 (October 1823): 160-61.

11. A study of the critical reception of a dozen industrial novels reveals that their reviewers were generally more interested in social and economic problems than in making literary judgments. See the Ph.D. dissertation (New York University, 1953) by David Shusterman, "The Victorian Novel of Industrial Conflict: 1832-1870." passim.

12. *Autobiography*, 2:226-28. V. S. Pritchett's statement that the book was "twenty years without a publisher" is thus not quite accurate. See his *The Living Novel* (New York, 1947), p. 51.

13. See, for example, his outburst expressing dislike for orthodox preachers and his tendency to throw things at his servant. *Annals of the Parish* in *The Works of John Galt*, ed. D. S. Meldrum and W. Roughead (Edinburgh, 1936), 1:164-66, 168. It is noteworthy that "Cayenne" was descriptive of choler as early as 1782: "His temper hot as Kayan, taste uncouth." *O.E.D.*

14. *Works*, 1:203-04. On his deathbed, Cayenne is also impious. *Works*, 2:48-50. According to Ernest Baker, Cayenne's blasphemies place him in the Smollett tradition. *The History of the English Novel*, 6 (New York, 1950), 236.

15. *Works*, 2:8-9.   16. *Works*, 2:11.   17. *Works*, 1:175.

18. Ray uses this designation in his classification of authors in the Sadleir collection. See his *Bibliographical Resources for the Study of Nineteenth Century English Fiction* (Los Angeles, 1964).

19. Whether John Kay (b. 1704), the much abused Lancashire inventor of the fly shuttle (1733)—the first of the inventions which were to revolutionize the textile industry—was an ancestor, I have been unable to determine.

20. Frank Smith, *The Life and Work of Sir James Kay-Shuttleworth* (London, 1923), pp. 24-25, 62, 92.

21. Quoted in R. J. Cruikshank, *Charles Dickens and Early Victorian England* (London, 1949), p. 87.

22. Smith, p. 342.   23. Smith, pp. 31-32.

24. Quoted in A. B. Hopkins, *Elizabeth Gaskell: Her Life and Works* (London, 1952), p. 206. Aside from Mrs. Gaskell, who came to Manchester upon her marriage, few of the novelists writing about manufacturers knew the industrial North at first hand. Kay-Shuttleworth, Geraldine Jewsbury, and the would-be novelist Elizabeth Stone are the only Lancastrians in this study. As a rule, these regional novelists tend not to be critical of industrial society. They express a belief in meliorism and have not that sense of a need for immediate action that characterizes the work of polemicists, such as Frances Trollope.

25. Quoted in Hopkins, pp. 167-68.

26. Quoted in Smith, p. 225.

27. *Scarsdale: Life on the Lancashire and Yorkshire Border Thirty Years Ago* (London, 1860), 3:241. I have used the three-volume first edition. Subsequent references to volume and page will be included in the text.

28. That the average early manufacturer had little knowledge and limited ideas outside his own sphere of activity was also Robert Owen's observation.

29. Cf. John Thornton's remark to Margaret Hale in Mrs. Gaskell's *North and South* [1855] (London, 1961), p. 118. "Cromwell would have made a capital mill-owner."

30. *The Uses of Diversity* (New York, 1921), p. 101.

31. In his study, *Religion and the Rise of Capitalism* [1926] (New York, 1958), R. H. Tawney notes that Puritanism had been associated with the counties engaged in textiles as far back as the time of Cromwell: "In Lancashire, the clothing towns—'the Genevas of Lancashire'—rose like Puritan islands from the surrounding sea of Roman Catholicism." p. 169. The most prominent eighteenth-century ironmasters also had a connection with Puritanism. p. 210.

32. R. H. Tawney's phrase. By way of justifying his study, Tawney affirms that making a connection between religious movements in the sixteenth and seventeenth centuries and a surge of economic activity in the Netherlands and England is not "the sinister concoction of a dark modern conspiracy, designed to confound Calvinism and Capitalism, godly Geneva and industrious Manchester in a common ruin." He adds that contemporaries first saw a connection between religious and economic radicalism in those centuries. Ibid, p. 9.

33. *Yeast: A Problem* (London, 1913), pp. 36-37. Restrictive legislation and civil disabilities, though gradually removed in the nineteenth century also circumscribed the careers of Nonconformists by denying them a role in public affairs until 1828 and forbidding them degrees from Oxford and Cambridge until the 1850s. Tawney, p. 209; G. Kitson Clark, *The Making of Victorian England* (Cambridge, Mass., 1962), pp. 38-39, 43.

34. Tawney, pp. 6-7.   35. Tawney, pp. 97, 200-01.

36. Tawney, p. 214.   37. Tawney, p. 226.   38. Tawney, p. 189.

39. *Le Roman Social en Angleterre: 1830-1850* [1904] (Paris, 1934), 2:110-11.

40. *Ribblesdale or Lancashire Sixty Years Ago* (London, 1874), 1:120-21. I have used the three-volume first edition, and as in my discussion of *Scarsdale*, subsequent references to volume and page will be included in the text.

41. Tawney, p. 211.   42. See note 32 above.

43. Tobias Smollett, *The Expedition of Humphry Clinker* [1771] (New York, 1929), pp. 39-40.

44. See Chapter 1, p. 12, note 38.

45. There are two other works dealing with the "horror of parvenuism" that I do not include in this study. They are "The Mill and the Manor (1844)," an anonymous tale that appeared in *Chambers' Edinburgh Journal* and Catherine Gore's *Cromer Hall: or Old Families and New*, the second of two novels gathered in her work, *Men of Business* (1846). In both works, parvenuism serves merely as the plot complication for a love story. The "parvenus" are in every way established and respectable manufacturers whose offspring become enamored of the children of aristocratic families whose sole objection to industrialists is a lack of pedigree. In the first work, the obstacle to marriage is overcome by the discovery of venerable ancestors for the industrialist; and in the second novel, Mrs. Gore permits her aristocrat to override parental authority.

Mrs. Trollope, whose work shall be discussed later in another connection, begins her factory novel, *Michael Armstrong* (1839-40) in the drawing room of her villainous millowner, the scene being designed to display his vulgarity. It is noteworthy, however, that Mrs. Trollope had this first installment in the press before she left London for her one brief trip to Manchester to gather material about factory life.

46. *Plebeians and Patricians*, 1:1-14. I have used the two-volume American edition published in Philadelphia in 1836, the same year that the work first appeared in England.

47. In *Table Talk* (1821-22) in *The Complete Works of William Hazlitt*, ed. P. P. Howe (London and Toronto, 1931), 8:104-5.

48. Hazlitt, *Works*, 8:105.

49. London, 1833, pp. 54-55, 60-61.

50. Peter Gaskell, p. 58.   51. Peter Gaskell, pp. 58-59.

52. Andrew Carnegie's appellation for the speculator also expresses the feelings of industrious Victorian businessmen on the other side of the Atlantic. The phrase is taken from his *The Empire of Business*, quoted in Irvin G. Wyllie's *The Self-Made Man in America* (New Brunswick, 1954), p. 78.

53. Susanne Howe, *Geraldine Jewsbury: Her Life and Errors* (London, 1935), pp. 2-3.

54. Howe, pp. 4-5.

55. "Geraldine and Jane," *TLS*, 28 (February 28, 1929) : 149.

56. *Memoirs of the Life of Sir Samuel Romilly, Written by Himself*, 2d ed. (London, 1840), 2:378-79.

57. *Marian Withers* (London, 1851), 1:21. I have used the three-volume first edition. Subsequent references to volume and page will be included in the text.

58. *The Industrial Revolution: 1760-1830* (London, 1962), p. 113.

59. Harriet Martineau, *History of the Thirty Years' Peace, A.D. 1816-1846* (London, 1911), 2:2,8. Also, Herman Jansonius, *Some Aspects of Business Life in Early Victorian Fiction* (Amsterdam, 1926), p. 168.

60. While the image of the captain of industry gradually approaches the ideal of the gentleman, that of the captain of finance pejorates. This latter phenomenon might be explained by the recurrence of another speculative mania only twenty years later, during the railway boom in 1845-46 when the nation went money mad once more.

61. *Harriet Martineau's Autobiography*, ed. Maria Weston Chapman (Boston, 1877), 1:98.

62. "Speculative Manias," *Chambers's Miscellany of Useful and Entertaining Tracts*, No. 126 (Edinburgh, 1874), 8:1-2.

63. *Yeast: A Problem* [1848] (London, 1913), p. 198.

64. "Hudson's Statue," *Latter-Day Pamphlets* (1850), in *Thomas Carlyle's Col-*

lected Works (London, 1870), 19:317-19. A satiric tale which illustrates how a rail-way was promoted is W. E. Aytoun's "How We Got Up the Glenmutchkin Railway, And How We Got Out of It," *Blackwood's Edinburgh Magazine*, 58 (October 1845): 453-66.

65. *Davenport Dunn: A Man of Our Day* (London, 1859), p. 683.

66. *Our Mutual Friend* [1864-65] (New York, 1964), pp. 136-37.

67. This nobleman devoted all of his revenue but £400 a year to his projects. Even at that, the Duke was at times forced to send his agent riding up and down the countryside to raise capital on his promissory notes. "Account of James Brindley: Canals," in George Lillie Craik, *The Pursuit of Knowledge Under Difficulties* (London, 1830), p. 329.

68. Jansonius, pp. 164-67.   69. Jansonius, pp. 182-83.

70. "The Nineteenth Century," *Fraser's Magazine*, 69 (1864): 482.

71. *The Life of Robert Owen by Himself* [1857] (New York, 1920), p. 47.

72. Owen, *Life*, p. 47.

73. *Hard Times* [1854] (London, 1957), p. 234.

74. For example, the *Life of George Stevenson* (1857), *Lives of the Engineers* (1861-62), *Industrial Biography* (1863), *Boulton and Watt* (1866). *Self-Help* (1859) includes brief biographies for purposes of illustration.

75. *Athenaeum*, No. 1244 (August 30, 1851), p. 921.

76. Hazlitt, *Works*, 8:103-4.

CHAPTER THREE

1. *Reasons for Contentment Addressed to the Labouring Part of the British Public* (London, 1793), pp. 5-7, 8, 22. See also Micah Balwhidder's sermon intended to keep his parishioners "contented with their lowly estate" in the year 1791. *Annals of the Parish* in *The Works of John Galt*, ed. D. S. Meldrum and W. Roughead (Edinburgh, 1936), 1:194. The Church of England was not a guiding force in the Industrial Revolution. By Paley's time the Church no longer had an independent influence over social institutions. It was possessed of a frame of mind that accepted the status quo of class relations, not questioning that economic laws which governed the acquisition of wealth were subject to the higher laws of moral obligation. As a consequence, in its connection with the established order, religion was "not its critic or its accuser, but its anodyne, its apologist, and its drudge." R. H. Tawney, *Religion and the Rise of Capitalism* (New York, 1958), p. 163. That the Established Church showed little understanding of the needs of the working people is evidenced in the clergyman's sermon in *Marian Withers*, 2:121-22.

2. *The Rioters* [1827] (London, 1842), p. 22.

3. The fear of foreign competition which would seem to be exaggerated by English manufacturers is not without a basis in fact. Describing the industrial activity of Julien Sorel's birthplace, a small town in a French province near the Swiss border, Stendhal writes: "It is not . . . the saw-mills [of the peasant class] that have enriched this little town. It is the manufacture of print cloth called 'Mulhouse'; from this has come the general prosperity which has rebuilt nearly every house in Verrières since the fall of Napoleon." *The Red and The Black* [1831] (New York, 1963), p. 3. Moreover, not the Manchester cotton lord only, but the Birmingham nailer also had competitors in France. The great nail factory of M. de Renal, (with its "twenty heavy

hammers" fed "bits of iron which are quickly transformed into nails,") made "many thousands of nails a day." *Ibid*, p. 4.

4. *Marian Withers*, 2:56-57.

5. Jane Marcet was a popularizer of many subjects, including philosophy, chemistry, domestic and political economy. She employed a dialogue form wherein a "Mrs. B." expounded on these subjects to her pupil "Caroline." John C. Nevill, *Harriet Martineau* (London, 1943), pp. 35-36. See also supplement to Ivanka Kovačević, *Industriski Proleter u Engleskoj Pripovednoj Prozi Prve Polovine XIX Veka* (Beograd, 1960), 2:7.

6. *Harriet Martineau's Autobiography*, ed. Maria Weston Chapman (Boston, 1877), 1:105. After an extensive search I have been unable to locate *The Turn-Out* (1829), a long short story devoted to the futility of strikes and the tyranny of trade unions over their members. The tale is summarized in Kovačević, "Supplement," 2:8-9.

7. Quoted in R. K. Webb, *Harriet Martineau: A Radical Victorian* (New York, 1960), p. 105. For the popularity of the science in the early 1830s and the oversimplification which was a result, see Webb, p. 102. For the relationship between the ascendancy, in the early nineteenth century, of the mathematical and physical sciences upon the deductive method of political economy, see G. von Schulze-Gaevernitz, *Social Peace*, trans. G. M. Wicksteed (London, 1893), p. 121; and J. L. and Barbara Hammond, *The Town Labourer, 1760-1832* (London, 1918), p. 203.

8. *Harriet Martineau's Autobiography*, 1:147. For her debt to Malthus, Adam Smith, and Ricardo through James Mill, see Mark Blaug, *Ricardian Economics* (New Haven, 1958), p. 131.

9. *The Hill and the Valley*, in *Illustrations of Political Economy* (London, 1834), 1:140.

10. *A Manchester Strike*, in *Illustrations of Political Economy* (London, 1834), 3:134-36.

11. Robert Heilbroner's phrase, from his useful survey of economic theory from Adam Smith to Keynes, *The Worldly Philosophers* (New York, 1961), p. 70.

12. Preface to *Illustrations of Political Economy*, 1:xiii.

13. *The Dickens World* [1941] (London, 1960), p. 74.

14. Webb, pp. 110, 133.

15. *Harriet Martineau's Autobiography*, 1:85-86.

CHAPTER FOUR

1. Several prominent Victorians from the middle classes were also unsympathetic toward both Harriet Martineau's fiction of political economy and the general principles of the science. John Stuart Mill thought Harriet Martineau had reduced the principle of laissez-faire to an absurdity "by carrying it out to all its consequences." Quoted in R. K. Webb, *Harriet Martineau: A Radical Victorian* (New York, 1960), p. 109. James Mill initially disapproved of her plan and at one point almost convinced her publisher that the proposed popularization be issued as nonfiction. *Harriet Martineau's Autobiography*, ed. Maria Weston Chapman (Boston, 1877), 1:128-29. The essence of John Gibson Lockhart's review of *A Manchester Strike* in his "Miss Martineau's Monthly Novels," *Quarterly Review* 49 (April 1833): 143-144, is, to borrow G. M. Young's succinct phrasing, that "Industrial England was neither overpopulated nor under-employed, but periodically over—and under—employed." *Victorian England: Portrait of an Age* (London, 1960), pp. 26-27.

Carlyle deplored the "Paralytic Radicalism" of political economy, that, on the eve of the "hungry forties," saw that nothing could be done about the existing state of affairs. *Chartism* [1839] in *Thomas Carlyle's Collected Works* (London, 1869), 10:409. Robert Owen argued that the political economists, by reasoning from a false principle and knowing little of human nature or society, had perverted reason. What was worse, they had persuaded the Government to make laws restricting the rights of working men while favoring the wealthy. *The Life of Robert Owen Written by Himself* [1857] (New York, 1920), pp. 177-79, 180.

2. "On Radical Snobs (1846)" from *Contributions to Punch* in *The Works of William Makepeace Thackeray* (London, 1898), 26:33.

3. Friedrich Engels, *The Condition of the Working Class in England* [1845], translated and edited by W. O. Henderson and W. H. Chaloner (Oxford, 1958), pp. 257-58.

4. "Manifesto of the Communist Party [1848]," in *Basic Writings on Politics and Philosophy: Karl Marx and Friedrich Engels*, ed. Lewis S. Feuer (New York, 1959), p. 18. A similar opinion of the political economist is expressed by one of Kingsley's Chartist tailors who encountered such a man while accompanying the Chartist petition to London: "He may have been a wise man. I only know he was a rich one. Everyone speaks well of the bridge which carries him over. Everyone fancies the laws which fill his pockets to be God's laws." *Alton Locke* [1849] (London, 1910), p. 110.

5. Introduction to Engels's *Condition*, pp. xxiii-xxiv.

6. Engels, *Condition*, pp. 167-68. In the Report of the Factories Enquiry Commission, Engels's editors note evidence of immorality among young workers but little support for Engels's accustation against factory owners. p. 168, n. 1.

7. Engels, *Condition*, p. 168. It is probable that Engels was familiar with Peter Gaskell's account of the sexual indecency of the early manufacturers and their sons described in his *The Manufacturing Population of England* (London, 1833), pp. 63-65.

8. Louis James, *Fiction for the Working Man, 1830-1850: A Study of the Literature Produced for the Working Classes in Early Victorian Urban England* (London, 1963), p. 10.

9. James, pp. 12-13, 27.   10. Quoted in James, p. 30.

11. Quoted in Margaret Dalziel, *Popular Fiction 100 Years Ago: An Unexplored Tract of Literary History* (London, 1957), p. 20.

12. Dalziel, p. 21.

13. Reynolds was a member of the middle classes who was interested in developing cheap fiction. Taking his inheritance of £12,000, he went to Paris and spent his fortune in journalistic enterprise. While there he became acquainted with the works of Eugene Sue and the revolutionary ideas of 1789. It was his interest in the latter which later led him to Radical political activism and a leading part in the Chartist agitation of 1848. He returned to London and in 1845 became the first editor of the *London Journal*. He left the *Journal* in 1846 in order to start his *Reynolds's Miscellany*, with the intention of covering the middle ground between periodicals devoted entirely to fiction and those written for instruction. He himself wrote extensively, producing thirty novels between 1841 and 1856, many of which were serialized after he started the *Miscellany*. One of these, *The Mysteries of the Court of London*, revealing the influence of Eugene Sue, was serialized over a period of ten years, 1846-56, and is said to be four and a half million words in length, though parts of it may have been the work of ghost writers. Dalziel, pp. 35-36; James, pp. 40-41.

14. *The English Novel: A Panorama* (Boston, 1960), p. 283.

15. Quoted in Dalziel, p. 36.   16. Dalziel, p. 36.

17. "Charity and Humour," in *The Works of William Makepeace Thackeray* (New York and London, 1898), 7:722.

18. Quoted in Dalziel, p. 43.   19. James, pp. 165-66.

20. Paul Pimlico, "The Manufacturer," *Reynolds's Miscellany* 2:NS (June 16-July 21, 1849); "The Factory Girl," *Reynolds's Miscellany*, 3:NS (Oct. 20-Nov. 24, 1849). Subsequent references to these tales will appear in the text. Each tale was serialized in six weekly parts and printed on triple-column pages. My references will include the month and day of the installment and the page number.

21. Dickens had praised the factory system at Lowell. The girls came from rural areas to work for a few years and then to return home with their savings. While at Lowell, they lived in dormitories under responsible supervision, had access to pianos, and published poetry in the *Lowell Offering*. *American Notes and Pictures from Italy* in *The Works of Charles Dickens* (London, 1898), 28:77-81.

22. At the turn of the century the charge of arbitrariness and partiality on the part of factory owners serving as justices of the peace in the manufacturing districts was common. G. von Schulze-Gaevernitz, *Social Peace*, trans. C. M. Wicksteed (London, 1893), pp. 19-20.

23. Reynolds himself may have been Paul Pimlico. The latter's Radicalism is similar to that of Reynolds as outlined by Louis James, pp. 166-67. For the uniqueness of the Pimlico-Reynolds attack on the rich viewed in relation to other writers of popular magazine fiction, see Dalziel, pp. 140-41. This last critic finds that, outside of Reynolds, other popular writers rarely exhibit an employer deliberately abusing an employee. Moreover, as a result of the agitation for a purified penny press which was at its height around 1850, even Reynolds' work after mid-century is subdued.

24. "Mary Barton," reprinted in his *Essays on Political and Social Science* (London, 1853), 1:377. This review originally appeared in the *Edinburgh Review* in 1849. For a general account of the controversial reception of the novel, see A. B. Hopkins, *Elizabeth Gaskell: Her Life and Work* (London, 1952), p. 52. For a full account of the same, see the chapter on *Mary Barton* in the Ph.D. dissertation (New York University, 1953) by David Shusterman, "The Victorian Novel of Industrial Conflict: 1830-1870."

25. Quoted in Hopkins, p. 81.

26. Cited in the headnote to the Chartist "National Petition (1839)" in *Voices of the Industrial Revolution: Selected Readings of the Liberal Economists and Their Critics*, edited by J. Bowditch and C. Ramsland (Ann Arbor, 1963), p. 112.

27. "National Petition (1839)" in Bowditch and Ramsland, p. 113. The Petition is better known as the Charter.

28. Ibid, p. 115.

29. *Thomas Carlyle's Collected Works* (London, 1869), 10:356-57. When Carlyle's philosophical position, stripped of his moral sense, is taken as a plan of action by the deranged John Barton, the consequences are tragic. For all his contempt for fiction, Carlyle, it is worth noting, considered *Mary Barton* a book "deserving to take its place above the ordinary garbage of Novels . . . a real contribution (about the first one) toward developing a huge subject which has lain dumb too long. . . ." Letter from Chelsea to the author of *Mary Barton* [1848], quoted in Hopkins, p. 82.

30. Engels, *Condition*, p. 91.

31. *The Manufacturing Population of England* (London, 1833), p. 57.

32. Peter Gaskell, p. 68.   33. Peter Gaskell, p. 63.   34. Peter Gaskell, pp. 63-64.

35. As a critic of industrialism, Peter Gaskell belongs to another faction of its enemies, the Tory reactionaries. In the novels of this study, the only sustained expres-

sion of this backward-looking point of view is Charlotte Elizabeth's *Helen Fleetwood* (1841), though her Victorian evangelical propriety prevents her from attacking sexual license directly. This group of critics should be differentiated from the Tory Radicals, such as Shaftesbury, Oastler, and Sadler, who having accepted the inevitability of industrialism, wanted reform; namely, factory legislation rather than a return to the past.

36. For a brief account of the diversity of progressive and reactionary elements among the Chartists, see Guy Chapman, "The Economic Background," in *The Victorians and After, 1830-1914*, ed. E. C. Batho and Bonamy Dobree (London, 1950), p. 130.

37. *The Opinions of William Cobbett*, ed. G. D. H. Cole and Margaret Cole (London, 1944), pp. 86-87.

38. *Opinions of William Cobbett*, p. 87.

39. Ibid. Dickens's Boffin, while only playing the part of a nouveau, succinctly phrases the relationship between a newly-arrived rich man and his employees as "either scrunch them, or let them scrunch you." *Our Mutual Friend* (New York, 1964), p. 514.

40. Raymond Williams, *Culture and Society 1780-1950* (New York, 1960), pp. 95-96.

41. *Mary Barton* [1848] (New York, 1958), p. 3. The following bibliographical procedure shall be employed in the discussion of each novel: the footnote to the first passage or phrase quoted from a novel will contain full bibliographical information. The remaining references to the novel will be cited in the text of this study.

42. For a concise account of the depression which in its entirety spanned the years 1836-42, see S. G. Checkland, *The Rise of Industrial Society in England, 1815-1885* (London, 1964), pp. 17-18.

43. "Communist Manifesto," p. 18. For historical evidence that Marx and Engels's "Manifesto" was, so to speak, a mirror more than a lamp, see Oscar J. Hammen, "The Spectre of Communism in the 1840s," *JHI*, 14 (1954), 404-20.

44. On this point, see R. H. Tawney's section, "The New Medicine for Poverty," in his *Religion and the Rise of Capitalism* (New York, 1958), pp. 210-26.

CHAPTER FIVE

1. "Michael Armstrong," *Athenaeum*, No. 615 (Aug. 10, 1839), p. 588. Frances Eleanor Trollope, *Frances Trollope: Her Life and Literary Work from George III to Victoria* (London, 1895), 1:301.

2. Preface to *The Life and Adventures of Michael Armstrong, the Factory Boy* (London, 1840), pp. iii-iv.

3. See especially such a work as Thomas A. Jackson, *Charles Dickens: The Progress of a Radical* (London, 1937), passim.

4. W. H. Hutt, "The Factory System of the Early Nineteenth Century," in *Capitalism and the Historians*, ed. F. A. Hayek (Chicago, 1954), pp. 161-63.

5. *The Condition of the Working Class in England* [1845], trans. and ed. W. O. Henderson and W. H. Chaloner (Oxford, 1958), p. 192.

6. Engels, *Condition*, p. 192.

7. *The Manufacturing Population of England* (London, 1833), p. 207.

8. Ibid, p. 208.

9. *Philosophy of Manufactures* [1835], quoted in Engels, *Condition*, pp. 189-90.

10. Quoted in R. K. Webb, *Harriet Martineau: A Radical Victorian* (New York, 1960), p. 110, n. 1.

11. Thomas Adolphus Trollope, *What I Remember* (London, 1887), 2:7-9.

12. The *OED* records that the word, "millocrat," first appeared in *Michael Armstrong*.

13. T. S. Ashton, *The Industrial Revolution: 1760-1830* (London, 1962), p. 153. S. G. Checkland, *The Rise of Industrial Society in England: 1815-1885* (London, 1964), p. 20. John W. Dodd, *The Age of Paradox: A Briography of England, 1841-1851* (New York, 1952), pp. 45-46.

14. Elgood Sharpton seems to have been modeled after Ellice Needham, the persecutor of the pauper apprentice, Robert Blincoe, whose sensational *Memoir of Robert Blincoe* was published in 1828 and reprinted in 1832 by John Doherty, a trade union pioneer whom Mrs. Trollope had met in Lancashire. W. H. Chaloner, "Mrs. Trollope and the Early Factory System," *VS,* 4 (1960): 164. For a summary of Blincoe's *Memoir,* which though an isolated case, was no doubt intended to indict the generality of millowners employing pauper apprentices, see Robert L. Heilbroner, *The Worldly Philosophers* (New York, 1961), pp. 102-3.

15. *The Life and Adventures of Michael Armstrong, the Factory Boy* (London, 1840), p. 118.

16. Until the Second Reform Bill, to working men a shift in power among the wealthy classes meant that new millocrat was but old aristocrat writ large. On this basis, Harold Transome the Radical candidate in *Felix Holt* (1866) offers the working man a choice. In his campaign speech, Transome explains that the millowners are "men who will be satisfied if they can only bring in a plutocracy, buy up the land, and stick the old crests on their new gateways. . . ." Transome continues, "I have had the advantage of considering national welfare under varied lights: I have wider views than those of a mere cotton lord." *Felix Holt, the Radical* [1866] (Edinburgh and London, n. d.), p. 182.

17. Frances Trollope, *Domestic Manners of the Americans* [1832] (London, 1927), p. 9.

18. Ibid, p. 40.   19. Ibid, pp. 59-67.

20. Anthony Trollope, *An Autobiography* [1883] (London, 1950), p. 33.

21. *The Manufacturing Population of England,* p. 50.

22. "To the Landowners. On the evils of collecting Manufacturers in great masses," *Political Register* (Nov. 20, 1824) in *The Opinions of William Cobbett,* ed. G. D. H. Cole and Margaret Cole (London, 1944), p. 180.

23. Peter Gaskell, pp. 7-8, 89.

24. See Peter Gaskell's panegyric of the country squire in Chapter One of this study, pp. 6-7, note 19.

25. Cobbett, *Opinions,* p. 174.

26. *Helen Fleetwood* [1841] (New York, 1844), p. 79.

27. At this point, Charlotte Elizabeth assails the depravity of the workers and the greed of their employers. The human heart is depraved and "the vile, the cruel, the body and soul-murdering system" of factory labor is the product of one of the most hateful forms of depravity—covetousness, which is the "prolific root of every ill that can unhumanize man, and render an enlightened Christian country the mark of God's most just and holy indignation provoking even Him to blot its place and name from among the nations of the earth." p. 95.

28. p. 105. Here the author cites Factory Inspector Leonard Horner's evidence given to the House of Commons in 1840.

29. *Le Roman Social en Angleterre: 1830-1850* (Paris, 1934), 2:157.

30. Quoted in Margaret Dalziel, *Popular Fiction 100 Years Ago* (London, 1957), p. 11.

31. *Personal Recollections by Charlotte Elizabeth* [1841] (New York, 1958), p. 3.

32. Ibid, p. 9.   33. Ibid.

34. "Novels are not objected to as they were; now that every sect in politics and religion has found their efficacy as a means, the form is adopted by all." *Blackwood's*, Oct. 1848, quoted in Kathleen Tillotson, *Novels of the Eighteen-Forties* (Oxford, 1954), p. 15.

35. Quoted in Edgar Johnson, *Charles Dickens: His Tragedy and Triumph* (New York, 1952), 1:225.

36. Letter to Dr. Southwood Smith (1840) in *The Letters of Charles Dickens*, ed. Walter Dexter (London, 1938), 1:282.

37. Lionel Stevenson, "Dickens's Dark Novels, 1851-1857," *SeR* 51 (1943): 398-409.

38. *Nicholas Nickleby* [1838-39] (London, 1957), p. 457.

39. *The Dickens World* [1942] (London, 1960), pp. 65-66.

40. Ibid, p. 74.

41. *The Claims of Labour. An Essay on the Duties of the Employer to the Employed* [1844] (London, 1845), p. 39, 153.

42. Ibid, p. 156.   43. Ibid, pp. 46-48.

44. W. R. Greg, "The Relation between Employers and Employed," reprinted in his *Essays on Political and Social Science* (London, 1853), 2:299.

45. Ibid, 2:301.

46. Quoted in House, *The Dickens World*, p. 65.

47. Quoted in Johnson, *Charles Dickens*, 1:289.

48. From "The Vulgarity of Little Nell" [1930] reprinted in *The Dickens Critics*, ed. George H. Ford and Lauriat Lane, Jr. (Ithaca, N.Y., 1961), pp. 153-54.

49. *Charles Dickens: The Progress of a Radical* (London, 1937), p. 110.

50. Johnson, *Charles Dickens*, 1:289.

51. Preface to *Nicholas Nickleby*, pp. xvi-xvii.

52. S. M. Ellis, *William Harrison Ainsworth and His Friends* (London, 1911), 1:339-42.

53. *Letters of Charles Dickens*, 1:445.

54. *Self-Help; with Illustrations of Character, Conduct, and Perseverance* [1859] (Chicago, 1881), p. 430.

55. Ibid, p. 431.

56. C. Whibley, *Lord John Manners and His Friends* (Edinburgh and London, 1925), 1:99.

57. Ibid, 1:102.

58. Quoted in Ibid, 1:103.   59. Quoted in Ibid, 1:104.

60. Ibid. Such a tribute to industry as well as character seems strange coming from Lord John Manners who was the author of, to use his own words, "two lines which clung to him through life like a burr":

> "Let wealth and commerce, laws and learning die,
> But leave us still our old Nobility."

Quoted in Whibley, 1:113.

61. Because his virulent attack upon Josiah Bounderby in this novel is more in the spirit of the 1840s than that of the peaceful 1850s and because Dickens' outlook is humanitarian, *Hard Times* is included in this chapter.

62. *Letters of Charles Dickens*, 2:554.

63. *Hard Times* [1854] (London, 1957), p. 63.

64. The opponents to Ashley's Factory Act of 1833 argued that the loss of two hours to be set aside for children's schooling would make for dreadful consequences on a national scale. The measure would destroy capital, undermine competition with foreign manufacturers, reduce the value of mills, ruin the power and wealth of England, enfeebling the country and making it a prey to foreign countries. "Factory Bill" in *Political Register* for June 7, 1833, reprinted in *The Opinions of William Cobbett*, p. 184. Cobbett ironically comments that the Bank of England and its credit, English shipping and agriculture are negligible when compared to the work of 300,000 small girls in Lancashire who are to be congratulated for holding England's prosperity, happiness, and independence in their hands, Ibid, pp. 184-85.

65. *Religion and the Rise of Capitalism* [1926] (New York, 1958), p. 221.

66. S. G. Checkland, *The Rise of Industrial Society in England: 1815-1885* (London, 1964), p. 219.

67. Reinhard Bendix, *Work and Authority in Industry: Ideologies of Management in the Course of Industrialization* (New York and Evanston, 1956), pp. 24-25. Even in America where opportunities were great, the self-made man has been more a myth than a reality. On this point, see Irvin G. Wyllie, *The Self-Made Man in America* (New Brunswick, N.J., 1954), p. 174. F. W. Gregory and I. D. Neu, "The American Industrial Elite in 1870's: Their Social Origins," in *Men in Business*, ed. William Miller (Cambridge, Mass., 1952), p. 204. For a curiously subjective comparison between the English and the American self-made man, in which the Englishman resembles the plebeian John Manford and the American James' Christopher Newman, see Nathaniel Hawthorne, *English Notebooks* [1856] in *The Works of Nathaniel Hawthorne* (Boston and New York, 1899), 8:241-42.

68. "A Note on *Hard Times* [1860]," in *The Dickens Critics*, pp. 47-48.

69. *William Langshawe, the Cotton Lord* (London, 1842), 1:182-83.

70. Henry Adams bears witness to the "showy suppers" that were characteristic of Lancashire hospitality. Arthur W. Silber, "Henry Adams' 'Diary of a Visit to Manchester,'" *AHR*, 51 (1945): 83.

71. "William Langshawe, the Cotton Lord" *Athenaeum*, No. 779 (Oct. 1, 1842), p. 846.

72. T. S. Ashton, *The Industrial Revolution: A Study in Bibliography* (London, 1937), p. 2.

73. Checkland, *Rise of Industrial Society*, pp. 120-22.

CHAPTER SIX

1. *Past and Present* [1843] (London, 1962), p. 135.

2. Ibid, p. 24.   3. Ibid, p. 140.   4. Ibid, p. 141.

5. Ibid, p. 140.   6. Ibid, p. 172.   7. Ibid, p. 183.

8. Ibid, pp. 185-86.   9. Ibid, p. 186.   10. Ibid, p. 201.

11. Ibid, p. 186.   12. Ibid, p. 201.   13. Ibid, p. 241.

14. Ibid, p. 261.   15. Ibid, p. 265.   16. Ibid, pp. 266-67.

17. Ibid, p. 271.

18. *Lord Beaconsfield* (New York, 1890), p. 92.

19. The choice of an Old English name for the manufacturer's son is not accidental.

Moreover, Millbank's daughter is given the name of Edith because, her father explains, "she is the daughter of a Saxon." *Coningsby, or the New Generation* [1844] (London, 1963), p. 137.

20. *Past and Present*, p. 129.

21. "The Norman Yoke," in *Democracy and the Labour Movement*, ed. John Saville (London, 1954), p. 11. Hill traces the theory from the *Mirrour For Magistrates* to a half-serious use in 1911.

22. Hill, p. 11. In this connection, a German historian observes, "Englishmen always try to put their demands in the form of a revival of ancient rights, however gross the historical error involved in such an attempt may be . . . not for fresh rights to be won, but for lost rights to be recovered." G. von Schulze-Gaevernitz, *Social Peace*, trans. G. M. Wicksteed (London, 1893), p. 51. According to L. G. Johnson, because of the work of Thomas Hardy and T. H. B. Oldfield, antiquarians writing at the turn of the nineteenth century, many of the members of the new manufacturing population knew more about pre-Norman England than about the England following the Revolution of 1688. Before the passage of the Reform Bill when the question of extending the franchise was in the air, Hardy and Oldfield looked back to the constitution of Saxon England. *The Social Evolution of Industrial Britain: A Study of the Growth of Our Industrial Society* (Liverpool, 1959), pp. 6-7.

23. A reviewer of Disraeli's second novel in the Young England trilogy said as much. He declared that Disraeli (who was the elder statesman and spokesman for Young England), Lord John Manners, and George Smythe had derived their views from Scott's romances. "Sybil; or The Two Nations," *Douglas Jerrold's Shilling Magazine*, 1 (Jan. to June, 1845): 557-65.

24. Disraeli's biographer, Froude, who also edited Carlyle's *Reminiscences* (1881) maintained that, at the outset of Disraeli's Parliamentary career, the opinions of the author of *Sybil* were those of the writer of *Past and Present*. See his *Lord Beaconsfield*, p. 92.

25. *Sybil, or the Two Nations* [1845] (Harmondsworth, 1954), p. 91.

26. The hatred of miners for colliery managers also appears in *Felix Holt*, where on election day, Spratt might have been killed had not Felix, to his own detriment, stepped in to turn the mob's fury in another direction.

27. *Great Britain from Adam Smith to the Present Day* (London, 1928), p. 378. For further evidence that Disraeli's information was not first hand, see Cazamian, *Le Roman Social*, 2:103; and Kovačević, "Proletarian Fiction," Supplement to her *Industriski Proleter*, 2:17.

28. His sole critic is a young factory girl who is bored by the singing classes and the schools at his establishment. pp. 93-94. One is reminded of the compulsory music and dancing that Humphry House mentions as the reason for some employees' leaving Robert Owen's model factory at New Lanark. *The Dickens World*, p. 66.

29. W. R. Greg convincingly undermines Young England's belief in uniting the "Two Nations" by a return to the vassal-master state. "The Relation between Employers and Employed," in his *Essays on Political and Social Science* (London, 1853), 2:271-72. Greg's premise is that the progress of civilization reveals a tendency toward the equalization of social conditions. According to Greg, there are three stages of employer-employee relations. The first master-slave; the second, master-vassal; and the third, a product of the nineteenth century, equality between both parties. He argues that Young England's efforts to revive the second stage are futile.

30. Carlyle's "Friend Prudence," who has worked at attaching his employees to

him by providing playgrounds, a concert band and "conversational soirees," comments, to Carlyle's great satisfaction, upon another manufacturer whose relation to his men is strictly cash-nexus: "I would not . . . exchange my workers for his with seven thousand pounds to boot." *Past and Present*, pp. 268-69.

31. *Past and Present*, p. 208.

32. Ibid, p. 212.   33. Ibid, p. 210.

34. Ibid, p. 211.   35. Ibid, p. 212.

36. *Culture and Society* (New York, 1960), p. 107.

37. Sheila M. Smith, "Willenhall and Wodgate: Disraeli's Use of Blue Book Evidence," *RES*, NS, 2 (1962), 368-84.

38. In an analysis of communist, socialist and anarchist thought between 1830 and 1848, O. J. Hammen notes the tendency to trace Marxian ideology back to specific individuals, thereby minimizing the part of the intellectual and emotional climate prevalent in radical circles. That Marx thought communism inevitable may have been due as much to the atmosphere of avant garde thought as well as to his study of economic trends. The accomplishment of Marx was his integration of these currents of thought in the 1840s into a system and proclaiming them eternally valid. Oscar J. Hammen, "The Spectre of Communism in the 1840's," *JHI*, 14 (1954): 404, 420.

39. Hammen, pp. 408-9.   40. Hammen, p. 411.   41. Hammen, p. 414.

42. Hammen, p. 415.   43. Hammen, p. 408.   44. Hammen, pp. 418-419.

45. *Victorian England: Portrait of an Age* (London, 1960), pp. 54-55, n. 2.

46. *Culture and Society*, p. 97. Williams's insight also helps to explain, in this case, why a social problem novelist who might naturally be expected to stick to contemporary evils, would use obsolete evidence: Mrs. Gaskell based her incident upon the notorious murder of Thomas Ashton, son of a "good" Manchester manufacturer, which occurred in 1831. The crime was committed by three workmen paid £10 by a workmen's secret society. Engels mentions the crime in *Condition*, p. 249; and a late Victorian chronicler writes that "the motive was not private vengeance, for Mr. Ashton was an amiable young man, but a desire to intimidate the masters generally." William E. A. Axon, *The Annals of Manchester* (London, 1886), p. 181.

47. *My Relations with Carlyle* [1887], quoted in Susanne Howe, *Geraldine Jewsbury: Her Life and Errors* (London, 1935), p. 178.

48. She departs from Carlyle only by way of demanding, in the light of his beliefs, a sphere of activity for woman. Carlyle's anti-feminist view was that "a woman's natural object in the world is to go out and find herself some sort of *man* her superior—and obey him loyally and lovingly and make herself as much as possible into a beautiful reflex of him!" Quoted in Howe, *Geraldine Jewsbury*, p. 105. Although *The Half-Sisters* was dedicated to Jane Carlyle, it is said that Carlyle, in his contempt for fiction, would not permit his wife to proofread the novel.

49. *The Half-Sisters* [1848] (London, 1854), p. 13.

50. That Alice Bryant is in part Jane Carlyle is a strong possibility. By way of consolation, Geraldine Jewsbury once wrote to Jane Carlyle, who was suffering nervous ailments in 1846, that most of her trouble stemmed from the lack of a regular occupation. Howe, *Geraldine Jewsbury*, p. 57.

51. *Sartor Resartus and Hero-Worship*. (London, 1929), p. 147.

52. Ibid, p. 148.   53. Ibid, p. 148.   54. Ibid, p. 149.

55. *Past and Present*, pp. 282-83.

56. *Sartor Resartus*, pp. 144-45.

CHAPTER SEVEN

1. S. G. Checkland, *The Rise of Industrial Society in England, 1815-1885* (London, 1964), p. 26. R. J. Cruikshank, *Charles Dickens and Early Victorian England* (London, 1949), p. 118.

2. Wanda F. Neff, *Victorian Working Women: An Historical and Literary Study of Women in British Industries and Professions, 1832-1850* (New York, 1929), pp. 78-79, 81, 112.

3. *Mervyn Clitheroe* [1851-1858] (London, 1870), p. 61. Ainsworth wrote his observation of "Cottonborough" in 1851. He postponed completion of this unsuccessful attempt at emulating *David Copperfield* until 1858.

4. Guy Chapman, "The Economic Background," in *The Victorians and After, 1830-1914*, ed. E. C. Batho and Bonamy Dobree (London, 1950), pp. 128-29. John W. Dodd, *The Age of Paradox: A Biography of England, 1841-1851* (New York, 1952), pp. 331-32. G. M. Young, *Victorian England: Portrait of an Age* (London, 1960), pp. 65-66. Despite the failure of the Chartist petitioners on April 10, 1848, Charles Kingsley, writing an address to working men in 1854, declared that the previous five years had been "years of progress for the good cause." He attributed this to the willingness of the holders of property "to be just to the workman." See his "Preface Written in 1854, Addressed to the Working Men of Great Britain," in *Alton Locke* (London, 1910), pp. 16-17.

5. Sidney and Beatrice Webb, *The History of Trade Unionism* (London, 1894), pp. 177-78, 206.

6. Appendix to Cruikshank, *Charles Dickens and Early Victorian England*, Chart. 5.

7. Thomas A. Jackson, *Charles Dickens: The Progress of a Radical* (London, 1937), p. 43.

8. See Gertrude Ward, "The Education of Factory Child Workers, 1833-50," *Economic History*, 3 (1935): 110-24, cited by Richard D. Altick, *The English Common Reader* (Chicago, 1963), p. 148.

9. *The English Common Reader*, p. 4, 293.

10. W. E. Houghton in *The Victorian Frame of Mind, 1830-1870* (New Haven, 1957), p. 43, quoting the Prince Consort and *The Times*. On this point, see also G. M. Young, *Victorian England*, p. 78; and Cazamian, *Le Roman Social*, 1:2.

11. This novel was serialized weekly in *The True Briton*, 1-2, NS, (June 9 to Oct. 20, 1853). Further references will appear in the text and will include date of the installment and page.

12. Fanny Mayne may have had Dickens in mind as the "maudlin sentimentalist," for she had previously criticized *Household Words* in a pamphlet entitled, *The Perilous Nature of the Penny Periodical Press* (1851). Although she acknowledged that Dickens's periodical, because of the talent behind it, stood apart from others, still *Household Words* supported separation of classes by making the poor feel that they were oppressed by the rich, who were supported by law and authority. M. Dalziel, *Popular Fiction 100 Years Ago* (London, 1957), p. 52.

13. As champion of a purified penny press, Fanny Mayne thus shows the pernicious effect upon the working man of such Radical papers as *Reynolds's Miscellany*. It might be added that the movement of which she was a part was probably responsible for making Reynolds alter the Radical tone of his weekly after 1850, and it also partly explains why there is so little Radical fiction in existence. Dalziel, *Popular Fiction*, pp. 46-54.

14. Her editorials were entitled "What I Saw and Heard in the Manufacturing

Districts. By a Friend of the People." For the point under consideration, see the following editorials: *The True Briton*, 2, NS (Nov. 17, 1853), 241-42; 2, NS (Dec. 1, 1853): 274-75.

15. Dalziel, *Popular Fiction*, p. 68.

16. *Lights and Shadows of English Life* (London, 1855), 1:215-16.

17. Quoted in Edgar Johnson, *Charles Dickens: His Tragedy and Triumph* (New York, 1952), 2:823.

18. *North and South* [1855] (London, 1961), p. 34.

19. *The Life of Robert Owen Written by Himself* [1857] (New York, 1920) p. 87.

20. A. L. Morton, *The Life and Ideas of Robert Owen* (New York, 1962), pp. 21, 38.

CHAPTER EIGHT

1. W. L. Burn, *The Age of Equipoise: A Study of the Mid-Victorian Generation* (New York, 1964).

2. *The Two Aristocracies* (Leipzig, 1857), 1:107.

3. Thackeray parodied her style and interests of the 1840s. See "Lords and Liveries," in his *Punch's Prize Novelists* [1847] (New York, 1853), pp. 72-87.

4. *The Silver-Fork School: Novels of Fashion Preceding Vanity Fair* (New York, 1936), p. 143.

5. Asa Briggs, "The Language of 'Class' in Early Nineteenth-Century England," in *Essays in Labour History*, ed. Asa Briggs and John Saville (London, 1960), p. 242. In his book-length study, *The Age of Improvement*, 1783-1867 (London, 1959), Briggs devotes a chapter to the balance of interests during this period.

6. *Bleak House* [1853] (London, 1962), p. 363.

7. *Charles Dickens and Early Victorian England* (London, 1949), p. 112.

8. "The Two Aristocracies" *Athenaeum*, No. 1549 (July 4, 1857), p. 852.

9. This novel was serialized in *The True Briton*, 2, NS (Oct. 20 to Dec. 20, 1853).

10. *Le Roman Social*, 2:34.

CHAPTER NINE

1. Quoted in Ralph E. Pumphrey, "The Introduction of Industrialists into the British Peerage: A Study in Adaptation of a Social Institution," *AHR*, 65 (1959): 10-11. The grandfather of the newly ennobled Lord Belper was Jedediah Strutt, the first to turn out ribbed stockings by machine (1758) and a subsequent partner of Arkwright. Samuel Smiles, *Self-Help* [1859] (London, 1876), pp. 214-15.

2. *The Age of Equipoise: A Study of the Mid-Victorian Generation* (New York, 1964), p. 254.

3. At the same time, Thackeray deplored Burke's influence when he wrote, "Lord-olatry is part of the English creed and English children are brought up to view the 'Peerage' as 'the Englishman's second Bible.' " *The Book of Snobs* [1846-47] in *The Works of William Makepeace Thackeray* (London, 1902), 14:16.

4. Quoted in *Self-Help*, p. 382.

5. Esmé Wingfield-Stratford, *The Making of a Gentleman* (London, 1938), p. 268.

6. Asa Briggs, *The Age of Improvement, 1783-1867* (London, 1959), p. 411.

7. Ibid, p. 412. Foreign observers have acknowledged that the gentleman is a purely English phenomenon. Taine, who visited England intermittently between 1861 and 1871 wrote that the French had no word for gentleman ("quite different from . . . the French *gentilhomme*") because they "have not the thing, and these three syllables, as used across the Channel, summarize the history of English society." *Notes on England*, trans. W. F. Rae (New York, 1874), p. 174. The modern German historian Wilhelm Dibelius has written the following encomium: "All England's other achievements pale by the side of this. It developed the idea of the gentleman more thoroughly and consistently than other nations have done, and by this gave an ethical idea of great—though certainly not unique—value to the world." *England, Its Character and Genius* (New York, 1930), p. 504.

8. From *Pre-Raphaelitism* [1851] quoted in Walter E. Houghton, *The Victorian Frame of Mind, 1830-1870* (New Haven, 1957), p. 187.

9. "The Language of 'Class' in Early Nineteenth-Century England," in *Essays in Labour History*, ed. Asa Briggs and John Saville (London, 1960), p. 69.

10. *An Autobiography* [1883] (London, 1950), pp. 39-40. Believing that the Civil Service should be manned by gentlemen, Trollope opposed the system of competitive examinations because it did not bring out the best sort of public servant. Aspirants to the Civil Service underwent a program of cramming that had little to do with education. Moreover, having passed the test, the successful candidate assumed that he was educated. But character, manners, and conduct could not be measured by such an examination. Ibid, pp. 37-40.

11. Ibid, p. 40.   12. Ibid, p. 294.

13. *Dr. Thorne* [1858] (Boston, 1959), p. 77.

14. See p. 101 for references to Scatcherd as a prophet inspired by the "rosy god" to communicate in "divine frenzies . . . with those deities who preside over trade transactions. . . ."

15. Dickens' "captain of finance," Merdle, also has difficulty, at his sumptuous dinners, making conversation on subjects other than railway shares. *Little Dorrit* [1855-57] (London, 1953), p. 241. Because of a lack of education, Commodore Vanderbilt exhibited similar feelings of social inadequacy. He once told a clergyman: "Folks may say that I don't care about education; but it ain't true; I do. . . . I've been to England, and seen them lords, and other fellows, and knew that I had twice as much brains as they had maybe, and yet I had to keep still, and couldn't say anything through fear of exposing myself." William A. Croffut, *The Vanderbilts and the Story of Their Fortune* (New York, 1886), p. 137, quoted in Irvin G. Wyllie, *The Self-Made Man in America* (New Brunswick, N.J., 1954).

16. *Anthony Trollope: Aspects of His Life and Art* (Bloomington, 1958), p. 45.

17. *Trollope: A Commentary* (London, 1927), p. 379. Trollope acknowledges that his brother sketched out the plot and adds that this was the only time that any one aided him in this way. *An Autobiography*, p. 115.

18. *An Autobiography*, p. 282.

19. *An Autobiography*, p. 210.

20. The notion that men with specialized talents were socially valuable is developed by G. Kitson Clark, *The Making of Victorian England* (Cambridge, Mass., 1962), p. 262.

21. *Self-Help*, pp. 397-98.

22. Ibid, p. 398.   23. Ibid, p. 398.

24. *Self-Help*, pp. 399-400.   25. Ibid, p. 406.

26. Louisa Parr, "Dinah Mulock (Mrs. Craik)," in *Women Novelists of Queen Victoria's Reign* (London, 1897), p. 248.

27. W. M. Parker, quoting an unspecified source in his "Introduction" to *John Halifax, Gentleman* (London, 1961), p. viii.

28. *John Halifax, Gentleman* [1856] (London, 1912), p. 11.

29. Quoted in Harold Nicolson, *Good Behaviour: Being a Study of Certain Types of Civility* (New York, 1955), p. 230.

30. G. Kitson Clark, *The Making of Victorian England* (Cambridge, Mass., 1962), pp. 254-55.

31. From his introduction to the second edition of *The English Constitution* (1872), quoted in Pumphrey, p. 13.

32. Kitson Clark, p. 255.   33. Ibid, p. 255.

34. *Good Behaviour*, p. 263.

35. *Victorian England: Portrait of an Age*, pp. 95-96.

36. *The Making of Victorian England*, p. 273.

37. Judging from a study of Cambridge alumni in the first half of the nineteenth century, the probability that manufacturers' sons sent to a university dominated by the landed classes would not enter business was great. Between 1800-49, none of the 5% of Cambridge students with business backgrounds took up business as a profession. H. Jenkins and D. C. Jones, "Social Class of Cambridge University Alumni of the Eighteenth and Nineteenth Centuries," *British Journal of Sociology* 1 (June, 1950): 99, cited by Reinhard Bendix in his *Work and Authority in Industry* (New York, 1963), p. 26, n. 12.

38. In America the classical curriculum was denounced as impractical both for a business career and for daily life. Wyllie, *Self-Made Man in America*, p. 103.

39. S. G. Checkland, *The Rise of Industrial Society in England, 1815-1885* (London, 1964), p. 295.

40. *The Age of Reform* (London and New York, 1962), p. 472.

41. *Mrs. Halliburton's Troubles* [1862] (London, 1877), p. 64.

42. In *Mildred Arkell* (1865), Mrs. Wood portrays William Arkell, another glove manufacturer, in much the same way as she did Thomas Ashley. Arkell, too, is "not only a thoroughly well-read classical scholar and an accomplished man . . ." (London, 1880), p. 3. The novel is a domestic drama in which Arkell's qualifications as a gentleman-manufacturer have little bearing outside of his family circle. In still another novel *A Life's Secret* (1867), the builder Henry Hunter is also involved in a domestic drama: he is preoccupied with his "life's secret," an earlier imprudent marriage.

43. Disagreement exists over the degree of the industrialist's commitment to the life of a country gentleman. In his account of the industrialist's tendency to drop out of city government, V. S. Pritchett writes that "the great moralizing industrialists rapidly turned into vegetative country squires, having moved to the country because "they hated the places where they made their money." See his "Exuberant Victorians" [review of Asa Briggs' *Victorian Cities*]," *New York Review of Books*, 5 (Sept. 30, 1965: 14. On the other hand, S. G. Checkland argues that industrialists did not effect a total separation from their source of wealth in the towns, for they often regarded their country estates merely as surplus assets. As a result, the industrialist as country gentleman did not involve himself in country life to the same degree as the "county families." *Rise of Industrial Society*, p. 289. For a convincing interpretation of more subtle

motives for desiring a place in the country, see G. M. Young, *Victorian England: Portrait of an Age*, pp. 84-85. Young maintains that the English bourgeoisie "had no tradition of civic magnificence," through which a wealthy town dweller might gain nationwide recognition.

44. Frances Collins, *Mortimer Collins: His Letters and Friendships, With Some Account of His Life* (London, 1877), 1:18.

45. Ibid, 2:35.   46. Ibid, 1:195.

47. *Marquis and Merchant* (London, 1871), 1:115.

Bibliography

I. BIBLIOGRAPHICAL STUDIES

Ashton, T. S. *The Industrial Revolution: A Study in Bibliography*. London, 1937.
Ray, Gordon N. *Bibliographical Resources for the Study of Nineteenth-Century English Fiction*. Los Angeles: School of Library Service, Univ. of Calif., 1964.

II. THE SOCIAL, ECONOMIC, AND INTELLECTUAL BACKGROUND

Adams, Henry. *The Education of Henry Adams*. 2 vols. New York, 1964.
Ashton, T. S. *The Industrial Revolution: 1760-1830*. London, 1962.
Axon, William E. A. *The Annals of Manchester*. London, 1886.
Bendix, Reinhard. *Work and Authority in Industry: Ideologies of Management in the Course of Industrialization*. (1956). New York and Evanston, 1963.
Blaug, Mark. *Ricardian Economics*. New Haven, 1958.
Boswell, James. *Life of Johnson*. London, 1953.
Bowden, Witt. *Industrial Society in England Towards the End of the Eighteenth Century*. New York, 1925.
Bowditch, J. and C. Ramsland, ed. *Voices of the Industrial Revolution: Selected Readings from the Liberal Economists and Their Critics*. Ann Arbor, 1963.
Briggs, Asa. *The Age of Improvement, 1783-1867*. New York, 1964.
Briggs, Asa. "The Language of 'Class' in Early Nineteenth-Century England," in *Essays in Labour History*, edited by Asa Briggs and John Saville. London, 1960. pp. 43-73.
Burn, W. L. *The Age of Equipoise: A Study of the Mid-Victorian Generation*. New York, 1964.
Carlyle, Thomas. "Hudson's Statue (1850)," in Vol. 19 of *Thomas Carlyle's Collected Works*. 30 vols. London, 1869. pp. 305-50.
————. *Past and Present* (1843). London, 1962.
————. "Chartism (1839)," in Vol. 10 of *Thomas Carlyle's Collected Works*. 30 vols. London, 1869. pp. 325-423.
————. *Sartor Resartus and On Heroes and Hero-Worship*. London, 1929.

Chapman, Guy. "The Economic Background," in The Victorians and After. Edited by E. C. Batho and B. Dobree. 2d rev. ed. London, 1950. pp. 128-41.

Checkland, S. G. The Rise of Industrial Society in England, 1815-1885. London, 1964.

Chesterton, G. K. The Uses of Diversity. New York, 1921.

Clark, G. Kitson. The Making of Victorian England. Cambridge, Mass., 1962.

Cobbe, Frances. "The Nineteenth Century." Fraser's Magazine 69 (1864) : 481-94.

Cobbett, William. The Opinions of William Cobbett, edited by G. D. H. Cole and Margaret Cole. London, 1944.

Craik, George Lillie. "Account of James Brindley: Canals," in The Pursuit of Knowledge Under Difficulties. London: Charles Knight, 1830. pp. 318-38.

Dibelius, Wilhelm. England, Its Character and Genius. New York, 1930.

Dodd, John W. The Age of Paradox: A Biography of England: 1841-1851. New York, 1952.

Emerson, Ralph Waldo. English Traits, Representative Men, and Other Essays. London, 1919.

Engels, Friedrich. The Condition of the Working Class in England (1845), translated and edited by W. O. Henderson and W. H. Chaloner. Oxford, 1958.

Fay, C. R. Great Britain from Adam Smith to the Present Day. London, 1928.

Gaskell, Elizabeth. The Life of Charlotte Brontë (1857). London, 1960.

Gaskell, Peter. The Manufacturing Population of England. London, 1833.

Greg, W. R. "The Relation between Employers and Employed," in Vol. 2 of Essays on Political and Social Science. 2 vols. London, 1853. pp. 252-302.

Hammen, Oscar J. "The Spectre of Communism in the 1840's," JHI, 14 (1953) : 404-20.

Hammond, J. L. and Barbara Hammond. "The Mind of the Rich," in The Town Labourer, 1760-1832. London, 1918. pp. 194-220.

Hawthorne, Nathaniel. English Note-Books. Vol. 8 of The Works of Nathaniel Hawthorne. 15 vols. Boston and New York, 1899.

Hazlitt, William. "On Thought and Action," in Table-Talk (1821-22). Vol. 8 of The Complete Works of William Hazlitt, edited by P. P. Howe. 21 vols. London and Toronto, 1931. pp. 101-13.

Heilbroner, Robert L. The Worldly Philosophers. rev. ed. New York, 1961.

Helps, Sir Arthur. The Claims of Labour. An Essay on the Duties of the Employer to the Employed (1844). London, 1845.

Hill, Christopher. "The Norman Yoke," in Democracy and the Labour Movement, edited by John Saville. London, 1954. pp. 11-66.

Houghton, Walter E. The Victorian Frame of Mind, 1830-1870. New Haven, 1957.

Hutt, W. H. "The Factory System of the Early Nineteenth Century," in Capitalism and the Historians, edited by F. A. Hayek. Chicago, 1954. pp. 160-88.

Johnson, L. G. The Social Evolution of Industrial Britain: A Study in the Growth of Our Industrial Society. Liverpool, 1959.

Kingsley, Charles. "Preface Written in 1854, Addressed to the Working Men of Great Britain," in Alton Locke. London, 1910. pp. 16-20.

Mantoux, Paul. The Industrial Revolution in the Eighteenth Century. New York and Evanston, 1962.

Martineau, Harriet. History of the Thirty Years' Peace, A. D. 1816-1846. 4 vols. London, 1911. 2.

Marx, Karl and Friedrich Engels. "Manifesto of the Communist Party (1848)," in Basic

Writings on Politics and Philosophy: Karl Marx and Friedrich Engels, edited by Lewis S. Feuer. New York, 1959. pp. 1-41.

Morton, A. L. *The Life and Ideas of Robert Owen*. New York, 1963.

Nicolson, Harold. *Good Behaviour: Being a Study of Certain Types of Civility*. New York, 1955.

Owen, Robert. *The Life of Robert Owen by Himself* (1857). New York, 1920.

Paley, William. *Reasons for Contentment Addressed to the Labouring Part of the British Public*. London, 1793.

Plumb, J. H. *England in the Eighteenth Century*. Harmondsworth, 1950.

Pritchett, V. S. "Exuberant Victorians." *New York Review of Books*, 5 (Sept. 30, 1965): 13-14.

Pumphrey, Ralph E. "The Introduction of Industrialists into the British Peerage: A Study in Adaptation of a Social Institution." *American Historical Review* 65 (1959): 1-16.

Romilly, Sir Samuel. *Memoirs of the Life of Sir Samuel Romilly, Written by Himself*. 3 vols. 2d ed., London, 1840. 2.

Ruskin, John. *Unto This Last* (1860) in *Unto This Last and Traffic*, edited by J. L. Bradley. New York, 1967.

Schulze-Gaevernitz, G. von. *Social Peace*, translated by C. M. Wicksteed. London, 1893.

Silver, Arthur W. "Henry Adams's 'Diary of a Visit to Manchester,'" *American Historical Review* 51 (1945): 74-89.

Smiles, Samuel. *Self-Help* (1859). London, 1876.

Smith, Henry Nash. *Virgin Land*. New York, 1957.

"Speculative Manias," No. 126 in Vol. 8 of *Chambers's Miscellany of Instructive and Entertaining Tracts*. 10 vols. Edinburgh, 1874.

Taine, H. A. *Notes on England*, translated by W. F. Rae. New York, 1874.

Tawney, R. H. *Religion and the Rise of Capitalism* (1926). New York, 1958.

Thackeray, W. M. "On Radical Snobs (1846)," in *Contributions to Punch*, Vol. 26 of *The Works of William Makepeace Thackeray*. 26 vols. London, 1898. pp. 333-35.

———. *The Book of Snobs* (1846-7), in Vol. 14 of *The Works of William Makepeace Thackeray*. 26 vols. London, 1902.

Toynbee, Arnold. *The Industrial Revolution* (1884). Boston, 1960.

Webb, Sidney, and Beatrice. *The History of Trade Unionism*. London, 1894.

Whibley, Charles. *Lordon John Manners and His Friends*. 2 vols. Edinburgh and London, 1925. 1.

Wingfield-Stratford, Esmé. *The Squire and His Relations*. London, 1956.

———. *The Making of a Gentleman*. London, 1938.

Woodward, E. L. *The Age of Reform: 1815-1870*. Oxford, 1939.

Wyllie, Irvin G. *The Self-Made Man in America*. New Brunswick, N.J., 1954.

Young, G. M. *Victorian England: Portrait of an Age*. London, 1960.

III. GENERAL LITERARY STUDIES

Altick, Richard. *The English Common Reader: A Social History of the Mass Reading Public 1800-1900*. Chicago, 1963.

Aydelotte, William O. "The England of Marx and Mill as Reflected in Fiction," *The Journal of Economic History*, Supplement 8 (1948), 42-58.

Cazamian, Louis. *Le Roman Social en Angleterre 1830-1850* (1904). 2 vols. Paris, 1934.

Gossman, Norbert J. "Political and Social Themes in the English Popular Novel—1815-1832." *Public Opinion Quarterly* 20 (1956). 531-41.

Jansonius, Herman. *Some Aspects of Business Life in Early Victorian Fiction*. Amsterdam, 1926.

Kovačević, Ivanka. "The Proletarian Fiction of the Industrial Revolution," Summary of *Industrijski Proleter U Engleskoj Pripovednoj Prozi Prve Polovine XIX Veka*. 2 vols. By Ivanka Kovačević. Beograd, 1960. 2. 44 pp.

Neff, Emery. "Social Background and Social Thought," in *The Reinterpretation of Victorian Literature*, edited by Joseph E. Baker. Princeton, 1950. pp. 3-19.

Neff, Wanda F. *Victorian Working Women: An Historical and Literary Study of Women in British Industries and Professions, 1832-1850*. New York, 1929.

Shusterman, David. "The Victorian Novel of Industrial Conflict: 1832-1870." Ph.D. dissertation, New York University, 1953.

Slagle, K. C. *The English Country Squire as Depicted in English Prose Fiction from 1740 to 1800*. Philadelphia, 1938.

Stevenson, Lionel. *The English Novel: A Panorama*. Boston, 1960.

Tillotson, Kathleen. *Novels of the Eighteen-Forties*. Oxford, 1954.

Williams, Raymond. "The Industrial Novels," in *Culture and Society: 1780-1950*. New York, 1960. pp. 94-118.

IV. FICTION

Ainsworth, W. H. *Mervyn Clitheroe (1851-58)*. London, 1870.

Aytoun, W. E. "How We Got Up the Glenmutchkin Railway, And How We Got Out of It." *Blackwood's Edinburgh Magazine*. 58 (October, 1845) : 453-66.

Brontë, Charlotte. *Shirley* (1849). London, 1962.

Collins, Edward James Mortimer. *Marquis and Merchant*. 3 vols. London, 1871.

Cooper, James Fenimore. *The Pioneers* (1823). New York, 1965.

Dickens, Charles. *Our Mutual Friend* (1864-65). New York, 1964.

———. *Little Dorrit* (1855-57). London, 1953.

———.*Hard Times* (1854). London, 1957.

———. *Bleak House* (1853). London, 1962.

———. *Martin Chuzzlewit* (1843-44). New York, 1965.

———. *Nicholas Nickleby* (1838-39). London, 1957.

Disraeli, Benjamin. *Sybil, or the Two Nations* (1845). Harmondsworth, 1954.

———. *Coningsby, or the New Generation* (1844). London, 1963.

———. *Popanilla* (1827). In Vol. 4 of *Novels and Tales By the Earl of Beaconsfield*. London, 1881.

Eliot, George. *Felix Holt, The Radical* (1866). Edinburgh and London, n.d.

Elizabeth, Charlotte. *Helen Fleetwood* (1839-40). In Vol. 2 of *The Works of Charlotte Elizabeth*. 3 vols. New York, 1844-45. pp. 43-184.

Galt, John. *Annals of the Parish* (1821). Vols. 1, 2 of *The Works of John Galt*, edited by D. S. Meldrum and William Roughead. 10 vols. Edinburgh, 1936.

Gaskell, Elizabeth. *North and South* (1855). London, 1961.

————. *Mary Barton* (1848). New York, 1958.

Gore, Catherine. *The Two Aristocracies.* 2 vols. in *Collection of British Authors,* Vols. 402-3. Leipzig: Bernhard Tauchnitz, 1857.

Gore, Catherine. *Cromer Hall: Or, Old Families and New.* In *Men of Capital* (1846). New York, 1849. pp. 45-140.

————. *Peers and Parvenus.* 3 vols. London, 1846.

"Hugh Vernon, The Weaver's Son," *The True Briton,* 2, NS (October 20 to December 29, 1853).

Jewsbury, Geraldine E. *Marian Withers.* 3 vols. London, 1851.

————. *The Half-Sisters* (1848). London, 1854.

Kay-Shuttleworth, Sir James Phillips. *Ribblesdale or Lancashire Sixty Years Ago.* 3 vols. London, 1874.

————. *Scarsdale; Life on the Lancashire and Yorkshire Border, Thirty Years Ago.* 3 vols. London, 1860.

Kingsley, Charles. *Alton Locke* (1849). London, 1910.

————. *Yeast: A Problem* (1848). London, 1913.

Lever, Charles *Davenport Dunn: A Man of Our Day.* London, 1859.

Lights and Shadows of English Life. 3 vols. London, 1855.

Martineau, Harriet. *A Manchester Strike* (1833). In Vol. 3 of *Illustrations of Political Economy.* 9 vols. London, 1834.

————. *The Hill and the Valley* (1832). In Vol. 1 of *Illustration of Political Economy.* 9 vols. London, 1834.

————. *The Rioters* (1827). London, 1842.

Mayne, Fanny. "Jane Rutherford; or the Miners' Strike," *The True Briton,* 1-2, NS (June 9 to Oct. 20, 1853).

"The Mill and the Manor." *Chambers's Edinburgh Journal,* Nos. 47-48, NS (Nov. 23-Nov. 30, 1844), 327-29; 338-41.

Mulock, Dinah Maria (Mrs. Craik). *John Halifax, Gentleman* (1856). London, 1912.

Pimlico, Paul. "The Factory Girl: A Tale in Six Chapters," *Reynolds's Miscellany* 3, NS (Oct. 20 to Nov. 24, 1849).

————. "The Manufacturer," *Reynolds's Miscellany,* 2 NS (June 16 to July 21, 1849).

Plebeians and Patricians. 2 vols. Philadelphia, 1836.

Smollett, Tobias. *The Expedition of Humphry Clinker* (1771). New York, 1929.

Stendhal, H. *The Red and the Black* (1831). New York, 1963.

Stone, Elizabeth. *William Langshawe, the Cotton Lord.* 2 vols. London, 1842.

Thackeray, W. M. *The History of Samuel Titmarsh and the Great Hoggarty Diamond* (1841). In Vol. 12 of *The Works of W. M. Thackeray.* 26 vols. London, 1898.

Trollope, Anthony. *Dr. Thorne* (1858). Boston, 1959.

Trollope, Frances. *The Life and Adventures of Michael Armstrong, the Factory Boy* (1839-40). London, 1840.

Wood, Mrs. Henry. *A Life's Secret* (1867). London, 1879.

————. *Mildred Arkell* (1865). London, 1880.

————. *Mrs. Halliburton's Troubles* (1862). London, 1877.

V. PRIMARY AND SECONDARY MATERIALS ON NOVELISTS AND THEIR WORKS

"Annals of the Parish." *Quarterly Review,* 25 (April, 1821): 147-53.

Baker, Ernest. *The History of the English Novel.* 10 vols. New York, 1950. 6.

Booth, Bradford A. *Anthony Trollope: Aspects of His Life and Art.* Bloomington, 1958.

Chaloner, W. H. "Mrs. Trollope and the Early Factory System," VS, 4 (1960), 159-66.

Chapman, Maria Weston, ed. *Harriet Martineau's Autobiography.* 2 vols. Boston, 1877.

Collins, Frances. *Mortimer Collins: His Letters and Friendships, With Some Account of His Life.* 2 vols. London, 1877.

Cruikshank, R. J. *Charles Dickens and Early Victorian England.* London, 1949.

Dalziel, Margaret. *Popular Fiction 100 Years Ago: An Unexplored Tract of Literary History.* London, 1957.

Dickens, Charles. *American Notes and Pictures from Italy.* Vol. 28 of *The Works of Charles Dickens.* 32 vols. London, 1898.

———. *The Letters of Charles Dickens,* edited by Walter Dexter. 3 vols. London, 1938.

Dixon, Hepworth. "Marian Withers." *Athenaeum,* No. 1244 (August 30, 1851), 920-21.

Ellis, S. M. *William Harrison Ainsworth and His Friends.* 2 vols. London, 1911.

Elizabeth, Charlotte. *Personal Recollections* (1841). In Vol. 1 of *The Works of Charlotte Elizabeth.* 3 vols. New York, 1844-45. pp. 1-126.

Froude, J. A. *Lord Beaconsfield* (1890). London and New York, 1914.

Galt, John. *The Literary Life, and Miscellanies, of John Galt.* 3 vols. Edinburgh, 1834.

Galt, John. *The Autobiography of John Galt.* 2 vols. London, 1833.

Greg, William Rathbone. "Mary Barton," in Vol. I of *Essays on Political and Social Science by W. R. Greg.* 2 vols. London, 1853. pp. 344-88.

Hopkins, A. B. *Elizabeth Gaskell: Her Life and Work.* London, 1952.

House, Humphry. *The Dickens World* (1942). 2d ed. London, 1960.

Howe, Susanne. *Geraldine Jewsbury: Her Life and Errors.* London, 1935.

Huxley, Aldous. "The Vulgarity of Little Nell (1930)," in *The Dickens Critics,* edited by George H. Ford and Lauriat Lane, Jr. Ithaca, N.Y., 1961.

Jackson, Thomas A. *Charles Dickens: The Progress of a Radical.* London, 1937.

James, Louis. *Fiction for the Working Man, 1830-1850: A Study of the Literature Produced for the Working Classes in Early Victorian Urban England.* London, 1963.

Jeffrey, Francis. "Secondary Scottish Novels," *Edinburgh Review* 39 (Oct. 1823), 158-96.

Johnson, Edgar. *Charles Dickens: His Tragedy and Triumph.* 2 vols. New York, 1952.

Lockhart, J. G. *Memoirs of the Life of Sir Walter Scott. Bart.* 7 vols. Edinburgh, 1837, 5.

———. "Miss Martineau's Monthly Novels," *Quarterly Review* 49 (April, 1833), 136-52.

Martineau, Harriet. "Preface," in Vol. 1 of *Illustrations of Political Economy.* 9 vols. London, 1832-34. pp. iii-xviii.

"Michael Armstrong," *Athenaeum* 615 (Aug. 10, 1839):587-90.

Nevill, John C. *Harriet Martineau.* London, 1943.

Parker, W. M. "Introduction," *John Halifax, Gentleman.* London, 1961. pp. v-xiii.

Parr, Louisa. "Dinah Mulock (Mrs. Craik)," in *Women Novelists of Queen Victoria's Reign.* London, 1897. pp. 217-48.

Pritchett, V. S. "A Scottish Documentary," in *The Living Novel.* New York, 1947. pp. 50-55.

Rosa, Matthew W. *The Silver-Fork School: Novels of Fashion Preceding Vanity Fair.* New York, 1936.

Ruskin, John. "A Note on *Hard Times* (1860)," in *The Dickens Critics,* edited by George H. Ford and Lauriat Lane, Jr. Ithaca, N.Y., 1961. pp. 47-48.

Sadleir, Michael. *Trollope: A Commentary.* London, 1927.

Smith, Frank. *The Life and Work of Sir James Kay-Shuttleworth.* London, 1923.

Smith, Sheila M. "Willenhall and Wodgate: Disraeli's Use of Blue Book Evidence," *RES* NS, 13 (1962), 368-84.

Stevenson, Lionel. "Dickens's Dark Novels, 1851-1857," *SeR* 51 (1943): 398-409.

"Sybil; or The Two Nations," *Douglas Jerrold's Shilling Magazine,* 1 (Jan. to June, 1845), 557-65.

Thackeray, W. M. "Lords and Liveries," in *Punch's Prize Novelists* (1847). New York, 1853. pp. 72-87.

———. "Charity and Humour," in Vol. 7 of *The Works of William Makepeace Thackeray.* 13 vols. New York and London, 1898. pp. 713-25.

Trollope, Anthony. *An Autobiography* (1883). London, 1950.

Trollope, Frances. *Domestic Manners of the Americans* (1832). London, 1927.

Trollope, Frances Eleanor. *Frances Trollope: Her Life and Literary Work from George III to Victoria.* 2 vols. London, 1895.

Trollope, Thomas Adolphus. *What I Remember.* 2d. ed. 2 vols. London, 1887.

"The Two Aristocracies," *Athenaeum,* No. 1549 (July 4, 1857), 852.

Webb, R. K. *Harriet Martineau: A Radical Victorian.* New York, 1960.

"William Langshawe, the Cotton Lord," *Athenaeum,* No. 779 (Oct. 1, 1842), 846.

Woolf, Virginia. "Geraldine and Jane," *TLS* 28 (Feb. 28, 1929), 149-50.

Index